Contents

Helion & Company Limited
Unit 8 Amherst Business Centre
Budbrooke Road
Warwick
CV34 5WE
England
Tel. 01926 499 619
Email: info@helion.co.uk
Website: www.helion.co.uk
Twitter: @helionbooks

Text © Tom Cooper, Albert Grandolini,
    Adrien Fontanellaz 2019
Colour profiles © Tom Cooper, David
    Bocquelet and Luca Canossa 2019
Maps © Tom Cooper 2019
Photographs © as individually credited

Designed & typeset by Farr out Publications,
    Wokingham, Berkshire
Cover design by Paul Hewitt, Battlefield
    Design (www.battlefield-design.co.uk)

Printed by Henry Ling Ltd., Dorchester,
    Dorset

ISBN 978-1-912866-29-8

British Library Cataloguing-in-Publication
    Data
A catalogue record for this book is available
    from the British Library

We always welcome receiving book
proposals from prospective authors.

Note: In order to simplify the use of this book, all names, locations and geographic designations are as provided in *The Times World Atlas*, or other traditionally accepted major sources of reference, as of the time of the described events. Arabic names are Romanised and transcripted rather than transliterated. For example: the definite article al- before words starting with 'sun letters' is given as pronounced instead of simply as al- (which is the usual practice for non-Arabic speakers in most English-language literature and media). For easier understanding of ranks of French Air Force and US Navy officers cited in this book, herewith a table comparing these with ranks in the Royal Air Force (United Kingdom):

Royal Air Force (of Morocco)	Royal Air Force (United Kingdom)	Armée de l'Air (France)	US Air Force (USA)
général d'armée aérienne	Marshal of the RAF	général d'armée aérienne	General of the Air Force
général de corps aérien	Air Chief Marshal	général de corps aérien	General
général de division aérienne	Air Marshal	général de division aérienne	Lieutenant-General
général de brigade aérienne	Air Vice Marshal	général de brigade aérienne	Major-General
colonel-major			Brigadier General
colonel	Air Commodore	colonel	Colonel
lieutenant-colonel	Group Captain	lieutenant-colonel	Lieutenant-Colonel
commandant	Wing Commander	commandant	
	Squadron Leader	commandant d'escadron	Major
capitaine	Flight Lieutenant	capitaine	Captain
premier lieutenant	Flying Officer	lieutenant	2nd Lieutenant
sous-lieutenant	Pilot Officer	sous-lieutenant	1st Lieutenant
adjutant-chef[1]	Master Aircrew	aspirant /major	Chief Master Sergeant

Abbreviations

4WD	Four-wheel drive
AB	Air Base
AdA	*Armée de l'Air* (French Air Force)
AdT	*Armée de Terre* (French Army)
AGLT	Air-Ground Liaison Team
AK	Automat Kalashnikova; general designation for a class of Soviet or former Eastern Bloc-manufactured assault rifles
ALAT	*Aviation Légère de l'Armée de Terre* (French Army Light Aviation)
AMIN	*Aéro Maroc Industrie*
AMG	*Atelier Magasin General* (General Workshop, main overhaul facility of the FRA)
AML	*Automitrailleuse Légère* (class of wheeled armoured cars manufactured by Panhard)
An	Antonov (the design bureau led by Oleg Antonov)
ANP	*Armée Nationale Populaire* (National Popular Army, Algeria)
APC	Armoured Personnel Carrier
ATGM	anti-tank guided missile
BA-FRA	*Base Annexe-FRA* (a sub-unit of the La'ayoun base, Royal Air Force of Morocco)
BCCP	*bataillon de parachutiste commando colonial* (Colonial Para-Commando Battalion, French Army)
BG	*bataillon de garnison* (Garrison Battalion, FAR)
BIM	*bataillon d'infanterie motorisé* (Motorised Infantry Battalion, FAR)
BISMAR	*bataillon d'infanterie de marine* (Marine Infantry Battalion, FAR)
BIS	*bataillon d'infanterie de secteur* (Sector Infantry Battalion, FAR)
BM	*bataillon méharis* (Méharis Battalion, FAR)
BN	*base navale* (Naval Base, FAR)
BP	*bataillon de parachutiste* (Parachute Battalion, FAR)
BRIMeca	*brigade d'infanterie mécanisée* (Mechanised Infantry Brigade, FAR)
BRIMoto	*brigade d'infanterie motorisée* (Motorised Infantry Brigade, FAR)
BSI	*bataillon de soutien intendance* (Battalion Support Group, FAR)
BSMAT	*bataillon de soutien matériel* (Hardware Support Battalion, FAR)
BSMUN	*bataillon de soutien munition* (Ammunition Support Battalion, FAR)
BSS	*bataillon de soutien sanitaire* (Sanitary Support Battalion: medical unit, FAR)
BT	*bataillon de transmission* (Signals Battalion, FAR)
CAP	Combat Air Patrol
CAS	Close Air Support
CASA	Construcciones Aeronáuticas SA (Spanish aircraft manufacturer)
CBU	cluster bomb unit
CIA	Central Intelligence Agency (USA)
CIFAS	*Centre d'Instruction Forces Aériennes Stratégiques* (Centre for Instruction of Strategic Forces, France)
CIPC	*Centre d'Instruction Pilotes de Combat* (Training Centre for Combat Pilots, FRA)
CMV	*commando marche verte* (Green March Commando, FAR)
CO	Commanding Officer or commander
COIN	counterinsurgency
COMINOR	Complexe Minier du Nord (iron mining company in Mauritania)
DGSE	*Direction Générale de la Sécurité Extérieure* (Directorate-General for External Security; French external intelligence agency operating under the direction of the French Ministry of Defence)
DIR	*détachment d'intervention rapide* (rapid intervention detachment, FAR; usually consisting of two squadrons of AML/Eland armoured cars)
DoD	Department of Defence (USA)
EAA	*Escadron d'Appui Aérien* (Air Support Squadron)
EAF	Egyptian Air Force (official title since 1972)
EALA	*Escadrille d'Aviation Légere d'Appui* (Light Attack Aviation Squadron)
EC	*Escadre de Chasse* (Fighter Wing)
ECM	Electronic countermeasures
EdA	*Ejercito del Aire* (Spanish Air Force)
ELAA	*Escadrille Légère d'Appui Aérien* (Light Air Support Squadron)
ELINT	Electronic intelligence
ELPS	*Ejército de Liberación Popular Saharaui* (Sahrawi Popular Liberation Army)
ERV	*Escadron de Ravitaillement en Vol* (Air Refuelling Squadron)
FAIM	*Force Aérienne Islamique de Mauritanie* (Islamic Air Force of Mauritania)
FAMET	*Fuerzas Aeromoviles del Ejercito de Tierra* (Spanish Army Aviation)
FAR	*Forces Armées Royale* (Royal Armed Forces of Morocco), also *Force Aérienne Royale Marocaine* (Royal Air Force of Morocco)
FLU	*Frente de Liberación y de la Unidad* (Front for Liberation and Unity, a quasi-insurgency of Sahrawis, organized by Morocco in 1975)
FRA	*Forces Royales Air* (Royal Air Force of Morocco, since the 1990s)
FRELISARIO	see POLISARIO
GAR	*groupe d'artillerie royale* (Royal Artillery Group of the FAR)
GARIM	*groupement aérien* (original designation of the Mauritanian Air Force, see FAIM)
GEB	*groupe d'escadron blindé* (armoured squadron/group, a FAR armoured unit ranging in size between a battalion and regiment, equipped with 50-60 MBTs, 30 APCs and reconnaissance vehicles)
GFT	*groupe de transport* (Transport Group, FAR)
GLS	*groupe léger de securité* (Light Security Group, FAR)
GTIA	*groupe tactique inter-armes* (Task Force, FAR)
GTr	*groupe transport* (Transport Group, FAR)

HA	Hispano Aviacion (Spanish aircraft manufacturer)			Democratic Republic)
HOT	*Haut subsonique Optiquement Téléguidé Tiré d'un Tube* (High Subsonic, Optical, Remote-Guided, Tube-launched; French ATGM)		**REC**	*régiment étranger de cavalerie* (Cavalry Regiment of the Foreign Legion, French Army)
HPM	*hôpital militaire* (Military Hospital, FAR)		**REI**	*regiment étranger d'infanterie* (Infantry Regiment of the Foreign Legion, French Army)
HQ	headquarters		**REP**	*régiment étranger parachutistes* (Parachute Regiment of the Foreign Legion, French Army)
HUMINT	human intelligence			
IADS	integrated air defence system		**RIAOM**	*régiment interarmes d'outre-mer* (Overseas Interarms Regiment, French Army)
IAP	international airport			
ICJ	International Court of Justice		**RICM**	*régiment d'infanterie chars de marine* (Marine Infantry Tank Regiment, French Army)
IFF	identification friend or foe			
IFR	in-flight refuelling		**RIMa**	*régiment d'infanterie de marine* (Marine Infantry Regiment, French Army)
IFV	infantry fighting vehicle			
IR	infra-red, electromagnetic radiation longer than deepest red light sensed as heat		**RIM**	*regiment d'infanterie motorisé* (Motorised Infantry Regiment, FAR)
Il	Ilyushin (the design bureau led by Sergey Vladimirovich Ilyushin, also known as OKB-39)		**RPG**	rocket propelled grenade
			RWR	radar warning receiver
INS	Instrumental navigation system		**RHC**	*Régiment d'Hélicoptères de Combat* (Combat Helicopter Regiment)
Km	kilometre			
LAAF	Libyan Arab Air Force		**SA**	Sud Aviation (French aircraft manufacturer)
LORAN	radio navigation system		**SA-2 Guideline**	ASCC codename for S-75 Dvina, Soviet SAM system
LOROP	long-range oblique photography (aerial reconnaissance method)			
			SA-3 Goa	ASCC codename for S-125 Pechora, Soviet SAM system
MANPADS	man-portable air defence system(s) – light surface-to-air missile system that can be carried and deployed in combat by a single soldier			
			SA-6 Gainful	ASCC codename for 2K12E Kvadrat/Kub, Soviet SAM system
MBT	Main Battle Tank		**SA-7 Grail**	ASCC codename for 9K32 Strela-2, Soviet MANPADS
MH	Max Holste (French aircraft manufacturer)			
MHz	Megahertz, millions of cycles per second		**SA-8 Gecko**	ASCC codename for 9K33 Osa, Soviet SAM system
Mi	Mil (Soviet/Russian helicopter designer and manufacturer)			
			SA-9 Gaskin	ASCC codename for 9K31 Strela-1, Soviet SAM system
MiG	Mikoyan i Gurevich (the design bureau led by Artyom Ivanovich Mikoyan and Mikhail i Gurevich, also known as OKB-155 or MMZ "Zenit")			
			SAM	surface-to-air missile
			SEAD	suppression of enemy air defences
MPA	maritime patrol aircraft		**SEPECAT**	*Société Européenne de Production de l'Avion d'École de Combat et d'Appui Tactique* (European Company for the Production of a Combat Trainer and Tactical Support Aircraft)
MRL	multiple rocket launcher			
MS	Morane-Saulnier (French aircraft manufacturer)			
Nav/attack	System used for navigation and to aim weapons against surface targets			
			SIGINT	signals intelligence
NCO	non-commissioned officer		**SLAR**	side looking radar
OAU	Organisation of African Unity		**SN**	*Sureté Nationale* (National Security Agency, Morocco)
OPEC	Organization of the Petroleum Exporting Countries			
			Technical	improvised fighting vehicle (typically an open-backed civilian 4WD modified to a gun truck)
ORBAT	Order of Battle			
OTU	Operational Training Unit		**TEL**	transporter-erector-launcher
PC/GMM	*poste de commandement groupe Makhzen mobile* (Mobile Makhzen Group Command Post)		**TF/TG**	task force or tactical group of the FAR (most such units consisted of a reinforced brigade, and thus frequently reached up to the size of a division)
POLISARIO	*Frente Popular para la Liberación de Saquia el-Hamra y Río de Oro* (Popular Front for the Liberation of Saquia el-Hamra and Río de Oro; FRELISARIO, colloquially POLISARIO)		**TFR**	terrain following radar
			US/USA	United States of America
			USAF	United States Air Force
			USD	United States Dollar (also US$)
PoW	prisoner of war		**USN**	United States Navy
QJJ	*al-Quwwat al-Jawwiya al-Jaza'eriya* (Algerian Air Force)		**USSR**	Union of Soviet Socialist Republics (or Soviet Union)
RAF	Royal Air Force (of the United Kingdom)		**VHF**	very high frequency
RAMa	*Régiment d'Artillerie de Marine* (Marine Artillery Regiment, French Army)		**WIA**	Wounded in Action
			ZACAO	*Zona Aérea de Canarias y Africa Occidental* (Aerial Zone of Canary Islands and Western Africa, EdA)
RAP	*Régiment d'Artillerie Aéroportée* (Airborne Artillery Regiment, French Army)			
RASD	*República Árabe Saharaui Democrática* (Sahrawi Arab		**ZSU**	*Zenitnaya Samokhodnaya Ustanovka* (Soviet-built self-propelled anti-aircraft artillery)

Addenda/Errata to *Showdown in Western Sahara*, Volume 1

FAR, FARM or FRA?

Several readers from Morocco have commented upon the use of the abbreviation 'FARM' (standing for *Forces Armeées Royale Marocaine*) as the designation of the Royal Moroccan Air Force. While stressing that the French is the, *de-facto*, official language of this service, they have provided clear and undisputable evidence that the actual official designation is 'just' the *Forces Royales Air*, i.e. FRA (for an example, see the colour section of this volume), while the official designation of the Moroccan armed forces is *Forces Armées Royales* (FAR). While taking care to correct the designation in most of our manuscript – based on its use in much of the specialised English-language press over the last 40 years – on a number of occasions the term 'FARM' was wrongly used in Volume 1.

Introduction and Acknowledgements

The idea for this book emerged as long ago as an evening in October 1987, when – inspired by a short article in a daily newspaper describing the geo-political situation in an apparently 'forgotten corner' of western Africa – one of the authors decided to go through his collection of related press releases. At the time, the conflict in question was rarely reported in the English language: at most it would capture the second page of major newspapers. Only occasionally, bigger articles were published in France and Spain. Detailed information was next to non-available: the few bits and pieces indicated deployments of Dassault Mirage F.1 fighter-bombers against 'Polisario guerrillas.' Reporting related to the geo-strategic issues of this war appeared more often and was quite clear: it began with Morocco, previously administered by the French and Spanish, before achieving independence in 1956; Mauritania following in 1960, and Algeria reaching this status only after a protracted and particularly bitter war against the French, in 1962. In between the three was a territory colloquially known as 'Spanish Sahara' and, later on, 'Western Sahara': as of 1975, this was one of the last few colonies on the African continent. Rather suddenly, the Spaniards withdrew, leaving the locals to sort out things amongst themselves: the last of the Spanish troops were not even out of this territory when the Moroccans marched in from the north, the Mauritanians from the south, and – apparently – the Algerians from the east. Moreover, what was widely described as a 'leftist insurgency' – and then one supported by Algeria, Libya, and the USSR – then launched a war against the Moroccan forces supported by France and the United States of America. Indeed, for nearly all of the 1980s, the war in Western Sahara was widely described as another of the many proxy-wars being fought all over the world at the time, but especially in Africa and Asia – always between the 'good' and the 'bad', between the 'East' and the 'West', and within the context of the Cold War.

On the first superficial look, the military history of that conflict could not have been any more confusing, and, perhaps, not interesting. Although wearing the official title of the Royal Armed Forces of Morocco (*Forces Armées Royale*, FAR), the Moroccan armed forces were driving Soviet-made T-54/55 main battle tanks (MBTs) – prompting questions like; why was an Arab monarchy operating Soviet-made weapon systems? Surely enough, by the time the war in Western Sahara reached its climax, in the early 1980s, the Moroccans were also equipped with US-made M48 MBTs and a miscellany of French-made armoured cars, while their acquisition of SK-105 Kürassier light tanks from strictly neutral Austria provoked a public outrage and a major political crisis in that country. Originally riding camels, the insurgents rapidly switched to the famous British-made Land Rover all-terrain vehicles: later on, they appeared driving Soviet-made BMP-1 infantry fighting vehicles (IFVs). By the mid-1980s, the impression created by reporting in the world-wide media

was that the situation in the air was quite similar: the Moroccans first flew Soviet-made MiGs, then US-made Northrop F-5A/B Freedom Fighters and F-5E/F Tiger IIs, and then French-made Dassault Mirages. The insurgency had no air power, but successfully fought back with Soviet-made 9K32 Strela-2 (best-known by its ASCC/NATO-codename 'SA-7 Grail') man-portable air defence systems (MANPADs). Moreover, ever heavier air defence systems of Soviet origin – including heavy surface-to-air missiles – began appearing, first in the form of systems like the 9K31 Strela-1 (ASCC/NATO-codename 'SA-9 Gaskin') and then the 2K12E Kvadrat (ASCC/NATO-codename 'SA-6 Gainful'), famous from the October 1973 Arab-Israeli War. Finally, the situation on the ground was generally described as a stalemate: reportedly, the Moroccans constructed a massive defensive wall, stretching for hundreds of kilometres. In turn, as one report about the downing of a Moroccan Mirage followed another, the deployment of Soviet-made SAMs appeared to have 'sealed the skies over Western Sahara' for Moroccan combat aircraft. While the resulting idea was thus that of the insurgency being well on the way to winning this war, in 1991 a ceasefire was announced – and accepted – by both sides, and the war appeared to be over, with most of its events remaining as mysterious as the many other secrets one might guess are hidden under the sands of the Sahara Desert.

The Sahara is certainly a fascinating part of the world for many foreigners. It might be a mysterious area, and it is perfectly possible that it still hides plenty of secrets, just as many of the details of the war fought in Western Sahara in 1975-1991 remain largely unknown to the present day. However, at least enough details are available to outline the flow of this conflict, point out the most important developments, explain their reasons, and thus describe the impact of the major weapon systems, strategy and tactics of all of the involved parties.

When doing that, it should be pointed out, up front, that this war is not actually over: the fighting ended with a cease-fire in 1991, but no peace deal was ever arranged, and the root reasons for the conflict have never been solved through any treaties. No doubt, the Moroccan authorities are in control over most of what they designated the 'Southern Provinces' and up to 40% of the native population. Indeed, some of the latter have not only accepted Moroccan rule but prefer it to that of any other party. Nevertheless, at least 50 per cent of the population of Western Sahara grew up in exile, foremost in the refugee camps of south-western Algeria. From there, a steady stream of reports about mass protests and violent confrontations has appeared in recent years: some pointing out the repression of the natives in Western Sahara by the Moroccans, others about a growing discontent among the younger generations of the Sahrawis that grew up in Algeria. The refugee camps in the Tindouf area have lately seen a series of kidnappings and infiltration attempts by groups associated with the Jihadism of al-Qaeda. Finally, at least from the Moroccan point of view, Western Sahara remains a major point of contention with Algeria.

As so often, any closer study of an armed conflict promptly shows that the affairs in question are far more than just another local power struggle. Indeed, no matter if one calls the area the Southern Provinces or Western Sahara, for reasons described in *Showdown in Western Sahara, Volume 1*, the fact remains that the history of this territory is directly related to the history of modern-day Morocco, Mauritania, Algeria, and even France and Spain – often to the point where it forms the foundation of these nations. Therefore, one of the crucial issues is an understanding of where the people living in this part of Africa have come from, their culture and their way of thinking: after all, their views of the world are shaped by their individual experiences as much as by the experiences of the group within which they grew up and live. It is for this reason that our methods of research are all-encompassing: while foremost concentrating on air forces, aircraft, and aerial warfare in this volume, we insist on presenting these against the backdrop of the socio-economic and geo-political context, and the developments on the ground. Neither wars, nor air wars happen in a vacuum, and even less so on their own: on the contrary, the socio-economic and geo-political background help to explain everything necessary to understand why the air forces are established and built-up in the way that they are, why they are equipped with specific types of aircraft and other equipment, why and how they are trained, how they are organized, and why and where they are deployed in combat.

Another aim of the effort that resulted in this project was the work on an earlier series of books covering the history of Arab air forces involved in the wars against Israel, when one of the aims was to find out why the Moroccan government failed to keep its promise of supporting Egypt and Syria during the October 1973 War through deployment of at least a squadron of its fighter-bombers. Related research eventually led to a wider reconstruction of the operational history of the Algerian, Mauritanian, Moroccan, and even the French and Spanish air forces in this part of the world – which was also provided in *Showdown in Western Sahara, Volume 1*.

While the first volume thus told the story of the emergence of local nations, of their mutual relations, of their military flying services, and of military flying in this part of Africa up to 1975, the aim of this volume will be to find out what happened in the air – and on the ground – once the Spaniards left the Spanish Sahara. While we do understand that the emergence of every publication of this kind represents a sort of an 'intervention', our intention is not to make accusations about the behaviour or politics of one or another of the involved parties, or to point out who is right and who is wrong. We do discuss political and diverse other agendas, but only as far as they are directly influential to the military-related issues. Instead, the aim of *Volume 2* is to provide the first coherent, English-language military history of an armed conflict that savaged much of this territory in the period 1975-1991, evaluate the use of air power, discuss the air forces and air defence forces involved, the aircraft types and their equipment, the reasons for and effectiveness of their deployment, and the lessons learned.

In the course of our related work, we were quickly forced into the conclusion that research with the help of official documentation was de-facto impossible. The official military archives of countries like Morocco, Algeria, and Mauritania, or even those of the Popular Front for the Liberation of Saguia el-Hamra and Río de Oro (*Frente Popular para la Liberación de Saguia el-Hamra y Río de Oro*, FRELISARIO, colloquially POLISARIO), are all kept well outside the public reach. Arguably, a few – more or less – 'officially sanctioned' publications have emerged over time. However, it is only in Algeria that some of these are based on documentation released to a handful of, literally, 'handpicked' historians, and then published in the form of articles in the official military magazine *el-Djeich*, or various other books (see Bibliography). A few memoirs released by different individuals of Moroccan origin over time are preoccupied with explaining the makings of internal Moroccan politics, and personal relations, and provide relatively few hard facts about the fighting in Western Sahara. Correspondingly, we found no other solution than to run most of our research in the form of oral history – through interviews with participants and eyewitnesses, and then to virtually glue together the bits and pieces of the story. Of immense help in this regard were several first-hand contacts we had made over time in three out of four of the key players in this drama, foremost researchers from (in alphabetic order) Algeria, Morocco and Western Sahara, whom we only feel free to name as K. H., P. A., E. C., H. B., and N. B. In this place, we would like to express our gratitude for their extensive help, and preparedness to spend literally days with helping us to prepare this volume. Further information and advice were provided by Dr. David Nicolle from Great Britain – who is currently working on a book-series about the first 50 years of military flying in what is known as the Arab world; by Laurent Touchard, from France; by Pit Weinert, from Germany; and Nour Bardai from Egypt; to all of whom we would like to forward our thanks in this place.

The third kind of information was obtained through cross-examining dozens of second- and third-hand sources – like the online archive (or the Electronic Reading Room) of the Central Intelligence Agency (CIA) of the USA, and then from books and periodicals in the French and Spanish languages, and a few in the English language. It is almost unnecessary to say that much of the information we have collected over time was rather contradictory – often even directly conflicting – in nature, even if based on primary research, and released by reputable sources. The very nature of contemporary military history is such that a truly 'complete and reliable' account of almost every war is impossible to produce: it is not the sheer volume of misinformation released over the years that causes problems, but military operations and combat experiences are sensitive topics and it regularly takes five or more decades before definite facts might become available. This is even more valid for a war that has actually never ended, and for military forces that are still operating essentially the same military equipment as back in the 1980s.

In our analysis, we went to great extents to avoid becoming dogmatic or taking sides. While we have no political axe to grind, and have taken care to keep the choice of language non-partisan, some inevitable observations are made in the analysis, which we trust are unlikely to be found disturbing by readers from 'either side of the tribune'. If we seem unduly harsh towards one or the other side, then it is primarily because of the availability of information at one or another point in time.

We have intentionally written and designed this book as one for a wide audience – intended to serve as a primer for researchers and enthusiasts alike – and hopefully as a source of inspiration for further, more detailed studies. It was written with journalists and modelmakers in mind, too: both for people not familiar with the subject matter and those with all sorts of familiarity with the subject. Our hope is that all the readers are going to find this volume enjoyable and informative reading and would be delighted to hear from readers with any suggested corrections or amendments.

Chapter 1
The Spanish Sahara

For at least the last 2,000 years, the western part of the Sahara has been one of the most desolate and sparsely populated areas on the Earth. Unsurprisingly, much of the recorded history of humanity in this area is related to the neighbouring countries, especially Morocco. Indeed, the relations between the local population and that of their powerful neighbour further north have played a crucial role in the fate of this territory and are certain to continue doing so for decades to come.

Early History

Western Sahara is positioned in north-western Africa, on the coast of the Atlantic Ocean. The area neighbours Morocco in the north, Algeria in the north-east, and Mauritania in the east and south. Geographically, it is divided into two regions: the northern panhandle, known by its Spanish name Saguia el-Hamra, with a low coast, deep gullies and large rises of the Ouarkziz Mountains; and the larger, flat area called Río de Oro in the south. The terrain is dominated by rocky plains, and is one of the most arid and inhospitable places on this planet: average temperatures during the summer – in July and August – are as high as 43-45°C (109-113°F), and rarely drop below 25-30°C (77-86°F) even during the winter in December and January. On the contrary, the areas away from the coast can get very cold in winter, when the thermometer rarely shows more than 0°C (32°F) by night. There is no permanent watering in nearly all of Western Sahara, although occasional flash floods do take place in the spring and cool offshore currents can produce fog and heavy dew. Rain is so rare that crops occupy less than one half of a per cent of this hyper-arid country, and nearly all food has to be imported. Further inland there is just enough water for seasonal grazing by the camels and goats herded there by local nomads for thousands of years.

The principal issue about the fate of this territory is closely related to its human habitation – most of which in turn is related to that of its neighbours: the western Sahara used to be a well-watered grassland with a great deal of wildlife in pre-historic times, but it had already gone through the transition into the arid phase by the time it was reached by the Phoenicians in the 5th Century BC and then the Romans. Thus, the population over the following thousands of years largely consisted of nomads in the plains of the north and semi-nomadic tribes in the south. The spread of Islam in the 8th Century CE found this area more sparsely populated than ever before, as many migrated to the towns of what is present-day Morocco. However, Islam re-vitalised trade, converting the area into the scene of a near-permanent and bitter struggle for the control of major trade routes towards the south.

In 1039, the area nowadays within the limits of Western Sahara was invaded by Almoravides – mostly Sanhaja Berbers from what is nowadays eastern Morocco. They established their ruling house in Marrakesh in 1062, and then created an empire stretching for 3,000 kilometres (1,900 miles), from modern-day Mauritania in the south, to Sevilla in modern-day Spain in the north. Precisely this period became the reason for most of the disputes regarding Western Sahara, and between Morocco and Algeria, of modern times: because Morocco traces its lineage from the Almoravides, it has irredentist claims to most of the territories in question, generally summarised as the 'Idea of Greater Morocco'. While often described as 'unrealistic' in the West and by most of Morocco's neighbours, this is a subject of not only serious emotions at home and abroad but has also been the official ideology and policy of successive Moroccan governments.

The Almoravides were swept from power by another Berber tribal confederation, the Almohads, who conquered all of modern-day northern Algeria, all of Tunisia and most of modern-day northern Libya, in the 12th Century. In turn, the Almohads lost most of their possessions by the 14th Century, when Maqil Arab tribes (also known as the 'Bani Hassan Arabs') migrated into north-western Africa (for example, the Oulad Dlim tribe from Himyari in Yemen has settled in the Dakhla area). While furnishing protection and supplies, they Arabised the Berbers and greatly intensified trade. In the course of near-constant wars with their neighbours, they leaned upon key oasis settlements and ports to develop a network of trade stations, which helped them eventually establish themselves in a position of dominance. Through intermarriage, the Arabo-Berber people known as Saharawi came into being, with their distinct Arabic dialect, Hassaniya, becoming the dominant mother-tongue of Western Sahara and Mauritania.

The Spaniards and the Portuguese opened the era of European conquests in the 15th Century. With the exception of the Spanish possession of Ceuta, all of their early attempts in the 15th Century were repulsed or abandoned. During the 19th Century, the United Kingdom and France began vying for influence in Morocco, and in 1860 Spain launched several small wars to bite off pieces of Moroccan territory, such as Tetuan and Ifni, and to enlarge Ceuta. In 1904, the British agreed to give France a free hand in Morocco in return for undisputed control of Egypt, and Spain was pacified through French agreement to recognize northern Morocco as a sphere of Spanish interest.

Further south, three representatives of the Oulad Bou Sbaa tribe and of the Society of Africanists and Colonists (*Sociedad de Africanistas y Colonistas*) signed a treaty that formed the legal basis for the Spanish conquest of Sahara in November 1884. A year later, in December 1885, the Spanish government placed Rio de Oro, Angra de Cintra, and Bay of the West under its protection and appointed the first commissioner, and two years later extended its jurisdiction for 150 miles (240km) inland, before – in 1900 – signing a convention with France that defined the border between the Spanish Sahara and the area that became known as the French-controlled Mauritania. To the present day, there is a dispute over whether it was under Moroccan sovereignty at the time the Spanish claimed it, or was it assigned to the Spanish only during the Berlin Conference of 1884-1885. What is certain is that the appearance of the Spaniards on this part of the Atlantic coast of Africa was promptly and stiffly opposed by the indigenous Sahrawis: preoccupied with the struggle for their own survival, Moroccan rulers usually played only an indirect role. On 30 March 1912, the Treaty of Fez secured Morocco as a French protectorate: six months later, Madrid and Paris then signed a treaty distributing West Africa between them.

Carving out an Overseas Province

On their arrival in Río de Oro, the Spanish found the area populated by two main groups: regardless if colloquially designated the 'Sahrawis', or referred to as 'Southerners' or 'Southern Berbers' in Morocco, these were the ruling Arabs and the nomadic Berber tribes, divided into a variety of tribes within a complex and highly stratified society. The dominating tribes were the Reguibat, Tekna, and Delim: the Reguibat comprised Arabized Berbers who spoke Hassaniya Arabic. They lived as nomadic herdsmen and inhabited the eastern half of the country (as well as parts of Algeria, Morocco, and Mauritania). The Tekna tribe was of mixed Arab and Berber origin, speaking a Berber dialect and living as semi-nomads in the northern part of the area (and in southern Morocco). The Delim were ethnically more Arab than the Reguibat or the Tekna: speaking Hassaniya Arabic they lived in the south-eastern part of the territory.[1]

The Spanish first established the settlements of Boujdour and Dakhla (subsequently renamed as Villa Cisneros) before moving further inland – only to encounter armed resistance. Disorganized at first, the Sahrawi resistance built-up gradually: by 1898, Sheikh Mohamed Mustafa Ma al-'Aynayn from Oualata (present day Mauritania) – who saw the European presence both as an intrusion of hostile foreign powers and a Christian assault on Islam – began agitating for an all-out uprising. Numerous Sahrawi tribes sided with him and began conducting raids against the Spaniards – and against the French in southern Morocco. Ma al-'Aynayn then established a 'ribat' (a base, retreat, or a small fortification) in Samara with the aim of using it as a springboard for attacks on the colonialists. In support of this effort, the Moroccan sultan Abdelaziz – meanwhile under massive pressure from the French – provided him with craftsmen, materials, financing and arms, and then appointed him a Qaid ('commander' or 'leader').[2]

While the Sultan of Morocco finally gave in to Paris, in 1904, Ma al-'Aynayn continued to resist. During the same year, he proclaimed a holy war ('jihad') and – claiming to be acting on behalf of the Sultan although the latter had no direct control over him, but then also entered into cooperation with the colonial powers – began seeking support from other European powers, including the German Empire. The result of his effort was a fighting force of around 6,000 that resisted the French and Spanish invasions of southern Morocco and Río de Oro. Emboldened by minor success, in 1910 Ma al-'Aynayn led his army north with the aim of toppling the new Sultan Moulay Abd el-Hafiz and uniting Morocco under his command. However, he was defeated by the French on 23 June 1910, and died only a few months later. Two years later, the French imposed the Treaty of Fez upon the Moroccans: according to this, Sultan Abd el-Hafiz preserved his family's position, but conceded most of his country's sovereignty to France as a protectorate. Nominally, this meant that France was to protect Morocco against external threats only. In practice, the French ruled absolutely, ignoring the Sultan and his ministers, and foremost failed to protect Morocco's territorial integrity: they granted Spain the right to enlarge its enclaves in northern Morocco and then grab another – the so-called Tafraya Strip – in the south, in addition to their control over Río de Oro.

Contrary to the Sultan of Morocco, the Sahrawis continued resisting. Ma al-'Aynayn's son, Ahmed al-Hiba (also known as 'The Blue Sultan') continued the legacy of his father. In 1912, he proclaimed a jihad and sparked a general uprising in the Spanish Sahara and southern Morocco. Widely recognized as the Sultan of Taroudannt, Agadir, and Dades and Draa regions, he was reinforced by thousands of tribal warriors: on 18 August 1912 he entered Marrakesh and was proclaimed a Sultan there, too. Keen to secure what they had gained through the Treaty of Fez, the French were alarmed at the possibility of al-Hiba undermining the legacy of their puppet-sultan. They rushed a column of 5,000 troops, supported by about a dozen each of field guns and machine guns, under the command of Colonel Charles Mangin, into a counterattack. On 6 September 1912, the two armies clashed in the Battle of Sidi Bou Othman, about 40 kilometres outside Marrakesh, where the tribal warriors were promptly subjected to the devastating firepower of the French Army. After suffering horrific losses, Hiba's forces withdrew south. Al-Hiba never gave up the struggle, however: his warriors continued to harass the Europeans until his death on 23 June 1919.

Free of organised resistance thanks to the French, the Spaniards continued their conquests: although struggling while vying for control of the entire area until establishing a garrison in Samara, and conquering the hinterland in 1934 – primarily through forcing previously nomadic inhabitants to settle within certain 'protected' areas, thus introducing urbanisation – they eventually managed to firm their grip over Río de Oro in the north, and Saguia el-Hamra in the south. In 1946, Madrid issued a decree that separated the Spanish Sahara from the Spanish Protectorate in Morocco, and a year later the first phosphate reserves were discovered.

The organised resistance of the Sahrawis was suppressed for only a generation. In 1947-1950, the long-simmering crisis between the French and the Moroccans culminated as Sultan Mohammed V – at that time primarily supported by the far-right, conservative, monarchist, and nationalist movement that developed into the Istiqlal Party (Hizb al-Istiqlal) – began openly challenging Paris. The French attempted to appoint a new Sultan only to cause mass unrest and an armed uprising in southern Morocco, further bolstered by a near-simultaneous uprising in neighbouring Algeria in 1954. Although their armed forces successfully suppressed the insurgency, the politicians in Paris were forced into a realisation that the game was lost: on 2 March 1956, they released Morocco into independence. Almost immediately, King Mohammed V and Crown Prince Hassan laid claims to the remaining Spanish possessions in Morocco, including the Río de Oro and Saquia el-Hamra. Local tribes then grouped into the Liberation Army that moved north to besiege the Spanish-Moroccan enclave of Ifni, provoking another French military intervention: de-facto abandoned even by King Mohammed V, the Liberation Army was defeated during the Ifni War of 1958, and the French and Spanish forces then also mopped up all of the Spanish possessions further south. Nevertheless, King Mohammed established himself as a national hero, and not only continued demanding Ifni, the Tafraya strip and Spanish-controlled areas in the south: indeed, when the French released Mauritania into independence, on 28 November 1960, he strongly protested and seriously contemplated an invasion of this country (whose nationalists had begun claiming stakes in the western Sahara about three years earlier). Although supported by the Arab League, the option of a Moroccan invasion of Mauritania proved unrealistic and was finally frustrated when the latter country was admitted to the United Nations (UN) in 1960. Tensions with Spain remained high until Madrid decided to formally return the Tafraya Strip in May 1958, and then also Ifni to Morocco, on 30 June 1969, though retaining Ceuta and Melilla in the north.[3]

Meanwhile, the Spanish colonial authorities not only settled most of the Sahrawi population in protected areas but united the territories of Río de Oro and Saquia el Hamra into the Spanish overseas province of Spanish Sahara in January 1958, and then launched a major attempt to improve the economic situation. Correspondingly,

A map of Spanish Sahara as published in the local press in the 1950s. (via Tom Cooper)

Phosphate mine of Bou Craa, as seen from space in 2000: the starting point of the conveyor-belt to el-Aaiún is visible in the left upper centre. In its latest version, the latter is capable of transporting 2,000 tonnes of phosphate rock per hour. (NASA)

in 1960 they granted rights to 17 foreign companies to explore suspected oil reserves. Instead of oil, the exploration found additional and extensive sources of high-grade phosphates in the Bou Craa region, southeast of el-Aaiún, and high-quality iron ore deposits near Agracha, in the north-east of the territory – opposite Tindouf in Algeria. Quantities of titanium, vanadium, bauxite, copper, zinc, manganese and uranium were also reported. The economic development resulted in dramatic changes within the diminutive native population of Spanish Sahara: the Spanish language became common and the Catholic faith became widespread, prompting Madrid to decide to retain the overseas province. Interpreting such developments as an affront, Morocco began deploying 'irregulars' – actually elements of its armed forces, reinforced by tribal warriors – in raids and kidnappings of foreign workers, eventually prompting the Spaniards to deploy up to 20,000 troops and significant contingents of the Spanish Air Force (*Ejército del Aire*, EdA) in the territory.[4]

Natural Resources

From this period onwards, not only Moroccan irredentism, or the emerging nationalism of the Sahrawis, but especially the issue of mineral wealth began to play a crucial role in the fate of Western Sahara. Certainly enough, it is superimposed over all other issues in some accounts, and downplayed or at least described as 'exaggerated' in other accounts. However, the laws of biology and physics, and known statistics all speak a very clear language.

All life on Earth, and so also all agricultural production, depends on phosphorus. The element is found in phosphate rock: the latter accounts for about one third of the phosphoric acid used to produce fertilizers (foremost

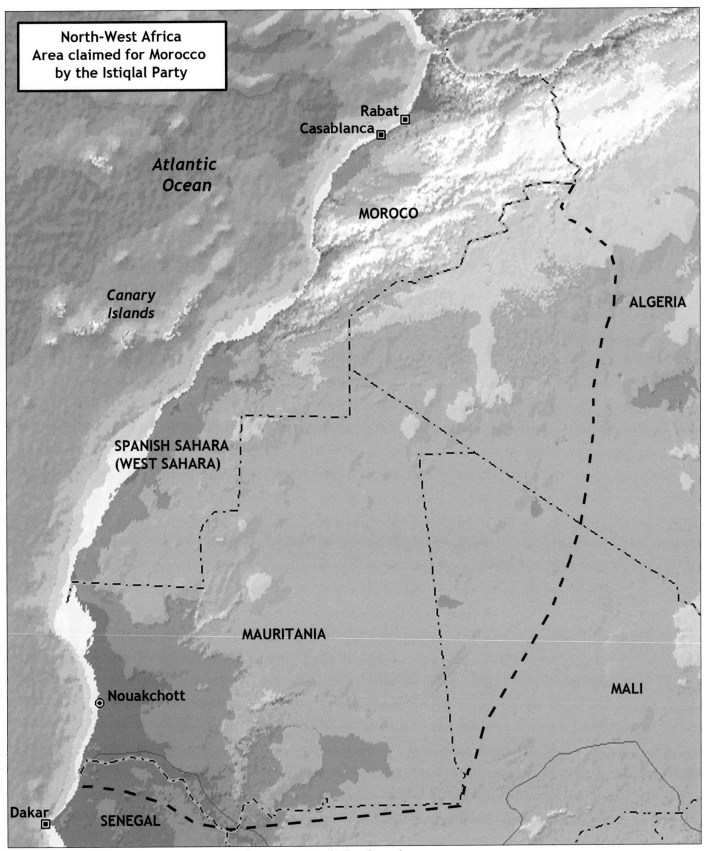

A map depicting the area claimed by Hizb al-Istiqlal for Morocco. (Map by Tom Cooper)

diammonium phosphate and triple superphosphate). The rapidly accelerating growth of the human population that began in the 1960s and 1970s created an ever-bigger demand for food, and thus for fertilizers. Known reserves of phosphate rock in major producing countries – mainly the USA and the People's Republic of China (PRC) – were constantly dwindling and extraction decreasing. Thus, a major new source of this vital mineral was more than welcome on the international markets, but especially so in North America and India.

The Spanish consortium Fosfatos de Bucraa S.A. (also known as 'Phosboucraa' or 'Fos Bucraa'), launched the extraction and exportation of the high-quality phosphate deposits from the mine at Bou Craa in 1972. This ran via the world's largest conveyor belt – stretching over 98 kilometres (61 miles) – to the port of el-

Aaiún. The mine initially had an annual production capacity of three million tonnes, but was estimated to be capable of an output of 10 million tonnes annually within 5-10 years if the necessary investments were made.[5] While this figure might appear diminutive under modern-day circumstances, it should be kept in mind that by 1973 the Spanish Sahara and Morocco accounted for no less than 17 per cent of world-wide production of phosphates. Ever since, this rate increased significantly: it reached 27 per cent by 1980, and then nearly 50 per cent by the end of the same decade. Indeed, by 1980, Morocco became the supplier of over 70 per cent of Western Europe's imports of phosphate rock and, when prices of that mineral boomed in 2008, the related income accounted for 33 per cent of the country's exports, earning US$5 billion. Presently, Morocco is estimated to be in control of over 85 per cent of the world's reserves of phosphate rock, and to have as much leverage in determining its prices as the Organization of the Petroleum Exporting Countries (OPEC) has over oil prices.[6]

Therefore, control over the sources of phosphate rock in Western Sahara is a factor that cannot be ignored: it is apparent that they played an important role in the events of 1975-1991, and ever since – and this irrespective of how diversified the Spanish, and then the Moroccan economies might have been then, or are nowadays.[7]

Stubborn Franco

Certainly enough, as of the 1960s and early 1970s many of the above-mentioned issues still lay in the future. To counter the Moroccan irredentism, in May 1963 Madrid created the Jama'a (or 'Djemma'), the General Assembly of the Sahara with 82 seats, which was supposed to represent Sahrawi interests, and held the first provincial elections: three representatives of the Jama'a then took their seats at the *Cortes Generales* (Spanish parliament). Disgusted, Morocco referred the issue of this territory to the UN, insisting on the history of its control over the territory. In 1964, the UN urged Spain to decolonize Spanish Sahara, but Franco remained stubborn. After publicly announcing the scale of phosphate deposits in the Bou Craa area, he set up a referendum in which the Sahrawis endorsed the Spanish occupation in 1966, and then increased the number of their seats in the Cortes to six. However, the Jama'a included only tribal leaders that collaborated with the Spaniards, and thus rapidly lost any semblance of credibility. Moreover, political demonstrations staged by a group of students naming themselves the Saharan Liberation Front, in June 1970, were brutally suppressed by the Spanish authorities, prompting the nationalists to start recruiting and organising an armed guerrilla organisation. In 1971, the first cell of Sahrawi armed resistance came into being in the form of FREPOLISARIO, which was then reformed as the POLISARIO in the course of a meeting of student activists of the Reguibat tribe at Ain Bentili on 10 May 1973. Ten days later, all seven POLISARIO members led by the organisation's second Secretary General, ran their first attack on the Spanish military in the territory. Later during the same year, the original cadre of the movement was reinforced by several members of the Delim tribe that had served with the Spanish Army and police and brought with them the first significant quantity of firearms and ammunition. While the Reguibat and the Delim were to carry the burden of the initial armed uprising, over time all of the Sahrawi tribes de-facto joined their uprising.

Meanwhile, in 1972, a new party became involved in this affair in the form of Colonel Muammar el-Qadhaffi, the Libyan leader, who announced he would back a liberation war in the Spanish Sahara and provided several – still rather small – shipments of firearms. The POLISARIO thus grew slowly and only gradually began

General Francisco Franco, as seen in 1969. His stubborn refusal to give up Spanish Sahara, but also his sudden demise in 1975, both proved fateful for the future of this territory – and that of the mass of its inhabitants. (Revista Argentina)

operating in small groups mounted on camels, and its primary means of activity consisted of mining desert tracks or ambushing small convoys. Unsurprisingly, on 26 January 1974, it suffered its first major setback at Guelb Lahmmar, when the Spanish forces managed to capture several of its insurgents. It was only after the second congress of the POLISARIO, held in late August of the same year, that the movement not only announced the goal of full independence, but also began receiving significant support from Libya. With the help of the latter, on 20 October 1974, it launched the first major attack that rendered the conveyor belt from Bou Craa to el-Aaiún inoperable.

This action took place only months after the military coup in Portugal of April 1974 (also known as the 'Carnation Revolution'): Lisbon's subsequent decision to grant its African territories independence convinced King Hassan II of Morocco that Spain would not wish to remain long as the only colonial power in Africa, and he once again pressed Madrid to pull out of the Spanish Sahara. On 29 August 1974, the government of Spain notified the UN Secretary General of its intention to hold a referendum on self-determination of its overseas province. Rabat promptly seized the opportunity to reassert its claims to the territory, aggressively arguing that the pre-colonial era Moroccan rulers intermittently exercised control over the area. Mauritania began voicing its own territorial claims, causing a brief period of tensions: a reconciliation was effected by September 1974, when Rabat and Nouakchott agreed to submit their case to the International Court of Justice (ICJ) for a legal opinion – which was actually a step initiated by Morocco out of a fear that the Sahrawis would opt for independence – while King

Hassan II convinced Madrid to postpone the referendum.

Although the Spanish dictator Franco was meanwhile aged, as of late 1974 he was still in control and thus Madrid remained stubborn. Determined to increase pressure, in November 1974 King Hassan II ordered a deployment of four battalions of the FAR – including a squadron equipped with French-made EBR.75 armoured cars, and another equipped with AMX-13 light tanks – to the border with Spanish Sahara. While most of these units were in their new positions by late December, the build-up was subsequently continued, eventually bringing the troop strength along the southern border to 20,000. Spain reacted promptly: in November 1974, the EdA reinforced its units in the area by detaching between eight and ten Northrop F-5A fighter-bombers and RF-5A reconnaissance fighters of its 21st Wing to Gando AB, on the Canary Islands. From there, a flight of four was regularly forward-deployed to el-Aaiún AB. The arrival of the F-5As greatly improved the reaction time of the EdA to any calls for help from the ground forces because these jets were much faster than old North American T-6Ds present at el-Aaiún since earlier times. Moreover, their pilots were trained for providing close air support by night, too. At least as important was the presence

An RF-5A of the 21st Wing at Gando AB. The Spanish-built RF-5As retained the combat capability of the F-5A (including two 20mm cannon installed in the hose), but flew their missions over southern Morocco unarmed: in the event that one was shot down or crashed, Madrid would thus be able to explain that the aircraft was on a 'routine training mission', and crossed the border 'due to a navigational mistake'. (EdA, via Albert Grandolini)

The pilot of one of the Spanish T-6Ds seen sitting below his mount, while on alert at el-Aaiún. (EdA, via Albert Grandolini)

of RF-5As, which flew low-altitude reconnaissance operations – frequently north of the Moroccan border. They enabled the Spanish commanders to precisely pinpoint positions of major FAR units and supply depots, and thus precisely estimate the possible routes of Moroccan incursions.

After bolstering its troop-presence in Spanish Sahara to about 21,000, on 16 January 1975 Madrid announced it would suspend the referendum and instead give evidence to the ICJ. The Spanish forces in the territory meanwhile included 5,000 from the Spanish Foreign Legion, and an entire mechanised brigade equipped with 35 M48A1 and 18 AMX.30 main battle tanks (MBTs), supported by French-made AML-60 and AML-90 armoured cars, M113 and Panhard M3 APCs, and M109 self-propelled howitzers. Moreover, a mobile Westinghouse AN/TPS-43 radar – one of the most advanced systems in the world at the time – was deployed at el-Aaiún for

early warning and ground control, while air defences of that air base, and the one at Villa Cisneros, were strengthened through the deployment of 16 40mm Bofors L40/70 anti-aircraft guns, 12 radar-directed 35mm Oerlikon 35/90 anti-aircraft guns, and an unknown quantity of 20mm anti-aircraft guns. While most of these troops and equipment were brought to Spanish Sahara by transport ships, aircraft such as Boeing KC-97L tankers of the 123rd Squadron (12 Wing EdA) also played an important role in this deployment.

Moroccan-Spanish Stand-Off

As the stand-off on the border between Morocco and the Spanish Sahara continued, not only POLISARIO guerrillas, but also regular Moroccan troops and then their proxies became involved in attacks on Spanish forces. On 22 January 1975, Rabat began deploying pseudo-Sahrawi insurgents disguised as the Front for Liberation

One of 16 Bofors L40/70 anti-aircraft guns deployed for protection of the Villa Cisneros airfield in late 1974. (EdA, via Albert Grandolini)

A T-54 of the 3°GEB as seen in position close to the border of the Spanish Sahara. (via E.C.)

in an attempt to avoid a direct military confrontation. On 26 March 1975, alleged Moroccan agents planted bombs at several Spanish military posts in Ceuta in northern Morocco. In April 1975, warships of the Moroccan Navy began harassing Spanish fishing vessels all along the coast of north-western Africa, forcing the Spanish *Armada* to escort trawlers with a permanent taskforce based in the Canary Islands. To enable them to intervene quickly, many of the Spanish warships carried Agusta-Bell AB.212 helicopters of the 3rd Squadron, or heavier Sikorsky SH-3D Sea Kings of the 5th Squadron Naval Aviation. It was in support of such operations that one of EdA's Hispano Aviacion HA-200D Saettta light strikers crashed into the sea, on 23 June 1975, killing its pilot, Captain Angel Feijoo Jimenez.

On 10 May 1975, a motorized infantry unit of the FAR crossed the border near Sequen, but quickly withdrew when overflown by a patrol of T-6Ds and two Bell UH-1H gunships. Only a day later, a unit of the *Tropas Nomadas* mutinied near Mahbes: the troops took 15 Spanish officers and other ranks hostage before defecting to the POLISARIO.[8] Despite an intensive search and rescue operation that lasted for three days and was supported by EdA T-6Ds (two of which made a search flight over northern Mauritania, too), Dornier Do.27s and UH-1Hs, the group managed to reach Tindouf in Algeria. The reason was relatively simple: although the POLISARIO still counted fewer than 1,000 active combatants, it already had a vast network of informants and supporters, with the help of which its small units were able to avoid the Spanish pursuit.

On 13 May, a Soviet-made 9K32 Strela-2 (ASCC/NATO-codename 'SA-7 Grail') portable air defence system (MANPAD) was fired from the Moroccan side of the border at a pair of UH-1Hs led by Captain Serra: both helicopters dived to very low altitude, thus evading this attack, which alarmed the Spanish authorities into providing all of their crews with additional training in evasion manoeuvres. Pilots of T-6Ds, who usually operated at low altitudes, decided to fly their 'observation passes' even lower, reasoning that this was the best protection against SA-7s: this in turn resulted in

and Unity (*Frente de Liberación y de la Unidad*, FLU) for what were little more than terrorist attacks. The first target was el-Aaiún, where three bombs were detonated, causing 37 casualties. The core of the FLU was a camel-mounted battalion home-based in Tantan, staffed by 257 Sahrawis – mostly defectors from units of the Spanish Army, commanded by Moroccan officers and non-commissioned officers (NCOs). By early 1975, the unit was reinforced to about 500 and expanded into four battalions. However, while the POLISARIO ran its hit-and-run attacks with great success, the Moroccan-sponsored quasi-guerrillas didn't. On 23 March the unit that attacked the Spanish outpost in Ambala was easily repulsed.

While the POLISARIO suffered its first combat fatalities in a clash with the Spaniards, Rabat next re-directed its efforts elsewhere several accidents, such as when one of the Texans hit the roof of an army vehicle, but managed to limp back home with a broken propeller. Later on, in October 1975, another T-6D collided with three camels while inspecting a caravan underway in the Cap Bojador area.

Elsewhere, in May 1975 the Spanish Police arrested a group of 14 members of the FLU in el-Aaiún: under interrogation, they admitted being organised and supported by Morocco. Finally, late the same month a bomb blew up a café in the Spanish enclave of Melilla, causing numerous injuries. Although the true nature of the FLU was thus revealed in public, on 4 June 1975, King Hassan II launched his quasi-guerrillas in an attack on Edcheria, which was easily repulsed – also thanks to close air support of EdA T-6Ds and HA-200Ds. Thus, three days later the Moroccans deployed a squadron of 46 regular troops to attack the Spanish outpost in Mabbe. Warned by timely intelligence, the position was reinforced by two complete infantry companies – including one from the 4th Regiment of the Spanish Foreign Legion. When the Moroccans attacked, they found themselves subjected to vastly superior firepower, including a well-planned mortar barrage, and then subjected to repeated air strikes of the T-6Ds and F-5As. Understanding their retreat route was cut, the survivors were then convinced by their Sahrawi guides – who were all the time in touch with the Spanish intelligence services – to surrender: the Spaniards thus captured all of their six light trucks, all 35 AK-47 assault rifles, 3 RPG-7 rocket propelled grenades, one 12.7mm machine gun and four SA-7 launchers with missiles. In the course of a subsequent press conference, Madrid thus fully exposed the direct Moroccan involvement in the escalating conflict.

Infiltrations continued, nevertheless, as did the insurgent activity. Indeed, when King Hassan ordered another attack, on 21 June, and his troops even briefly occupied the village of Tah that night, they were quickly forced to withdraw by a counterattack by motorised Spanish troops supported by two UH-1Hs and two T-6Ds. On 7 July 1975, the Spaniards ran a sweep searching for guerrillas in the area around Tins, west of Guelta Zemmour, where their ground forces were supported by two Bell OH-58s, three UH-1Hs, and one Aerospatiale SA.316B Alouette III gunship. The latter was damaged when one of its doors suddenly fell off and was forced to limp back to base. The operation bore no success. On 22 July 1975, a patrol of three UH-1Hs escorted by another Alouette landed troops near the Hagunia River to search for a group of FLU infiltrators. Three

SH-3D Sea Kings of the 5th Squadron of the Spanish naval aviation, on board the Armada's sole aircraft carrier, *Dedalo*, in 1975. (Albert Grandolini Collection)

days later, while searching for a group of Moroccan infiltrators that had attacked the Spanish outpost near Samara, four T-6Ds led by Captain Avila found a group of around 20 vehicles about two kilometres south of the border. The Moroccans promptly fired two SA-7s: Captain Avila led his formation into a hard dive towards the

AMX.30 MBTs of the Spanish Army moving into positions along the border with Morocco in early 1975. (Albert Grandolini Collection)

One of several groups of Moroccan Army troops captured by the Spaniards in early 1975. (Albert Grandolini Collection)

deck, avoiding both missiles, and reported the attack. However, as the T-6Ds turned back to open fire, they were recalled and ordered to let the Moroccans escape. On 27 July, a flight of four HA-200Ds, supported one OH-58 and two UH-1Hs in quelling another Moroccan attack on the Tah outpost. On 4 August, the Spaniards had to repel a Moroccan attack on the Hawzah oasis, which caused three casualties, and on 10 August they launched a search operation for a reported group of infiltrators in the Lagunia area, that was to go on for nearly three weeks. One of the Alouette IIIs involved in the latter operation crashed on 12 August, due to a sudden loss of power, but its pilot, Captain Arroba, and the gunner, Sergeant Perez, survived. Eight days later, the Moroccan infiltrators were finally cornered and – after a series of air strikes – forced to surrender. On the same day, 20 August, a radar contact was detected some 20 kilometres inside Spanish airspace, and a patrol of two T-6Ds was vectored to investigate. They detected a lonesome Agusta-Bell 205 that promptly turned around and flew to the north: the Spanish subsequently assumed that this was used for dropping supplies to infiltrators – a task for which the Moroccans subsequently also deployed their MH.152 Broussard light transports.

Actually, by September, the FAR restricted its operations inside Spanish Sahara to laying mines on the main roads – which usually hit civilian vehicles. Spanish military casualties thus remained limited: five troops were killed by a mine in the Tah area on 24 June, and two were killed by another mine near Haunia on 2 October, another vehicle was destroyed and one soldier killed by a mine near Tammboscal on 18 October.

Grand Finale

Ultimately, both the incursions by Moroccan regulars and the FLU left little lasting impression upon Madrid – principally because the politicians there were preoccupied with different issues, but also because their armed forces and security agencies easily prevented or overpowered most of the attacks. Left on his own, the last governor of the Spanish Sahara, General Frederico Gomez de Salazar, became convinced that the Moroccans were about to invade, and thus decided to change his strategy. Instead of maintaining forward defences, starting from 4 October 1975, he withdrew his forces 10 kilometres (6.2 miles) from all the outposts along the border, thus creating a 'no mans land', while concentrating his most powerful units for the protection of urban areas along the coast. El-Aaiún was thus defended by no less than two brigade-sized task forces (Task

Force Lince, in the north, and Task Force Gacela, in the east), each centred on a regiment of the Spanish Foreign Legion. The third task force consisted of paratroopers supported by tanks and self-propelled artillery and was kept in reserve in case the Moroccans breached the defences. In turn, the Spanish armed forces left both the coastal road leading to the border, and the road linking el-Aaiún with Hagunia lightly protected: these areas were heavily mined and screened by two battalions of mechanised infantry, supported by armoured cars and artillery.

Salazar's further actions were overtaken by developments on the diplomatic scene, starting from 12-19 May 1975, when a UN mission to Spanish Sahara encountered mass manifestations of public support for the POLISARIO – and clear opposition to unification with either Morocco or Mauritania. Madrid was now in a quandary: with Franco's terminal illness rendering him incapable of arbitrating between diverse wings of his government, there was a growing uncertainty about what action to take. To his successors, there appeared to be two solutions:

1) grant independence to the Sahrawis while hoping these would install a government that would safeguard the Spanish economic pre-eminence, or at least respect the possession of the Bou Craa mine, or,

2) expect what was perceived as a 'left-leaning' POLISARIO, supported by a 'revolutionary' and 'socialist' Algeria, and an openly anti-Western Libya – both of which were widely perceived as Soviet clients – to accede to power.

In the typically short-sighted fashion of so many Western governments – especially so during the Cold War – the faction arguing for the need to 'contain the spread of Communism in Africa' won the day. On 23 May 1975, Madrid announced its intention, '… to transfer the territory in [the] near future to any countries of the area fulfilling legitimate aspirations over it, but by respecting the aspiring sovereignty of its inhabitants.'

To say that this contradictive statement caused chaos would be an understatement. While diplomats were setting up one meeting after the other in the UN's HQ in New York, and Spanish representatives established direct contacts to the POLISARIO's representatives in Algiers, the uncertainty over the future led to mass desertion of the Sahrawi troops still serving with the *Tropas Nomadas* and the Police: most went straight to the insurgency, together with their weapons. Unsurprisingly, the POLISARIO was the first to react: with the help of local inhabitants, in early June 1975 it attacked and secured the Spanish outpost in Guelta Zemour, with the *Tropas Nomadas* offering only minimal resistance before changing sides. As a consequence of this affair, Madrid then ordered a disbandment of all the remaining units staffed by the natives, thus driving even more of the Sahrawis into the hands of the POLISARIO.

Sensing a threat to his designs, in September 1975 King Hassan II raised the stakes by ordering the deployment of the two most-powerful armoured formations of his army: the 1° and 3° Armoured Squadrons (*groupe d'escadron blindé*, GEB) to the border,

King Hassan II of Morocco, as seen in 1981. (Dutch National Archives)

each equipped with Czechoslovak-made T-54 MBTs.[9] This was a threat that the Spaniards took very seriously because they expected the Moroccan T-54s to be equipped with infra-red sights for nocturnal operations – which the FAR's MBTs lacked.[10] Still, once the Spaniards convinced themselves, they acted consequently: the EdA's T-6D pilots received a crash course in night attacks on enemy armour, under the guidance of Do.27s that acted as forward air controllers (FACs), and with the use of 88mm unguided rockets. Once the pilots were ready, their commanders staged a fire-power demonstration at the Amsequir firing range (about 20 kilometres from el-Aaiún), during which the T-6Ds also deployed napalm bombs, while Alouette IIIs used French-made AS.11 anti-tank guided missiles. Even then, this was a mere face-saving measure, because Madrid soon lost heart and decided to withdraw: the arrival of the 1° and 3° GEB on the border set the stage for the showdown in Western Sahara.

Chapter 2
Moroccan Armed Forces of the mid-1970s

As much as the external and internal pressure in Spanish Sahara had been building-up for decades, when the situation exploded in late 1975, related developments took nearly everybody by surprise. One exception was King Hassan II of Morocco, whose position was actually quite ironic. Although making the above-mentioned claims to not only all of the Spanish possessions in Morocco, Spanish Sahara, and to Mauritania and parts of Algeria and Mali since at least 1956, and despite traditional – and quite extensive – support by France and the USA, he knew very well that the Moroccan Armed Forces (*Forces Armées Royale*, FAR) were hopelessly out of condition to launch, run and win a major war against the Spanish armed forces in the western Sahara. The reasons for this were the developments of the previous few years.

Take, then Give
As described in *Volume 1*, officers of the Royal Armed Forces of Morocco (*Forces Armées Royale*, FAR) had staged two coup attempts against King Hussein II, in 1971 and 1972. As a consequence, all the cautious and protracted development of the FAR since 1956 was ruined in a matter of less than 14 months: especially after the third coup attempt, the Army and the Royal Air Force (*Forces Royales Air*, FRA) were subjected to a series of draconic purges, with traumatic consequences. Hassan II abolished the positions of Minister of Defence and Major-General of the FAR, took over direct control of the armed forces, disbanded all brigade-sized formations of the army, and even an entire air base (essentially a 'wing') of the FRA. Ultimately, the armed forces lost nearly all of their top commanders and administrators, and hundreds – if not thousands – of officers and other ranks. Indeed, this process reached such proportions that US intelligence assessments from early 1973 questioned the ability of the FAR to resist any Algerian military invasion for longer than

a few days.[1]

Of course, preoccupied with running the country, King Hassan II lacked the time to care about the reform and then every-day operations of his armed forces. Therefore, the latter affairs were actually in the hands of Major-General Ahmad Dlimi, who was in control of all three branches – army, air force, and navy – from the General Command in Rabat.[2]

Over the following two years, Dlimi took care to completely re-organize the FAR. Until the coup attempt of July 1971, the army was organized into five military regions (Rabat-Kenitra, Taza, Agadir, Meknes and Marrakesh), each with its own headquarters (HQ) and largely autonomous from the General Command in Rabat. Major ground units were organized into two infantry divisions, six manoeuvre brigades (each with one tank, one infantry and one artillery battalion), and three specialist brigades. After the coup, all the military regions, both divisions and all six manoeuvre brigades were disbanded, and all the remaining units subjected to the direct control of the General Command. The only brigade-sized units left intact were the Royal Guard Brigade, the 1st Paratrooper Brigade, and the Light Security Brigade. Instead of military districts, three principal commands – all subjected to the General Command (also General Staff) – were created:

- the Command Element controlled the army units, the navy and air force;
- the Directorate of General Studies advised and coordinated senior staff officers responsible for drawing up overall defence plans; and
- the Logistics Command, responsible for supporting and supplying all the units.[3]

Officer training was run by the Royal Military Academy at Meknes (all cadets were required to complete their first year there,

Table 1: FAR Equipment (Ground Forces), 1975[9]		
Type	Quanttity	Notes
M48	50	US-origin, MBT
T-54	50	USSR-origin, MBT
AMX-13	120	French-origin, light tank
EBR.75	36	French-origin, armoured car
AML-60/90	50	French-origin, armoured car
M3	40	US-origin, half-track APC
OT-62/64	95	Czechoslovak-origin; tracked and wheeled APCs, respectively
UR-416	30	German-origin, wheeled APC
M114	18	US-origin, 155mm howitzer
AMX-105	30	French-origin, self-propelled (tracked) 105mm artillery piece

The most important units of the FAR during this period were the Royal Guard Brigade and the 1st Paratrooper Brigade. Staffed by officers and other ranks subjected to ferocious training, they served not only the purpose of bodyguards for the king and his family, but also as a rapid intervention force. The work of both units was supported by the 11,000-strong *Sûreté Nationale*, the top intelligence service responsible for internal security and political intelligence and including a 3,000-strong 'reserve police'. The third linchpin of the de-facto 'praetorian guards' of the Moroccan king was the 30,000-strong Maghzen, a 'popular militia': consisting of three elements (administrative, municipal, and mobile commands), the Maghzen were armed with light firearms only – foremost Beretta-designed sub machine guns manufactured under licence in Morocco – and usually described as 'poorly-equipped and led'. However, this force proved its worth whenever deployed for its primary purpose, which was suppression of any kind of internal unrest.[6]

The rest of the FAR was foremost a 'force in being' that had to 'redeem itself' after all the shame of 1971 and 1972.

Moroccan troops with one of the T-54s acquired from Czechoslovakia in the late 1960s, during their deployment in Syria on the north-eastern side of the Golan Heights, in October 1973. Most of the veterans of this experience were subsequently grouped into the 3°GEB, one of the two primary armoured units of the FAR. (via E.C.)

irrespectively of the branch to which they were assigned), and was heavily dependent on foreign assistance (especially in the case of the air force and the navy), while all conscripted personnel were trained at centres in el-Hajeb, Sidi Slimane, and Ben Guerir. Higher military educational facilities were available in the form of the General Staff School at Kenitra, the NCO Academy at Ahermoummou (Meknes), the Artillery School at Fez, the Paratroop Training Centre at Rabat/ Sale AB, Signal School at Rabat, the material School at Casablanca, the Lycee Militaire at Kenitra, and the Engineering School at Tetouan.[4]

By 1975, the 60,000 troops assigned to the army were dispersed into a large number of – nominally – independent battalions, each with a specialised role, and frequently organised in not only an unusual, but even a fashion unique to Morocco. The purpose of this structure was to prevent any of the commanding officers (COs) establishing their own power base and thus threatening the king's rule again. Therefore, there was next to no coordination and very little lateral coordination between specific units. Indeed, the chain of command was kept intentionally complex with the aim of making any further coup attempt at least difficult, if not impossible to organize and run.[5]

Theoretically the strongest amongst the manoeuvre units were the above-mentioned armoured squadrons, each of which was usually equipped with between 35 and 60 MBTs, 30 armoured personnel carriers (APCs), and various reconnaissance vehicles (for a list of heavy weapons systems of the FAR as of the mid-1970s, and their quantities, see Table 1). However, the mass of manpower was organized into static, sector infantry battalions (*bataillon d'infanterie de secteur*, BIS) and garrison battalions (*bataillon de garnison*, BG), which were infantry formations responsible for the protection of specific towns (for a list of Moroccan military unit designations and their abbreviations, see Table 2). Even far more powerful and – nominally – mobile units, for example the 6th Motorised Infantry Regiment (*6° régiment d'infanterie motorisée*, 6° RIM), had strict orders not to move outside their garrisons without explicit orders from Rabat. Moreover, while having their organic transportation companies, they lacked the vehicles necessary to move the entire unit and its equipment at one time.[7]

It was only later during the war in Western Sahara, that the FAR began assembling and then operating brigade-sized formations again (for an order of battle of the FAR ground units deployed in the Western Sahara since 1975, see Table 4). The fact was that

Table 2: FAR Unit Abbreviations[10]

Abbreviation	French Designation	Notes
Place d'armes	Military HQ	HQ responsible for all military operations in the geographic area assigned to it, usually – but not always – located in the largest local urban area
Secteur	Sector	HQ responsible for operational duties in the given geographic area; could – but not necessarily – include numerous sub-sectors
BA-FRA	base aérienne FRA	air base
BA-annexe	Base aérienne annexe	forward base of the FRA, usually subordinated to the nearest BA-FRA
BG	bataillon de garnison	garrison battalion
BIM	bataillon d'infanterie motorisée	motorised infantry battalion
BISMAR	bataillon d'infanterie de marine	marine infantry battalion
BIS	bataillon d'infanterie de secteur	sector infantry battalion
BM	bataillon Méharis	Méhari battalion
BN	base navale	naval base
BP	Bataillon de parachutiste	parachute battalion
BRIMeca	brigade d'infanterie mécanisée	mechanised infantry brigade
BRIMoto	brigade d'infanterie motorisée	motorised infantry brigade
BSI	bataillon de soutien intendance	battalion support group
BSMAT	bataillon de soutien munition	hardware support battalion
BSMUN	bataillon de soutien matériel	ammunition support battalion
BSS	bataillon de soutien sanitaire	medical support battalion
BT	bataillon de transmission	signals battalion
CIPC	Centre d'Instruction Pilotes de Combat	Training Centre for Combat Pilots (fighter-weapons school of the FRA)
CMV	commando marche verte	Green March Commando (special forces unit)
FAR	Forces Armées Royale	Royal Armed Forces (of Morocco)
FRA	Forces Royales Air	Royal Air Force of Morocco (official title since 1990s)
GAR	groupe d'artillerie royale	royal artillery group; first GAR was established in 1976
GEB	groupe d'escadron blindé	armoured squadron or group
GFT	groupe de transport	transport group
GLS	groupe léger de sécurité	light security group
GMM	Groupe Mahsen mobile	Maghzen Mobile Group
GTIA	groupe tactique inter-armes	task force
GTr	groupe de transport	transport group
HPM	hôpital militaire	military hospital
MIR	regiment d'infanterie mécanisée	mechanised infantry regiment
PC/GMM	poste de commandement groupe Mahsen mobile	Mobile Group's Command Post
RIM	regiment d'infanterie motorisée	motorised infantry regiment

instead of keeping the armed forces busy with their regular routine military training, for much of this period Dlimi had the FAR constructing roads, bridges, dams, housing, schools, dispensaries, hospitals, and irrigation systems, and every year providing civilian-type of training for up to 7,500 recruits. These efforts were at least reasonably successful: contrary to earlier times, the armed forces eventually began enjoying considerable support and prestige with the population. On the negative side, due to the lack of qualified officers and funding, but also because of the rampant corruption within its higher-ranks, much of the ground forces were suffering from the lack of logistical support: spare parts and tyres for vehicles were especially rare.[8]

Safran Mirages

The FRA of the mid-1970s was commanded by Colonel Mohammad Kabbaj, the virtual saviour of King Hassan II during the coup of 1972. Kabaj controlled a force of about 3,000 men via three small departments (Operations; Personnel and Training, Materiel and Supply; and Inspection). His biggest problem was the lack of trained pilots and ground crews and he dedicated most of his efforts to its reconstruction and making it self-reliant: as a result of the August 1972 coup attempt, over 200 airmen – the bulk of the operational fighter force at Kenitra AB – was arrested: the number of pilots qualified for Northrop F-5A/B Freedom Fighters dropped from 21 to 5.[11]

With the help of extensive financing provided by Shah Reza

Pahlavi II of Iran, and US advisors, the FRA of 1973-1975 trained enough technicians to develop a fairly good maintenance capability for piston-powered aircraft and helicopters in the form of the General Workshop (*Atelier Magasin General*, AMG) at Casablanca/Anfa airfield. The work of the AMG was supported by French advisors, who provided instruction on Douglas C-47 transports, while the Belgian company SABENA was providing advice in maintenance of Fairchild C-119 Boxcar transports. With the serviceability of both types in gradual decline due to their age and wear, and with Iranian and financial backing, in 1974, Rabat secured the delivery of six Lockheed C-130H Hercules medium transports and six Beech King Air light transports. Despite protracted negotiations, the first round of talks with Washington regarding an acquisition of Northrop F-5E/F Tiger II fighter-bomber was concluded unsuccessfully. Rabat thus turned to France and in December 1975 placed an order for 25 Dassault Mirage F.1CH fighter-bombers, 38 Aerospatiale SA.330 Puma transport and assault helicopters, 6 Aerospatiale SA.342K and 6 SA.342L Gazelle attack helicopters, and 10 Swiss-made AS.202 Bravo basic trainers. The deliveries of all these aircraft, helicopters, associated ground equipment and armament, as well as training of the necessary Moroccan personnel (almost exclusively run in France) lasted from 1976 until 1979. Training of pilots necessary to fly all these aircraft and helicopters progressed very slowly, was partially controlled by the army, and was very comprehensive: the Moroccans insisted on quality instead of quantity, but also on the reliability of their future pilots, and thus all air force officers had to undergo their first year at the Royal Military Academy, before receiving two or three years of specialised training at the Air Academy or foreign schools. The French trained about 30 Moroccan cadets a year at the Royal Air Academy, while about 100 French advisors served at various Moroccan air bases; the Americans maintained a small training mission responsible for converting and advising F-5 pilots and ground crews at Rabat/Sale and Marrakesh; while an Italian team provided pilot and maintenance instruction for helicopter-crews.[12]

Additional F-5A/Bs

To bridge the gap caused by earlier attrition of available F-5A/Bs and RF-5as and until deliveries of Mirage F.1s, in 1975 Morocco requested delivery of additional F-5A/Bs from the USA. With the production of these meanwhile being closed on behalf of that of the F-5E/F Tiger IIs, and Washington proving unwilling to deliver any of the latter, Rabat was forced to look elsewhere. The nominal 'first address' in such case at the time was Iran: however, even this country – which has already donated two of its F-5As to Morocco, a year earlier – could not provide Freedom Fighters any more. The reason was that when Tehran arrived at the decision to replace its F-5A/Bs by F-5E/Fs, in late 1973, an agreement was reached with Washington to re-deliver them to various US allies. Correspondingly, almost all of the Iranian F-5A/Bs were resold to the USA, which promptly had them re-routed to South Vietnam (Operation Enhance Plus, within which 34 F-5As and 7 F-5Bs were sent to Saigon), Jordan (30 F-5as and 9 F-5Bs), Ethiopia (6 F-5As and 1 F-5B), and other countries. Eventually, the solution was found in Jordan: promising the delivery of brand-new F-5E/Fs financed by Washington, the US representatives convinced the local authorities to withdraw their F-5A/Bs and re-deliver them to Greece and Morocco. Related negotiations lasted several months, but eventually Amman agreed to provide six of its F-5As to Rabat, in February 1976. The sole jet fighter-bomber unit of the FRA thus received crucially important reinforcement just at the time it needed it the most.[13]

Overall, and despite the additional F-5As, as of 1975, the Moroccan air force was still largely equipped as three years earlier, even though its organisation was significantly different (for details on the FRA's order of battle as of 1975, see Table 3). Its primary fighter-bomber unit – a small squadron based at Meknes AB, further depleted by the necessity to convert many of its most-experienced pilots to the Mirages – still flew some 16-17 remaining Northrop F-5A/Bs and at least 1 RF-5A. The secondary fighter-bomber unit – which also acted as the fighter-weapons school and advanced training asset of the air force – operated North American T-28S Trojans/Fennecs and Fouga CM.170 Magisters from Meknes AB: because the T-28s were meanwhile all badly worn out, they were to see no action in the following war at all. Indeed, they were withdrawn from service in 1978, and all their pilots converted to F-5s.[14]

The backbone of the transport capacity was provided by a unit flying C-130Hs, another C-119Gs and C-47s, and a light transport squadron that still flew old Max-Holste MH.1521 Broussards, all based at Rabat/Sale AB. Finally, the helicopter squadrons flew a mix of Agusta-Bell AB.205s, Agusta-Bell 206s, and Boeing-Meridionali CH-47C Chinooks, while the Air Force Academy at Marrakesh operated a mix of Bell 205s, North American T-6Gs, and CM.170 Magisters. The AMG maintained a stock of 28,000 spares and 26,000 gallons of fuel, and thus served as the main supply depot for the entire air force, which – thanks to the Iranian sponsorship – was run with the help of computers. On average, 80 per cent of fighters and other combat aircraft were fully mission capable, while the in-commission rates for transports, trainers, and utility types were at about 60 per cent.[15] An order of battle for the FRA as of 1975, is provided in Table 3.

HQ	Base	Squadron	Aircraft Type & Notes
BA-FRA 1	Rabat/Sale	*Escadre d'Hélicoptère*	40 AB.205A, 2 AB.206A; 2 AB.212, 40 SA.330, 6 CH-47C on order
		Escadron de Liaison	12 MH.1521, 6 Beech King Air, 1 Gulfstream II
BA-FRA 2	Meknes/ Bassatine	*Escadron Borak*	15-16, then more than 30 F-5A/B, 1-2 RF-5A
		Escadron Panthère	21 T-28S, 22 CM.170
BA-FRA 3	Kenitra	*Escadron de Transport*	6 C-130H, 2 KC-130H on order
		Escadron de Transport	8 C-119, 10 C-47
BA-FRA 5	Sidi Slimane	*Escadron Assad*	Undergoing conversion to 50 Mirage F.1CH for delivery in 1978
BA-FRA 6	Ben Guerir	*Escadron Anti-Char*	Undergoing conversion to 12 SA.342 for delivery in 1976
Air Force Academy	Marrakesh	*Ecole de Pilotage*	10 AS.202, 12 T-6G, 12 T-34C, AB.206A, T-6G, CM.170

Table 3: FRA Order of Battle, 1975-1976[16]

When the USA refused to deliver Northrop F-5E/F Tiger II fighter-bombers, Morocco purchased 25 Mirage F.1CH interceptors from France instead (CH stood for 'Chasseur Hassan'). This photograph shows the second example manufactured for Morocco during a test-flight in France, prior to delivery. (Dassault, via Albert Grandolini)

Morocco began acquiring Lockheed C-130H Hercules transports in 1974, when an order for six (out of an eventual 19) was placed. Notable is that as of the 1970s, the Moroccan C-130s wore markings in the form of their construction number on the fin, the last two of which were repeated on the forward fuselage. (Albert Grandolini Collection)

The FRA's fleet of C-119 Boxcar transports was down to eight intact examples as of 1975, and these began showing their age: by the end of the decade, they – and the remaining C-47s – were all withdrawn from service and subsequently replaced by a total of 14 C-130s and 3 Dornier Do.28 Skyservants. (Albert Grandolini Collection)

Together with slightly older AB.205s, 38 Aerospatiale SA.330 Pumas were to form the backbone of the FRA's helicopter fleet in the late 1970s and through the 1980s. (Albert Grandolini Collection)

Conclusions

As of 1975, the Moroccan armed forces were still recovering from the blows they had received in the aftermath of the coup attempts of earlier years. For example, although totalling about 60,000 troops, the army included fewer than 1,000 officers. The situation was only partially solved by the creation of the rank of a *sous-officier*: similar to the French rank of *adjutant*, this was, technically, both a top non-commissioned officer rank, and the lowest officer rank, and thus 'in between'. Indeed, the *sous-officiers* bore the brunt of responsibility for everyday operations of the ground forces during the war in Western Sahara of 1975-1990, and even to fly fighter-jets of the air force. The reason was that their training was cheaper and shorter, and they were available in sufficient numbers. For example, those assigned to the air force did not attend the Meknes academy, did not receive leadership training nor tactical training as part of their military instruction, but 'only' underwent a two-year pilot training course (on average 15 were trained every year). Due to insistence on quality, average washout rate was at nearly 40 per cent.[17]

Even though the mass of the FAR troops were poorly-trained, the few officers that were around were not only trained to the highest standards possible, but some of those serving with major armoured and mechanised formations also possessed actual combat or at last near-combat experience: even though the second unit of that type arrived in Egypt only much too late, at least the personnel of the mechanised brigade of the FAR deployed in Syria took part in the high-intensity battles for the Golan Heights of the October 1973 Arab-Israeli War. The officers and other ranks of the 1st Parachute Brigade were to lead

The Mirage F.1CH was originally equipped as an interceptor with a secondary capability to deploy free-fall air-to-ground ordnance. Correspondingly, its primary armament was to consist of Matra R.530F air-to-air missiles (one of which is visible under this example, serial 133, photographed during flight-testing in France), and Matra R.550 Magic infra-red homing, short-range missiles. Eventually, the Moroccans acquired relatively few R.530Fs, and had their F.1CHs equipped with US-made bombs. (Dassault, via Albert Grandolini)

At least 10 C-47s were still operated by the Kenitra-based *Escadron de Transport* of the FRA as of 1975. (Photo by Jacques Guillem)

One of the former Jordanian F-5As (the serial is unreadable, but the aircraft was coded as 'D'), as seen at the ramp of el-Aaiún AB, in early 1976. (via N.B.)

US, but even Czechoslovak intelligence reports of that period repeatedly stressed that even though they often lacked basic knowledge about the equipment on which they were trained, the Moroccans were willing students, quick learners, and skilled warriors.[18]

However, higher up the chain of command, the FAR was not only organized and commanded in a fashion where its diverse units could not cooperate effectively: it lacked a semblance of a counterinsurgency (COIN) doctrine, had no idea about such proven concepts as that of 'hearts and minds', and joint-exercises including the air force and the ground forces were rarely conducted. Despite all the purges, such massive differences developed between various FAR high-ranking officers of the mid-1970s, that for much of the early period of the Moroccan involvement in Western Sahara, these were almost as preoccupied with petty bickering as with fighting the Sahrawi insurgency. Finally, already insufficient at earlier times, the entire support infrastructure of the FAR was further weakened by the necessity of supporting what was to follow, even more so because Morocco remained completely dependent on foreign sources – primarily France and the USA – for aircraft, electronic and communication equipment, most of its armament and ammunition, and all other associated support items. The result was that the Moroccan armed forces operated as an ill-commanded and poorly supplied occupation force, entirely unable to counter constantly improving guerrillas early during the following war.[19] They were not the only ones to pay the price for these deficiencies.

not only the take-over in Spanish Sahara, but also the Moroccan and then the French military interventions in Zaire of 1977 and 1978 (better known as Shabba I and Shabba II). Similarly, the sole F-5A/B squadron of the air force was deployed to Egypt in November 1973, and flew combat air patrols over the south of that country, and then the Red Sea, where it nearly clashed with the Israeli air force on at least one, perhaps two occasions. Unsurprisingly, not only

Chapter 3
All Against All

On 15 October 1975, the UN mission to Spanish Sahara issued a report in favour of Sahrawi self-determination, arguing that an overwhelming majority of the Sahrawis were in favour of independence and that the POLISARIO was by far the most important political movement in the territory. Only a day later, the ICJ followed by announcing its ruling that, even if Morocco did have a significant historical title – which the court found it did not have – the native Sahrawi right of self-determination was still paramount over all of Rabat's claims. Moreover, the court rejected both the Moroccan and Mauritanian claims to sovereignty over the Sahara as a territory belonging to no-one, and concluded it belonged to its inhabitants, the Sahrawis.[1] To say that these announcements prompted nearly all of the involved parties into hurried decisions with far-reaching consequences, would be an understatement.

Marche Verte

King Hassan II of Morocco was the first to react – and then in an entirely different manner than was expected. Ignoring most of the ICJ's ruling, he interpreted the rest to his advantage; ignoring US concerns about the possibility of drawing his country, and then Algeria and Mauritania into a costly and protracted armed conflict, and ignoring the latent weaknesses of his armed forces and his country's economy, he decided to gamble. Late on 16 October 1975, and after reaching Marrakesh together with his military staff, he announced what became known as the 'Green March' (*Marche Verte*): a mass, public demonstration with the strategic aim of forcing the Spanish to hand over the territory to Morocco. Correspondingly, after reaching an agreement with the Mauritanian government to take over and partition Spanish Sahara, he ordered a 'spontaneous' concentration of civilians to march on the border. Utilising nationalist and irredentist aspirations to achieve internal unity Hassan II managed to obtain support even from the major oppositional parties of the Moroccan political scene, in turn strengthening his own position: on 30 October, the first out of an eventual 300,000-350,000 Moroccans converged on Tafraya. The Moroccan authorities supported their gatherings through providing 7,813 trucks, while the FAR provided logistics for the huge mass of people in the form of tents, blankets, 17,000 tonnes of food, 23,000 tonnes of water, 2,590 tonnes of fuel, 200 ambulances and 470 military doctors. Helicopters of the FRA were also fully mobilized with C-47s, C-119s, and C-130s also ferrying in the supplies from bases in northern Morocco. Eventually the affair reached a point where even Moroccan military officers criticised

Participants in the *Marche Verte* moving on the border of Spanish Sahara, waving Moroccan flags – while 'escorted' by one of the FRA's Agusta-Bell 206s. (N.B. Collection)

A rare image of supplies for the participants in the *Marche Verte* being unloaded from a C-130H Hercules transport of the FRA in late October 1975. (via N.B.)

In addition to supplies, FRA transports – like this C-47 – were used to haul such propaganda material as photographs of King Hassan II. (via N.B..)

A formation of EdA Mirage IIIEE fighter-bombers from the 112th Squadron, as seen during their transfer flight to Spanish Sahara, in late October 1975. (EdA, via Albert Grandolini)

helicopters. The latter began flying armed patrols along the border – usually in cooperation with UH-1Hs – by 26 October. By 2 November, the EdA's assets in Spanish Sahara were reinforced through the arrival of 12 Mirage IIIEEs of the 111th and 112th Squadrons.

The first patrol of EdA T-6Ds to reach the border on the morning of 6 November 1975 quickly found out that the abandoned Spanish outpost of Sah was already occupied by FAR troops. Further concentrations of Moroccan troops were subsequently discovered at Hursl Sahlod and Temboscal, north of Hagunia, while Broussard light transports and several Moroccan military helicopters were airborne. Fearing an all-out invasion shielding behind the civilians, and seeking for ways to avoid bloodshed, General Salazar then ordered his troops to withhold fire, even to guide civilians around the minefields. Although Spanish pilots of Mirages, F-5As, HA-200Ds, T-6Ds and diverse helicopters were put on alert and sat in their cockpits ready to counterattack, no such orders were issued: instead, the movement of the civilians was constantly monitored by several Do.27s and OH-58s. Early in the evening, their crews finally reported that the marchers had stopped shortly after the border and showed no intention to press forward.

this 'plundering' of their own logistics depots at the cost of affecting the FAR's operational capabilities for a possible military offensive in Western Sahara. Nevertheless, the Green March went on. On 6 November 1975, the mass of civilians carrying Moroccan and Qoranic banners calling for the 'return of the Moroccan Sahara', photographs of King Hassan II, and escorted by FAR troops, reached and then crossed the border.[2]

Initially at least, the Spanish reaction to King Hassan's announcement was as stubborn as always. While the diplomats from Madrid attempted to dissuade Rabat from launching such an operation, the Spanish Navy dispatched its Task Force 90 – including the amphibious assault ship *Galicia* and more than 20 other warships (20 amphibious vessels, 4 destroyers, 2 frigates, 1 corvette, and several patrol boats and submarines) – to el-Aaiún. Once there, the ships landed a battalion of Spanish Marines and a Rapid Intervention Force of the Army, supported by eight Bell AH-1G Cobra attack

Madrid Accord

However, while the tensions between Morocco and Spain thus reached their maximum, the widely publicised Green March eventually broke the Spanish resistance: Franco was meanwhile dying (he passed away on 20 November 1975), the country's political future uncertain, and despite overwhelming military and logistic superiority vis-à-vis Morocco, there was no desire for another colonial war in Africa. On 9 November 1975, Madrid agreed to open negotiations for relinquishing Spanish Sahara, and Hassan II announced that the marchers would return to Tafraya. Following hurried negotiations, and in complete ignorance of the UN and ICJ findings, and the demands of the Sahrawis, on 14 November 1975 the Spanish, Moroccan, and Mauritanian representatives signed the Madrid Accords: a treaty according to which Spain was to end its presence in the territory of Spanish Sahara, and transfer

A Moroccan T-54 crossing the northern border to Spanish Sahara in mid-December 1975. Notable is the large turret number (3922) applied in white. (via N.B.)

T-54s of the 1° and 3°GEB of the FAR were followed by motorised troops, usually mounted on Land Rovers or, as in this case, Mercedes UNIMOG trucks. (via N.B.)

Mauritanian troops mounted on Land Rovers entering Spanish Sahara from the south in late December 1975. (Albert Grandolini Collection)

the Madrid Accords. While the Spanish Prince Juan Carlos vowed to defend the Sahara from Moroccan invasion, a few days earlier, on 6 November 1975 the Spaniards evacuated La Guera in the course of a 48-hour-long operation. The place was promptly taken over by the insurgency. Whether informed about this development or not, while withdrawing civilians involved in the Green March, King Hassan II ordered the FAR into an all-out advance. The troops of the 1st Parachute Brigade reached el-Aaiún on 11 December 1975, and a formal ceremony of lowering the Spanish flag and raising that of Morocco was quickly organized. The first clashes with the POLISARIO followed only shortly after. By then, up to 15,000 FAR troops – including the T-54-equipped 1° and 3° GEB – had crossed the border. In the south, the Mauritanians followed in fashion two weeks later: on 17 December, they occupied Lagouira, before moving on Tichy and La Guerra, both of which were taken after a siege that lasted nearly two weeks, despite relatively feeble resistance from a few insurgents and activists. Subsequently, the Mauritanians drove all the way to Dakhla, which became the centre of what was termed the 'New Territory' by the government in Nouakchott. Neither development was monitored with any kind of satisfaction by officers of the Spanish armed forces: on the contrary, they felt humiliated and some threatened to take things into their own hands. However, cooler heads prevailed: what greatly helped was a separate agreement for an exchange of prisoners with the POLISARIO, that had been reached on 21 October.[3]

Spanish Evacuation

For better or worse, the Spanish were soon on their way out of the territory. Run as an operation code-named Swallow (Golondrina), their evacuation was launched on 23 November 1975. The first to go were the civilians and military personnel from Hausa, Farsia and Jdairia, followed by those from Edcheria and Mahbes. Samara, a crucial garrison along a route regularly subjected to insurgent ambushes, was evacuated in the course of Operation Suzana, on 26 November: the column of no fewer than 320 vehicles of the 7th Regiment of the Spanish Foreign Legion was protected by a pair each of Do.27s, T-6Ds and UH-1Hs, and one Alouette. While scouting the retreat route, Spanish pilots first detected a large concentration of FAR troops on the northern bank of the Hamra River, and then a smaller group of camouflaged vehicles on its southern side. However, by the time an RF-5A, followed by another pair of T-6Ds called to provide additional support had reached the area, fighting erupted between the Moroccans and POLISARIO insurgents. The first shots of the future war for Western Sahara were thus fired well before this conflict officially began. Ignoring the battle, the Spaniards extricated their troops without any losses, collecting another column from Hagunia as they went. Once in el-Aaiún, some of the soldiers were flown out with the help of EdA transports – the fleet of which was meanwhile fully mobilised – while others embarked aboard the ships waiting off the coast: CASA C.207s,

administrative responsibilities – even if not the sovereignty – of this territory to Morocco and Mauritania, in return for retaining a 35 per cent share in the Bou Craa mine. With this treaty, Madrid was left with 60 days to evacuate the bulk of its forces and about 10,000 Spanish colonists from the Sahara. Furthermore, on Moroccan insistence, the treaty stipulated that all the public infrastructure and military installations were to be transferred to their control, 'in situ', while on Spanish insistence, all the military installations were to be taken over by the Moroccans only once they had vacated them.

In reality, not only the POLISARIO but especially the Moroccans and Mauritanians rushed to exploit the situation and to pre-empt

A pair of FRA T-6Ds at Villa Cisneros as seen in January 1976 (see the colour section for details on their colours and markings). Notable in the rear is a row of Moroccan AB.205s. (Albert Grandolini Collection)

A Spanish pilot posing with an FRA T-6G at Villa Cisneros airport in January 1976. Notable is that the engine cowling and wing-tips are painted in day-glo orange, and the armament of the aircraft in the background, the latter including pods for twin machine guns, and 3in (76mm) unguided rockets. (via Albert Grandolini)

A still from a video showing a row of FRA F-5As on the tarmac of el-Aaiún AB in early 1976. In the foreground is one of the former Jordanian jets, behind it one of Moroccan – still in its silver-grey livery (for details of the latter, see the colour section of the Volume 1). (via N.B.)

meanwhile withdrawn from the territory, four T-6Ds remained at el-Aaiún until the end of January 1976: their pilots thus witnessed the arrival of the first FRA aircraft, including C-47s and C-130Hs, T-6Gs and CM.170 Magisters, and several AB.205s. Moreover, they witnessed the deployment of several Moroccan T-6Gs at Villa Cisneros. Spain officially put an end to its presence in Sahara on 28 February 1976. Certainly enough, and with the help of bases in the Canary Islands, its armed forces kept a watchful eye on the developments there for a while longer.[4]

Security Operation in the Southern Zone

Indeed, the first units of the FRA deployed in Western Sahara almost as soon as the Moroccan ground forces had secured el-Aaiún – in what Rabat cynically declared to have been a 'security operation in the Southern Zone', but was soon to become an all-out war.

The commander of the first Moroccan detachment at this air base was Major Ali Najab, an F 5A pilot trained in the USA and then in Iran, before serving a tour as instructor-pilot for CM.170s and F-5s at the Air Force Academy in Marrakesh. Najab recalled:

I had been appointed the head of a detachment of 12 aircraft and 15 pilots deployed at el-Aaiún. We encountered lots of difficulties because that airfield was not constructed to accommodate fighter jets. The runway was very short. We had no navigational aids on the ground and were forced to use roads for navigation, and search for the enemy with our eyes. Our army was poorly prepared and poorly armed: some units were still equipped with weapons dating from the times our country was released into independence. We were suffering from the lack of coordination with the army. Our means of communication were different: we had UHF radios, the army had HF radios. This was a major problem because pilots had trouble distinguishing the enemy from our troops in the combat zone. The weather was characterised by strong sandy winds that often made flying impossible. The air force was also traumatised by the two coup d'états: the army was all the time

C-47s, DC-4s and C-130Hs, and also civilian airliners, were used to pick up troops and civilians from larger airfields, while lighter de Havilland Canada DHC-4 Caribous and CASA C.202 Aviocars were used to do so from shorter airstrips and the last remaining outposts. Nearly all of their operations were protected by combat aircraft, and at least one HA-200D is known to have been written off in the course of related operations, when it crashed on landing in el-Aaiún, in late December 1975.

The Spanish airbridge was maintained well into early January 1976, by when the aircraft were used to evacuate even the dead from the local graveyards. While the mass of the EdA aircraft were pointing the finger at us and treating us in a condescending fashion. Furthermore, King Hassan II's orders made it clear that the future of Sahara was related to the future of our entire state. Thus, there was immense pressure upon us.[5]

The arrival of the Moroccan troops caused a deep trauma for almost everybody involved: as the FAR units advanced ever deeper into Western Sahara, they either hit mines planted by the insurgents that were also involved in trying to take over positions vacated by the Spanish, or ran into dozens of small ambushes. Alone during the first week of January 1976, the POLISARIO claimed to have set on fire a section of the conveyor Belt from Bou Craa to el-Aaiún several hundred metres long, to have killed 104 Moroccan troops, wounded another 100, and taken 15 prisoner. Furthermore, the insurgents reported the destruction of 17 Moroccan trucks, 2 jeeps, 3 tanks, and 1 helicopter, and also to have caused 18 fatalities

Pilots of the Escadron Panthère with one of their CM.170s, as seen at el-Aaiún AB in June 1977. While the nearby capital of Western Sahara was renamed Laayoune by the Moroccans, the airport was named after King Hassan II and integrated into the air force's organisational structure as BA-FRA 4. (N.B. Collection)

FRA C-130Hs played a crucial role in supporting the deployment of Moroccan troops into Spanish Sahara in December 1975. (Albert Grandolini Collection)

and 26 wounded to the Mauritanians. Finally, US sources in Rabat reported that at least one of the FRA C-119s involved in supporting the forces deployed in Western Sahara crashed under unknown circumstances.[6]

As the losses quickly mounted, the poorly-trained and undersupplied Moroccan troops reacted with atrocities – prompting a flood of reports about widespread murder, rape, and pillaging. Regardless if fake, as claimed by Morocco, or true, these prompted thousands to flee – although the POLISARIO initially instructed everybody to stay put: by January 1976, about 40,000 people of the already diminutive population of a mere 74,954 – mostly women, children and the elderly – fled to the refugee camps in the interior of the Sahara. Up to 20,000 gathered in Guelta Zemmour, which was still under insurgent control, while about 15,000 converged on Tifariti.[7]

Rapidly expanded, the POLISARIO soon proved a major challenge to the Moroccan domination: indeed, the flight and suffering of dozens of thousands of civilians, followed by reports of air strikes and the deployment of napalm bombs on their camps in the east of the country causing hundreds of casualties, resulted in an explosion of Sahrawi nationalism. Nearly all of the natives that used to serve with the Spanish forces had meanwhile joined the insurgency, swelling the ranks of the POLISARIO to a force of about 2,500 combat-tested warriors with unrivalled knowledge and natural mastery of the terrain. In a matter of days, they not only occupied dozens of positions vacated by the Spaniards, but then

As the Moroccans and the Mauritanians entered the country, and with the Spanish in withdrawal, the Sahrawis rallied to the POLISARIO, the ranks of which quickly swelled through the influx of experienced and well-trained soldiers of the *Tropas Nomadas* in particular. (Albert Grandolini Collection)

began applying the ages-old practice of *al-ghazi* or *razzou* – 'the raid' – against the Moroccans and Mauritanians, in the form of highly-effective, surprise assaults from multiple directions, followed by retreat before the enemy could hit back. Unsurprisingly, Najab commented:

Our military strategy early on was to secure as much territory as possible and then settle down. We paid a high toll because of the mines laid by the POLISARIO. Movement on the ground was heavily hampered and thus support by our transport aircraft was very important during the first six months of this operation.

Although forced to withdraw from most of the population centres, the insurgents were quick to re-attack the Bou Craa conveyor belt (inoperable since 20 October 1974) on 11 December 1975 and again in early January 1976, causing so much damage that it remained out of operation for the next six years. Still, not only the Moroccans and Mauritanians, but also the mass of contemporary foreign observers quickly dismissed the ability of the Sahrawi nationalists to confront two foreign military forces – and to survive. For example, the US ambassador in Rabat wrote to Washington: '…even though [the] guerrillas' needs [are] probably few, [they] would not seem capable of standing up for long against relative Moroccan military might and in a highly inhospitable environment where spotting from [the] air [is] relatively easy…'[8]

Similarly, the International Institute for Strategic Studies (IISS), predicted, 'a quick end of an armed rebellion'.[9] And still, these were not the first grave mistakes by all the involved parties in this war and by far not the last.

Battles of Amgala

The Moroccan and Mauritanian militaries were not the only ones to enter Western Sahara in late 1975. As Moroccan air strikes on their camps continued, ever larger numbers of Sahrawis fled over the border into Algeria – and then the Algerian military also moved in. Contrary to what many contemporary reports stipulated, the Algerians did not want to get involved in the war: the task of the units of the National Popular Army of Algeria, (*Armée Nationale Populaire*, ANP) deployed inside Western Sahara was to set up two transit points for Sahrawi refugees: one near the watering place of Amgala, and the other at Tifariti. Each of the two spots was controlled by one logistic battalion, which were there to provide food, medical aid and water to refugees.[10]

Despite their rivalry with Morocco, the acquisition of Soviet-made arms, extensive US and French military aid provided to Rabat, and publicly announced support for the independence of Western Sahara, the Algerians decided to respect the Treaty of Solidarity and Cooperation King Hassan II and President Boumedienne signed in 1968. Moreover, although generally being considered a Soviet client state in the West, the Algerians were selling most of their oil and gas to the USA: therefore, they were not the least keen to provoke Morocco, and even less so its allies in France and the USA. The Moroccans, on the other hand, considered everybody who disagreed with their ideas of greater Morocco as an enemy, and strongly suspected the Algerians as masterminds of what happened next. With both parties deploying their forces inside Western Sahara, a clash became unavoidable.[11]

On 21 January 1976, a pair of FRA F-5s were flying a reconnaissance sortie over the area of Dakhla, when one of them was shot down, apparently by one of the first SA-7s that reached the POLISARIO. The pilot, Ahmed Ben Boubker, seems to have ejected, but subsequently went missing. From the Moroccan point of view, there could be no doubt about the culprits. Ali Najab exclaimed along the official Moroccan line of the time:

> Then we experienced our first clashes with Algerians because Boumedienne had sent his military units into the eastern and south-eastern part of the Sahara. The conflict thus began with Algerians, not with the secessionists.

Dakhla, however was well outside Algerian reach at the time.

Moreover, when questioned about Moroccan claims that it was the Algerian 'SA-6s' that had shot down Boubker's F-5A, as often insisted by the Moroccans, all Algerian sources pointed out the same fact:

> Even later on, in 1978-1979, we still did not know how to use our SAM-sites. We had specialists, people trained on such systems in the Soviet Union, but all of their experience was theoretic. When we received SA-3s, these were brand new to us and it took us three-four years of intensive training until we reached the point at which we were able to open fire on simulated targets. Even then, during our first exercises, our lack of experience was showing. Our batteries were ready; our crews knew from what direction the MiGs towing the target would approach; we had the perfect timing. And still, we were so inexperienced that in many cases we missed the target. It was not before 1988-1989 – when we bought Mirach target drones from Italy – that our training became much more realistic. The situation was the same with regards to our Army units equipped with SAMs. Therefore, shooting down any of Moroccan fighter jets in 1976 – and for most of the 1980s – was practically impossible for us.[12]

According to unofficial Algerian and Moroccan sources, what happened next was that during the night from 26 to 27 January 1977, detachments from the 28°, 29°, 42° and 59° Sector Infantry Battalions (*bataillon d'infanterie de secteur*, BIS) of the FAR first re-deployed from Bou Craa to Samara. Once there, the Moroccans re-organised their units into Task Force A and Task Force B, and then continued south, apparently by-passing the Algerian unit at Amgala – before suddenly turning east and then launching a pincer-attack. Facing a vastly superior enemy, the company of armed troops led by Lieutenant Ahmad Gaid Salah abandoned its positions, leaving the 41st Logistics Battalion of the ANP (*41° bataillon de logistique*), commanded by Captain Lounes Arib, on its own. The result was unavoidable: the ANP unit was largely destroyed, losing over 200 killed, dozens of wounded, and 106 captured.[13]

The next morning, surviving Algerians were pursued by the aircraft and helicopters of the FRA, forward deployed at Samara airfield. Reportedly, the Moroccans then flew air strikes on an Algerian artillery unit that was in the process of deploying near Gara Fogara in northern Mauritania, and dispersed it, too.[14]

Furious, Algerian President Houari Boumedienne did seriously consider launching an invasion of Morocco in retaliation. However, his military advisors were quick in explaining to him that because significant contingents of the ANP were still deployed in Egypt (where they had been since 1973), or were in the process of being transferred back to Algeria, the armed forces lacked the necessary strength. Meanwhile, the Commander of the 2nd Military Region (Oran), Chadli Bendjedid, and Minister of Foreign Affairs, Abdelaziz Bouteflika (both of whom were Boumedienne's relatives) offered alternative ideas: Bendjedid suggested engaging Morocco in a kind of cold war, while Bouteflika recommended diplomatic action. At this point in time, Egypt became involved as a mediator – and then especially in regards of the second ANP unit deployed inside Western Sahara: the unit that secured Tifariti, an oasis 138km (86 miles) from Samara and 15km (9 miles) north of the Mauritanian border. This was meanwhile surrounded by Moroccan troops, and regularly overflown by FRA F-5As. On the basis of reconnaissance photographs brought back by the later, the General Command in Rabat assessed its strength as about 2,100 troops and 120 vehicles. Informed that the situation was about to escalate if the

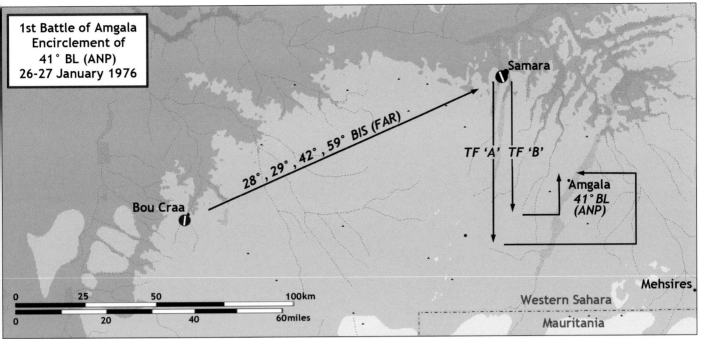

A map of the Moroccan attack on the Algerian logistics battalion at Amgala on the night of 26 to 27 January 1976. (Map by Tom Cooper)

Moroccans attacked the second ANP battalion, Egyptian president Anwar el-Sadat sent his Vice, Hossni Mubarak, as a mediator. Mubarak first travelled to Algiers, only to find Boumedienne enraged by Moroccan threats, explaining his troops would be on Algerian soil, and accusing the Egyptian of 'treachery'. Left without a choice, Mubarak flew to Rabat to meet King Hassan II. Of course, they promptly showed him reconnaissance photographs taken by FRA RF-5As, and the location of Tifariti on the map – about 300 kilometres (186,5 miles) inside Western Sahara. The Egyptian eventually returned to Algiers, and then managed to arrange an agreement: the Algerian unit was left to evacuate Tifariti – apparently together with about 15,000 Sahrawi civilians – without further fighting, by 6 February 1976.[15]

Determined to avenge the *blamage,* or humiliation, of Amgala, as soon as the troops and civilians were safe, Boumedienne ordered the ANP to demonstrate Algerian determination and the ability to hit back – even if in discrete fashion. This is how it came to be that although the Algerian

An AB.205A (foreground), and an SA.330 Puma of the FRA, as seen at the Bou Craa airfield: together with much bigger installations of this kind left behind by the Spaniards at el-Aaiún, Dakhla/Villa Cisneros and Samara, this airfield became one of the major forward operating bases of the FRA. (N.B. Collection)

Insurgents with the wreckage of what they claimed was the first Moroccan aircraft they had shot down: if so, this would be the F-5A flown by Ahmed Ben Boubker, on 21 January 1976. (via H.B.)

Gauging by the serial number visible on the fin of this F-5A, this was certainly the wreckage of Ahmed Ben Boubker's jet, shot down on 21 January 1976, near Amgala. (via K.H.)

Air Force (*al-Quwwat al-Jawwiya al-Jaza'eriya*, QJJ) had a squadron each of MiG-17s and MiG-21s deployed at Tindouf AB, instead of air strikes the ANP deployed only a commando battalion led by Colonel Zerguini. Wearing POLISARIO insignia, Zerguini's troops drove all the way to Amgala and there is little doubt that they took the Moroccans by surprise late on 14 February 1976. While Algiers strenuously denies any kind of involvement until this day, multiple unofficial Moroccan sources admit that the 6°BIS, FAR, which meanwhile garrisoned Amgala, was de-facto wiped out.[16] Most of the Algerian prisoners were liberated and returned to their homeland, leaving Moroccans like Ali Najab to report a typical, yet widespread error: 'During the famous battle of Amgala, we destroyed an entire battalion and captured 106 Algerians. A few days later, Algerian units came back, but we launched air strikes and forced them away'.[17]

Regardless of countless claims and counterclaims ever since, as far as is known, the two battles of Amgala from January and February 1976 remained the only direct clashes between the ANP and the FAR during the entire war in Western Sahara.[18]

Sahrawi Declaration of Independence

Certainly enough, the two battles of Amgala signalled no end to the Algerian involvement in this conflict. On the contrary, as Algiers let ever more Sahrawis into its territory, several large refugee camps came into being in the desert of the Tindouf area – and the POLISARIO quickly assumed command over all of them. This was not the least welcomed by local Algerians: not only that the insurgents all spoke Arabic that was difficult to understand, or Spanish, which the Algerians did not understand, but they also all regularly carried their firearms, and frequently behaved like an occupation force, while both the ANP and the local police maintained only minimal presence in the town. Correspondingly, there was little the Algerian authorities were able to do about the insurgent behaviour. Unsurprisingly, over the following years a de-facto para-state came into being in this part of Algeria, similar to the situation in southern Lebanon occupied by the Palestinian Liberation Organisation and diverse other factions around the same time, as explained by a retired officer of the ANP:

> Nowadays, the situation in their [Sahrawi; authors' note] camps in Tindouf isn't the same as before. Now the Sahrawis are forbidden to move with their weapons on hand, and they have to behave correctly to our people in Tindouf. But, back in the 1970s situation was different. When they came, they would speak to us in Arabic, but to each other in a language which we did not understand: Spanish…

Having secured safe bases inside Algeria, the POLISARIO was in a position to take several important steps. On 27 February 1976, it declared the Sahrawi Arab Democratic Republic (*República Árabe Saharaui Democrática*, SADR). Generally, members of the POLISARIO could be described as Arab nationalists, but there were at least three major ideologies amongst them. The dominant, moderate, pro-Algerian group included Secretary General Abdel Aziz, his Deputy Bachir Mustapha Sayed al-Ouali, the majority of the members of the Executive Committee, and the Politburo. Other identifiable groups were a pro-Libyan wing – some of whose members had leftist tendencies – and a much smaller group of hard-line Marxists. With regards to military-related affairs, the leadership of the POLISARIO was also divided. In September 1980, the hard-line faction – including the Secretary General and his Minister of Defence (Ibrahim Ghali Ould Mustapha) – favoured greater use of armed force to achieve independence, while a more moderate group – including the Prime Minister (Mohammed Lamine Ould Ahmed) – favoured greater emphasis on political dialogue and compromise.[19]

While the POLISARIO thus formalised its position as a political party and a government in exile, at the same time it took care to formalise the status of its combatants. Thus came into being the Sahrawi Popular Liberation Army (*Ejército de Liberación Popular Saharaui*, ELPS). The commanders of the ELPS promptly embarked on a major effort to increase the capabilities and combat effectiveness of their force, and promptly found a willing ally in Libya. Initially, Tripoli shipped relatively small amounts of small arms, primarily including different versions of the AKM 7.62mm assault rifles and DShK (or 'Dushka') 12.7mm heavy machine guns. By 1976, rocket-propelled grenades (RPGs), B-10 and B-11 recoilless rifles, 120mm mortars, and then the first shipments of SA-7 man-portable air defence systems (MANPADs) followed. Most of the armament and related ammunition was shipped via Oran in Algeria. On arrival in POLISARIO camps in the Tindouf area, nearly all of these were mounted on Land Rover four-wheel-drives (4WDs) – so-called 'technicals' – the availability of hundreds of which boosted its offensive power by several magnitudes.

The POLISARIO's Art of War

Knowing their forces were far too small and too weak to risk a direct confrontation with their enemy, the POLISARIO's leaders made it clear right from the start, that their campaign was unlikely to lead to a decisive military victory. While originally carefully avoiding attacks on enemy military bases – only the smallest of outposts were attacked during the first half of 1976, and then only after extremely careful reconnaissance – gradually, the ELPS converted its primary task to that of making the presence of Mauritanian and Moroccan troops in Western Sahara unbearable. For a while, it went through a 'learning by doing' phase, during which it ran a myriad of smaller raids against enemy supply lines. Although securing several villages in eastern areas of Western Sahara, like Tifariti, in April 1976, the Sahrawis quickly learned to avoid occupying territory or even spending too much time within captured military strongpoints: instead, they would attack and then disappear into the desert, only to re-attack at some other point. To further improve its freedom of action and minimalize the disadvantages of the lack of cover in the desert, the insurgency created large buffer zones between their own outposts in the eastern parts of Western Sahara, and enemy positions further west. Along the eastern fringe of these zones, it constructed a large number of well-concealed supply depots. With the help of these it gradually developed the capability of subjecting the Moroccans and the Mauritanians to a steady stream of assaults, each of which degenerated enemy capabilities and sapped morale,

A column of ELPS technicals navigating a desert track between the hills of northern Western Sahara. (Albert Grandolini Collection)

A Moroccan AMX-13 light tank knocked out by the insurgents in 1976. (Albert Grandolini Collection)

while improving those of the insurgency. Further east, and with help of the allied Touareg, the ELPS constructed several well-concealed forward supply depots in north-western Mali, well stocked with water, fuel, food and ammunition provided by Libya. Thanks to these, its columns became capable of raiding Dakhla on the Atlantic coast (held by the 15° BIS of the FAR as of 1976), and Nema in Mauritania – both originally well outside its reach. By the end of 1976, the ELPS was thus free to move virtually at will all over Western Sahara, southern Morocco, and northern Mauritania, and then opened the next phase of its war: a period during which it began setting up ambushes for supply convoys of the Mauritanian and Moroccan armed forces. Such operations were usually centred on heavily mining the roads and surrounding areas: when an enemy column hit one of the mines, it would be subjected to quick, often small-scale, hit-and-run attacks. Precise figures for the Moroccan casualties in a series of such ambushes set up in late 1976 and early 1977 remain unavailable; those for Mauritanian casualties even more so. However, contemporary US intelligence estimates cited the FAR's monthly casualty rate as 'approximately 10 to 20 killed in action'.[20]

While precise details about every single ambush and the Moroccan and Mauritanian reactions to these remain elusive, the few available

figures indicate the ELPS' ability to perfect these tactics – but also the ferocity of its attacks, and the enemy's reactions. By April 1977, the POLISARIO claimed to have shot down at least 18 combat aircraft and two transports of the Royal Air Force of Morocco and the Islamic Air Force of Mauritania (*Force Aérienne Islamique de Mauritanie*, FAIM). Furthermore, the insurgency reported having destroyed or captured more than 600 Moroccan military vehicles, while causing more than 4,200 deaths, 2,800 wounded, and to have captured 96 enemy troops; similarly, it may have caused up to 1,600 deaths, 900 wounded, and captured 16 Mauritanian soldiers. Indeed, even contemporary US intelligence reports reported the average monthly casualty rate of the FAR as 'between 100 and 200 killed, wounded, or captured'.[21]

On the other side, the POLISARIO's losses were frequently reported – and sometimes even admitted by the insurgents – as 'heavy', but details remain elusive. The primary reason was that the insurgents never left their casualties on the battlefield: if necessary, when in a hurry, they would catch bodies of their fallen with a hook, and then 'tow' them away behind their vehicles. This tactic became particularly efficient, because amongst the Moroccans it created the impression they were fighting 'ghosts', or at least an enemy that was 'invisible' and 'never suffering casualties'.[22]

Into Mauritania

Meanwhile, the POLISARIO decided to concentrate on defeating the Mauritanians first. Modelled along French patterns, the Mauritanian armed forces of 1976 counted only about 7,000 reasonably well-trained but inexperienced officers and other ranks. The involvement in Western Sahara prompted Nouakchott to introduce the draft and to rapidly expand its ground forces in particular: most of these were organized into motorised infantry battalions, supported by companies of French-made armoured cars like AML-90s. Like the Moroccans, the Mauritanians also introduced the rank of *adjutant-chef* to – at least partially – replace the lack of qualified officers. However, this was far from enough – because their forces were tasked with protection of a country twice the size of France, while supported by only minimal logistical and communication capabilities. As such, Mauritania was clearly the weaker of the POLISARIO's two opponents – and thus an obvious target. As in their campaign against the Moroccans, the insurgents did not seek to actually defeat the Mauritanian military in a set-piece battle, or to capture major population centres, but to weaken the government to a degree where they would have no other choice but to seek peace. For this purpose, and with the help of forward supply depots in Mali, the ELPS became capable of running operations against the trains hauling iron ore from mines in the Zouérate area. Initially, the insurgents operated in small groups and in their usual fashion, in the form of harassing attacks that utilised the element of surprise and made good use of the terrain to launch quick, sharp assaults, before quickly withdrawing.

The ELPS launched its first attack into Mauritania on 19 April 1976, when a small unit knocked out a train on the railway of the Complexe Minier du Nord (COMINOR), constructed to transport iron ore from the mines in the Zouérate area to the port of Nouadibou. However, this operation remained the last of its kind for a while longer, because on the same day the Moroccan Army – supported by sustained air strikes by FAR F-5s and CM.170s – overran Guelta Zemmour. Falling back upon its forward supply bases in Mali, the ELPS returned to Mauritania in early June 1976, by deploying multiple columns totalling about 100 vehicles and 600 combatants in the direction of Nouakchott. One of the units was detected by patrolling Mauritanian aircraft while still approaching the target zone, and the operation was thus aborted. Moreover, while withdrawing towards the north, the insurgents were pursued and repeatedly harassed by FAIM BN-2s armed with gun-pods and unguided rockets. Finally, shortly before reaching the Algerian border, on 9 June 1976 the main column was cut off by a squadron of Moroccan AML-90 armoured cars, and lost a number of combatants, including el-Ouali Mustapha Sayed, the POLISARIO's prestigious and charismatic Secretary General.[23]

In need of a new leader and sensing the requirement

The port of Nouadibou, the endpoint of the COMINOR railway, as seen from a French air force aircraft in December 1977. (AdA, via Albert Grandolini)

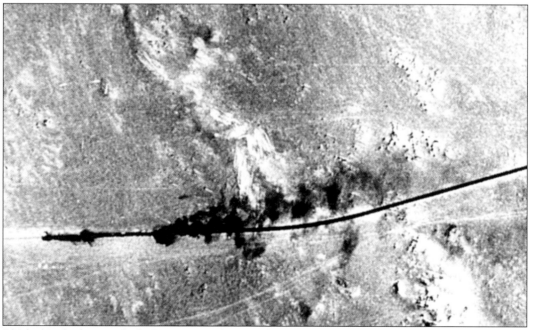

A high-altitude photograph of a COMINOR train burning after a raid in late 1977. (AdA, via Albert Grandolini)

A low-altitude, close-up reconnaissance photograph showing three locomotives of a COMINOR train. (AdA, via Albert Grandolini)

The first line of defence of Mauritania consisted of only a handful of British-made BN-2 Defenders (an armed variant of the BN-2 Islander), operated by the FAIM. In addition to gun-pods, these could be armed with Swiss-made Oerlikon Sura-FL unguided rockets, clearly visible in this pre-delivery photograph. (Albert Grandolini Collection)

to reorganize in the light of a rapidly developing situation, on 26 August 1976 the POLISARIO staged its third congress. In addition to the election of Mohammed Abdelaziz as a new Secretary General, the movement then arrived at the decision to intensify its operations against Mauritania. Of course, organising and running such a campaign proved anything other than easy, and took time – foremost necessary to acquire additional arms and supplies from Libya, and distribute these to forward supply depots. The longer it took the harder it became to drive all the way into Mauritania, because meanwhile the local military was getting better organised and prepared. The successful interception of the ELPS' first raid on Nouakchott had not been achieved for nothing: it was the result of very intensive operations by the FAIM. However, intensive operations exposed the aircraft and their crews to many risks, and the insurgents were quick in exacting revenge. For example, early on the morning of 29 December 1976, one of only three Britten-Norman BN-2 Defenders operated by the Mauritanians at the time was hit by an SA-7 while underway over the Bir Moghrein area, and shot down. The death of the crew – including Lieutenant Sidi Mohammed Ould Heyine, Sous-Lieutenant Ely O Nayaa and Sergeant-Chief Mohammed el-Hafedh O. Zegrar – was severely felt within the FAIM, which at the time still totalled under 150 officers and other ranks.[24]

The next large ELPS operation in Mauritania was launched only on 1 May 1977, but then in spectacular style. After restocking at their bases in Mali, multiple columns totalling between 60 and 110 vehicles and some 300-500 insurgents converged on the mining town of Zouérate. Although counting about 1,000 men – and thus considered the 'best protected piece of real estate in the country' – the local garrison was taken by surprise, and effectively overrun. The ELPS thus went on to damage the local airport – where two aircraft of unknown type were destroyed – and then the nearby mine. Finally, it drove into the European quarter, killed two French citizens and took a further six as hostages before withdrawing, only two hours after the start of its attack.[25]

To say this raid caused panic amongst foreign (primarily French) workers in Mauritania would be an understatement: nearly all 400 of them promptly left the country, in turn causing a major interruption in iron mining. Not only Mauritania and Morocco, but also France eventually reacted with outrage. Initially mindful of the popularity of Algeria and the Sahrawi insurgency within leftist circles in France, the government of the conservative-liberal French President Valéry Giscard d'Estaing first entered secret negotiations with the POLISARIO. However, when these failed, and the insurgents launched new raids, d'Estaing ordered the deployment of a flight of SEPECAT Jaguar A fighter-bombers to Ouakam Airport, near Dakar – the principal reception and staging base of French forces in western Africa.[26]

High Defence Committee

Although knowing such a measure was likely to become unpopular within the ranks of its armed forces, the 1 May raid on Zouérate shocked the Mauritanian government into signing a new security assistance agreement with Paris, stipulating the deployment of about

70 French military advisors to assist in training and equipment-maintenance for its military, meanwhile expanded to about 13,000. Moreover, on 13 May 1977, Nouakchott signed a joint defence and cooperation agreement with Rabat, granting permission for the deployment of 9,000 Moroccan troops inside Mauritania, especially in the Zouérate area. Deployed within the framework of Operation Fanon, the first two battalions of the FAR arrived on board C.160 Transall and Nord Aviation N.2501 Noratlas transports of the French Air Force (*Armée de l'Air*, AdA) directly in Zouérate, only a day later.[27] During the following weeks, and under guidance of French instructors, Moroccan construction companies began expanding the airfield facilities at Nouakchott, Nouadibou, Atar and Bir Moghrein

A column of 106mm recoilless rifle-armed Land Rovers of the Mauritanian Army. (Albert Grandolini Collection)

Driss Bahaji, the Moroccan F-5A pilot injured during the take-off for the FRA air strike on the ELPS major supply depot in north-western Mali in July 1977. He died in hospital a few days after the crash. (via E.C.)

to enable basing of their air force. As soon as these were ready, the FRA deployed a detachment of 18 aircraft – including F-5As (based at Nouadibou, near the strategically important port), T-6s, and Broussards (based at Bir Moghrein) – and a few helicopters, while the FAR concentrated two infantry battalions in Zouérate, one in Atik, and, starting in early 1978, another one in Ajouit.[28] Henceforth, the anti-ELPS operations of Morocco and Mauritania were coordinated through the High Defence Committee, a joint body consisting of top officers from both forces – and several French advisors – that met once a month, and in which the Mauritanians found themselves in the position of a 'junior partner'.[29]

Of course, this was all still 'too little too late'. On 3 June 1977, the ELPS drove another of its units from Tindouf over nearly 1,000 kilometres (621 miles), all the way to Nouakchott, and shelled the city with recoilless guns before withdrawing virtually unmolested. Undertaken during the annual summit of the Organisation of African Unity (OAU) in Libreville, Gabon, this attack caused immense embarrassment to Mauritanian President Ould Daddah, first and foremost.[30]

The first to react this time was – once again – the FRA, even though its related operation remained almost entirely unknown in public until the present day. On the basis of satellite intelligence provided by the USA, the General Command in Rabat ordered two pairs of F-5As into action against the main ELPS supply depot in north-western Mali. Each loaded with a pair of AIM-9B Sidewinder air-to-air missiles, two drop tanks, and five US-made Mk.82 bombs installed on a multiple-ejector

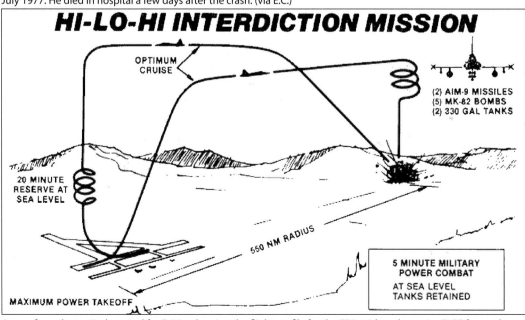

HI-LO-HI INTERDICTION MISSION

OPTIMUM CRUISE

(2) AIM-9 MISSILES
(5) MK-82 BOMBS
(2) 330 GAL TANKS

20 MINUTE RESERVE AT SEA LEVEL

550 NM RADIUS

5 MINUTE MILITARY POWER COMBAT
AT SEA LEVEL
TANKS RETAINED

MAXIMUM POWER TAKEOFF

A scan from the tactical manual for F-5As, showing the flight profile for the FRA raid on the major ELPS forward supply depot in north-western Mali in July 1977. (via Tom Cooper)

Different versions of the Land Rover played perhaps the most prominent role in the Western Saharan War for much of the 1970s and well into the 1980s: the vehicle replaced the camel as the primary mount of the insurgency, where it was usually crudely painted in sand or grey, and mostly used as a 'technical', armed with a Soviet-made 14.5mm ZPU-2 twin-barrel machine gun (left). The Moroccan Army also made extensive use of this vehicle (including Spanish-made Land Rover Santanas) – as mounts for 106mm recoilless rifles (right). Their camouflage colours usually consisted of sprayed spots or disruptive patterns in olive green or any other shades of green or brown that were available, brushed around the vehicle. (Artworks by David Bocquelet)

During the 1980s, the FAR gradually replaced its worn-out Land Rovers with such vehicles as US-made Ford M151 MUTT jeeps, frequently used to carry a launcher for the BGM-71 TOW ATGM (left side). Another type that became a frequent sight was the Mercedes UNIMOG, the chassis of which was often used to carry heavier weapons, like the ZPU-2 (right side), or – later on – the 23mm ZU-23 twin-barrel automatic anti-aircraft gun. (Artworks by David Bocquelet)

In the late 1970s and through to the early 1980s, Morocco acquired a total of 243 VAB/VMO, 12 VTM, 68 VAB PC, 20 ECH and 49 VAB BCI (all with 6x6 drive). The last of these – dubbed Toucan – was a wheeled infantry fighting vehicle equipped with a 20mm cannon, and was usually issued to the mechanised infantry battalions of the FAR. Most of the Moroccan VABs were painted in dark sand colour (with a strong orange touch), and they regularly received the insignia of the task force to which they were attached, such as two vertical white lines (Ouhoud), or – as shown here – the white letter 'Z' (Zellaka). (Artwork by David Bocquelet)

i

In order to replace its old EBR.75 armoured cars and AMX-13 light tanks, in 1978 Rabat placed an order for 108-111 Austrian-made SK-105 Kürassier light tanks, equipped with a 105mm high-velocity rifled gun. The type entered service with at least three armoured squadrons (GEBs), deployed to bolster the three task forces established in 1979: Ouhoud, Arrak and Zellaka. While usually left in their dark sand overall, some examples received a camouflage pattern in dark earth, as shown here. (Artwork by David Bocquelet)

The Soviet-made 9K31 (ZRK-BD Strela-1, ASCC/NATO-codename 'SA-9 Gaskin') was the first 'heavy' SAM to enter service with the ELPS, in 1979. The system consisted of four missiles in their containers installed atop the BRDM-2 armoured reconnaissance vehicle. It remains unclear if the POLISARIO/ELPS received the older 9M31 missiles with uncooled infra-red seekers and a range of 6.5km, or the more advanced 9M31M missiles with a cooled seeker, and a range of 8km. Generally, ELPS SA-9s were painted in a dark sand colour overall (reminiscent of the colour of cardboard), which was frequently enhanced through the addition of a disruptive pattern of olive green. The box-like missile containers were usually left in olive green overall. (Artwork by David Bocquelet)

The heaviest and most notorious SAM-system deployed by the ELPS was the 2K12 Kvadrat (ZRK-SD Kub, better known by its ASCC/NATO-codename 'SA-6 Gainful'). First delivered either by Cuba or Libya, the system was pressed into service in October 1981 and quickly gained notoriety for downing at least two Moroccan combat aircraft during the famous battle for Guelta Zemmour. As far as is known, most of the tractor-erector-launchers of the ELPS-operated SA-6 systems were painted in dark sand (similar to the cardboard colour), upon which disruptive patterns were applied in diverse shades of dark green. (Artwork by David Bocquelet)

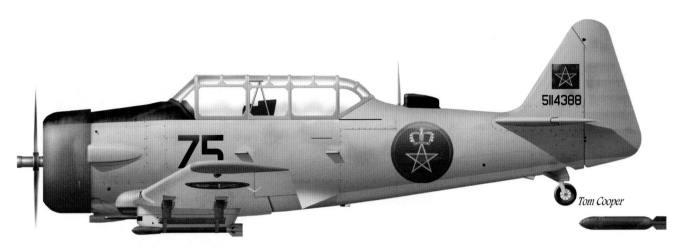

Morocco received about 50 T-6s of various marks, mostly directly from the USA under MAP or similar schemes, but also a batch of armed T-6Gs from France in the late 1960s. They served as basic and advanced trainers – but also as light COIN-strikers – at the Air Force Academy in Marrakesh. While usually left in bare metal overall at earlier times, the aircraft assigned to the detachment deployed to el-Aaiún AB in early 1976 were all painted in dark sand on upper surfaces and sides, and light grey on undersides. All had their engine cowlings and wing-tips painted in day-glo orange, and fin flashes, and roundels in six positions. Complete US FY-serials were applied in black on the fin, and the 'last two' of their construction number below the front cockpit. Their armament consisted of two underwing pods, each containing twin 7.62mm guns, launch rails for up to six 127mm unguided rockets and hardpoints for a total of two 50kg bombs. Alternatively, rockets could be replaced by a hardpoint for two 50kg bombs under each wing. (Artwork by Tom Cooper)

Morocco acquired a total of 24 ex-West German Fouga CM.170R Magister jet trainers in the late 1960s. All were overhauled in France before delivery but retained their camouflage pattern in RAL 7012 Basaltgrau and RAL 6014 Gelboliv on top surfaces and sides, and RAL 9006 Silber Metalic on undersurfaces. Roundels were worn in six positions, while small black serials (230 in this case) were applied on the rear fuselage. Some had their noses painted in yellow, as shown here. Although serving as jet trainers at the Air Force Academy in Marrakesh, all were operated by the *Escadron Panthère* as COIN-strikers and are known to have seen frequent deployments to el-Aaiún in the late 1970s. They were usually armed with a pair of 7.62mm machine guns in the nose, a pair of 127mm unguided rockets on each inboard pylon and light bombs on each of the outboard underwing pylons. (Artwork by Tom Cooper)

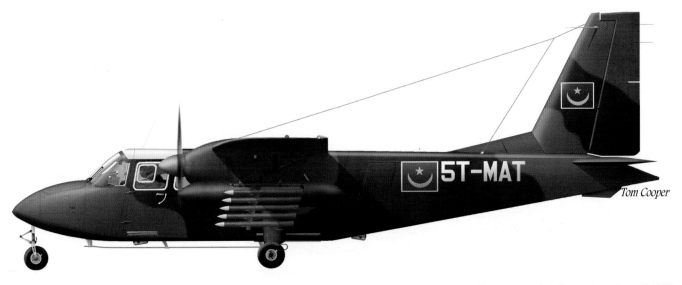

Mauritania originally acquired three BN-2A-21 Islanders (construction numbers 587, 747, and 765) in 1975. These received civilian registrations 5T-MAV, 5T-MAS and 5T-MAT, respectively. The second batch (construction numbers 574, 576, 577, 786, 787, and 793) followed in 1977-1978 and is known to have received registrations 5T-MAY, 5T-MAZ, 5T-MAA, 5T-MAU, 5T-MAQ, and 5T-MAR. At last three of the Mauritanian BN-2s were confirmed as being shot down in the 1976-1978 period, and it is possible that some of the aircraft from the second batch received one or two registrations of the first three. All were painted in dark brown (BS381C/450 or FS20095) overall, with a camouflage pattern in dark green (BS381C/641) and had the cockpit roof painted in white. National markings and registrations were applied on the rear fuselage and the fin only. Mauritanian Defenders were usually armed with 80mm Oerlikon Sura-FL rockets, or pods for 7.62mm machine guns. (Artwork by Tom Cooper)

About a dozen F-5A/Bs and RF-5As made the *Escadron Borak* the FRA's premier fighter-bomber unit of the 1970s. By this time, the aircraft had received a prominent VHF-aerial on the spine and were all camouflaged in the Flogger camouflage pattern consisting of tan (FS 30400), dark brown 8FS30140), and dark green (FS34079) on top surfaces and sides, and light grey (FS36622) on undersurfaces. Roundels were applied in six positions, and the 'last five' of the US-FY-serial number in black on the fin. The aircraft identified as deployed in Western Sahara also wore codes – shown in the insets – in black on the top of the fin, together with much larger fin flashes than usual. Notable is the serial 01381, belonging to an F-5A originally delivered to Jordan. The main artwork shows an F-5A as configured for the long-range strike on the ELPS forward supply depot in north-western Mali in July 1977: with five Mk.82 bombs on the MER under the centreline, AIM-9B Sidewinders on wing-tips, and a pair of drop tanks on the outboard underwing pylons. (Artwork by Tom Cooper)

The constantly growing threat from ELPS-operated SAMs led to the FRA having a requirement to establish its first dedicated reconnaissance and electronic-warfare unit. This became possible with the acquisition of 20 F-5As from Jordan in 1976 and became the Escadron Erige, the insignia of which is shown inset. This was equipped with at least two RF-5As, and several F-5Bs: these initially flew only photo and visual reconnaissance missions but both variants were eventually equipped with US-made AN/ALR-66 radar-warning receivers, thus also becoming capable of detecting the activity of the radar-supported SAM-systems. As far as is known, they never flew any kind of direct attack sorties, but could still be equipped with the same armament as F-5As, including US-made M117, Mk.82, Mk.83 and Mk.84 bombs. Later on, this unit frequently cooperated with Falcon 20 bizjets of the Escadron de ECM/ELINT. (Artwork by Tom Cooper)

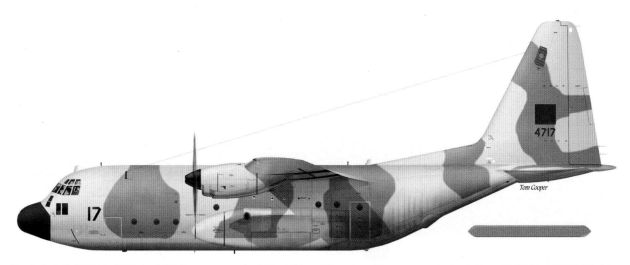

Following the first six C-130Hs in 1976, by 1982 Morocco acquired 11 additional Hercules of the same variant, and two KC-130Hs (4907/CNA-OR and 4909/CNA-OS). Furthermore, the last two C-130Hs (4888/CNA-OP and 4892/CNA-OQ) were modified into early warning aircraft and airborne command posts through the addition of Nadir SLAR-pods (one of which is shown in the inset). All wore the same standardised camouflage pattern consisting of light sand and light earth on top surfaces and sides, and light grey-blue on undersurfaces. Roundels were applied in six positions, and the construction-number originally served as the serial, applied on the rear fuselage (until replaced by the 'civilian' registration, in the 1977-1978 period). Two Moroccan Hercules were lost during the war in Western Sahara: 4537/CNA-OB crashed in 1976, while the aircraft shown here – 4717/CNA-OH – was shot down by ELPS SA-6s in October 1981. (Artwork by Tom Cooper)

The forty Italian-built Agusta-Bell 205As acquired by Morocco were originally painted in light sand and dark brown on top surfaces and sides, and had the undersides of the cabin painted in light grey. Black codes (shown is CN-AJT) and national markings were applied on the boom and the fin only: two-digit serials were usually applied on the nose, sometimes repeated low on the fin, always in black. Some had a cargo winch atop the right forward side of the cabin, while others were armed – usually with LAU-3A pods for 2.75in/68mm unguided rockets, sometimes with the XM59 weapons systems including the Browning M2 machine gun. The entire fleet was flown by the *Escadre d'Hélicoptère*: home-based at Rabat/Sale AB, this maintained regular detachments at el-Aaiún, Bou Craa, Samara and Dakhla airports. (Artwork by Tom Cooper)

Morocco acquired a total of 30 SA.342L and SA.342M Gazelle attack and reconnaissance helicopters. HOT-armed SA.342Ls – like the example shown here – saw intensive service during the later phases of the war, when they proved highly effective thanks to the stand-off range of their ATGMs. All were painted in light sand and light earth (with a strong touch of orange) overall. They wore national markings on the boom and the fin, construction number in black on the top of the fin and the 'last two' of their full registration (CNA-CR in this case) on the boom. Inset is shown the insignia of the FRA *Escadron Anti-Char*, home-based at Ben Guerir since 1978. (Artwork by Tom Cooper)

The primary assault and transport helicopter of the FRA became the 38 Aérospatiale SA.330B Puma helicopters acquired from 1975. Grouped into the *Escadre d'Hélicoptère* together with AB.205As, AB.206As and CH-47Cs, they saw intensive service in Western Sahara. Except for at least four SA.330Ls assigned to the *Gendarmerie Nationale*, all wore a standardised camouflage pattern in light sand and light earth overall. National markings were applied on the cabin's side and the fin only, while registrations were worn in black on the boom. The Moroccans did work on developing a gun-ship variant, equipped with 20mm cannon and a 12.7mm heavy machine gun, but related efforts were abandoned as soon as Gazelles became available. (Artwork by Tom Cooper)

Starting in 1978, the backbone of the Moroccan fighter-bomber fleet became the Mirage F.1CH. The first operational unit was the Sidi Slimane-based *Escadron Assad* (insignia inset). All Moroccan F.1s wore the same standardised camouflage pattern consisting of Brun Café (dark sand, FS30475), Khaki (FS36134), and Gris Vert Fonce (dark green) on top surfaces and sides, while undersurfaces were in light blue-grey (FS35189). The F.1CH variant was originally armed with Matra R.550 Magic Mk.I (lower left corner) and Matra R.530 air-to-air missiles, but during the war almost exclusively flew air-to-ground strikes armed with Mk.81 and Mk.82 bombs (shown installed underwing are parachute-retarded Mk.82s) or Matra F.4 pods for 68mm unguided rockets (lower right inset). Roundels were applied in four positions, and serials in black high on the fin: the latter were in the range 125 to 169. (Artwork by Tom Cooper)

The batch of 14 more advanced Mirage F.1EHs fighter-bombers (serials in range 156 to 169) followed starting in December 1979, and they were mostly assigned to the *Escadron Atlas* (insignia inset). Like earlier F.1CHs, this variant soon received locally manufactured chaff and flare dispensers applied low on the rear fuselage (directly above ventral fins) and was then adapted to carry Italian-made ELT-555 ECM-pods (shown inset, in the right lower corner). This example is illustrated as armed with four South African-made Mk.82 bombs with Daisy Cutter fuse-extenders. Inset in the lower left corner is shown a South African-made Mk.84 bomb with a Jupiter fuse: the heaviest weapon deployed by Moroccan F.1s in Western Sahara. (Artwork by Tom Cooper)

The final sub-variant of the Mirage acquired by Morocco was the F.1EH-200, equipped with in-flight refuelling probes (serials 170 to 175). Like earlier F.1CHs and F.1EHs, it also received chaff and flare dispensers on the lower rear fuselage. Most of F.1EH-200s were operated by the *Escadron Iguider*, a unit largely unknown outside Morocco and specialised in reconnaissance operations (insignia is shown in the upper left inset). For such operations, the aircraft could be equipped with COR-2 (lower left inset) and Harold reconnaissance pods, but also with the AMIN-manufactured Hares pod, containing a LOROP camera (shown as installed on the centreline). This aircraft is shown in the standardised camouflage pattern applied on all Moroccan Mirage F.1s, regardless of their sub-variant. (Artwork by Tom Cooper)

Morocco originally requested 24 Fairchild OV-10As, but only 6 were delivered under the same contract that finally secured the deliveries of F-5E/Fs starting in 1981. All six aircraft in question – BuAerNos 155397, 155404, 155425, 155433, 155462, and 155491 – were from the secondhand stocks of the US Marine Corps. They were assigned to the FRA's *Patrouille Maritime*, which worked up with the support of a team from the US Marine Corps, and primarily served reconnaissance purposes, including maritime patrols. Indeed, the first of two OV-10As that the Moroccans lost over Western Sahara were shot down near Dakhla while on maritime patrol missions. All six aircraft were painted in medium green overall. Their armament consisted of four 7.62mm machine guns installed internally, and LAU-3/M260 or similar pods for 2.75in/68mm unguided rockets. Overall, the Moroccans proved not particularly enthusiastic about their Broncos, and all were in storage by the mid-1990s. (Artwork by Tom Cooper)

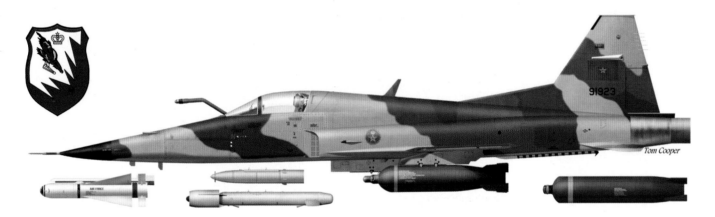

The 14 F-5Es originally acquired by Morocco had US FY-serial numbers 79-1920 to 79-1925, and 79-1932 to 79-1941, and were painted in the standardised Flogger camouflage pattern consisting of tan (FS 20400), dark brown (FS30140), and dark green (FS34079) on top surfaces and sides, and light grey (FS36622) on undersurfaces. The four two-seat F-5Fs (79-1942 to 79-1945) wore the same camouflage pattern but are not known to have been ever deployed in combat. The FRA usually used the 'last five' of their US FY-serials as its serial number (for example 91921, 91934, 91936 etc.). The type arrived armed with a standard complement of Mk.81 and Mk.82 bombs, but the *Escadron Chahine* (insignia in the left upper inset) also deployed 300 AGM-65B Maverick electro-optically guided missiles (bottom left inset), AAQ-8 IR-countermeasures- and ELT-555 ECM-pods (bottom centre), CBU-58s (shown underwing) and CBU-71s (lower right inset). (Artwork by Tom Cooper)

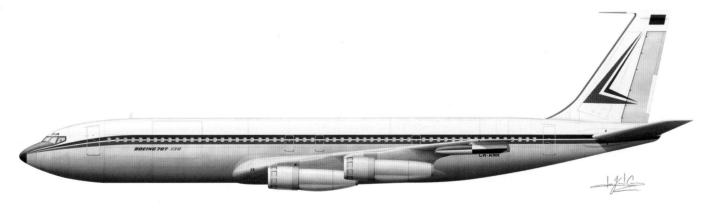

A reconstruction of the sole Boeing 707-320C acquired by the FRA and converted into a tanker by the AMIN: CN-ANR was the last airliner of this prolific series, originally manufactured as a B707-720 prototype. Its livery was quite simple and consisted of white on the top fuselage and the fin, while the rest of the aircraft was painted in light gray, and the engine gondolas left in their bare metal overall. Cheatlines on the fin were in Moroccan national colours: red and green. In addition to expanded internal fuel tanks, it was equipped with Beech 1080 IFR-pods, installed on wing-tips and usually painted in white and red. The aircraft was eventually sold to Omega Air, which subsequently re-sold it to the Israeli air force. (Artwork by Luca Canossa)

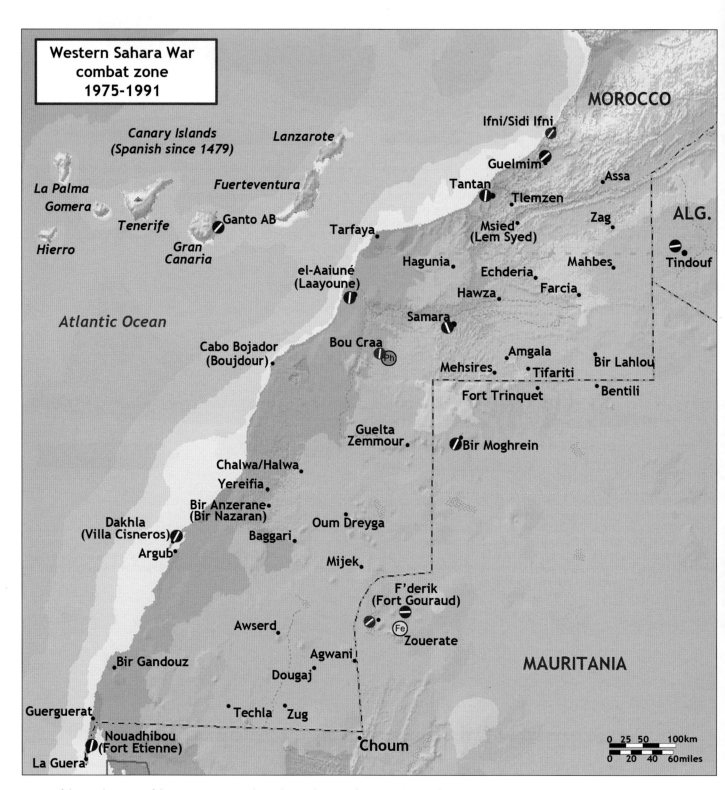

Western Sahara War combat zone 1975-1991

MOROCCO

Canary Islands (Spanish since 1479)

Lanzarote

Ifni/Sidi Ifni

Guelmim

Assa

La Palma

Gomera

Fuerteventura

Tantan

Tlemzen

ALG.

Zag

Hierro

Tenerife

Ganto AB

Gran Canaria

Tarfaya

Msied (Lem Syed)

Mahbes

Tindouf

Hagunia

Echderia

Atlantic Ocean

el-Aaiuné (Laayoune)

Hawza

Farcia

Samara

Cabo Bojador (Boujdour)

Bou Craa

Ph

Amgala

Bir Lahlou

Mehsires

Tifariti

Bentili

Fort Trinquet

Guelta Zemmour

Bir Moghrein

Chalwa/Halwa

Yereifia

Bir Anzerane (Bir Nazaran)

Oum Dreyga

Dakhla (Villa Cisneros)

Baggari

Argub

Mijek

F'derik (Fort Gouraud)

Awserd

Zouerate

Fe

MAURITANIA

Agwani

Bir Gandouz

Dougaj

Guerguerat

Techla

Zug

0 25 50 100km

Nouadhibou (Fort Etienne)

Choum

0 20 40 60miles

La Guera

A map of the combat zone of the war in Western Sahara, during the period 1975-1991. (Map by Tom Cooper)

A still from a rare video showing one of FAIM's BN-2s in flight, together with details of the camouflage pattern applied on its top surfaces. The Defender proved a highly reliable and well-armed aircraft, but also vulnerable to ground fire – and especially to the SA-7s operated by the ELPS. (Albert Grandolini Collection)

An AML-90 armoured car of the Mauritanian Army: the vehicle was painted in sand overall and wore small 'registration plates' applied low on the front and the rear of its hull. (Albert Grandolini Collection)

rack (MER) under the centreline hardpoint, the fighter-bombers launched from Guelmim airport in southern Morocco. Guided by a Gulfstream II business jet carrying Colonel Kabbaj in person, they first landed in Samara to refuel. After refuelling, the F-5As rolled to the runway for take-off in the direction of their target, when tragedy struck: the heavily loaded jet piloted by Lieutenant Driss Bahji suffered the failure of one of its tyres: the aircraft overshot the runway, caught fire and exploded. Miraculously, Bahji was recovered from the burning wrack: tragically, three days later at the military hospital of el-Aaiún, he died due to a penicillin allergy. Led by the Gulfstream II with Kabbaj on board, the remaining three aircraft continued their mission, and – reportedly – delivered a precise attack, completely demolishing what the Moroccans considered the 'main' and 'only' ELPS supply base in north-western Mali.[31]

Ambush for FAIM

Certainly enough, the High Defence Committee took nothing for granted. Accepting the fact that such air strikes could not be undertaken with the necessary frequency, it had to expect the insurgents to continue their raids into Mauritania. Correspondingly, it ordered both the FAIM, and the FRA units deployed in Morocco into intensive reconnaissance patrols, intended to detect and warn of any further raids. As usual, details of the resulting developments remain scarce (indeed, those about operations of the Moroccan air force in Mauritania are entirely unknown). The few indicating their intensity and nature became known only when a Mauritanian historian obtained one of the military reports and posted a summary of its content online.[32] On 16 July 1977, the FAIM was requested to help the garrison of Zouerate, after this was raided by an ELPS unit including about 25 Land Rovers. Commandant Mohammed Ould Bah Ould Abdel Kader, Sous-Lieutenant Fall Mahdoud and Private 2nd Class Ahmed O. Mohammed Abdallahi (observer) took off in a BN-2 Defender. It was around 13:00 when the crew finally sighted tracks left by

ELPS vehicles. Short on fuel, the crew landed on Zouérate to refuel, and then took-off again, following tracks that led in the direction of Tourine. Around 17:30, while underway at very low altitude, the crew found itself confronted with a virtual ambush: well-concealed, the insurgents suddenly opened fire with heavy machine guns. When the pilot attempted to avoid by executing an emergency climb, the ELPS fired an SA-7. The missile scored a direct hit, the impact of which ripped apart one engine and threw the observer out of the aircraft: not wearing a parachute, Abdallahi was killed. Kader somehow managed an emergency landing in the desert: he and Mahdoud buried themselves in the sand and – thanks to the sandstorm that covered the area – evaded capture by the insurgents that converged on the crash site a few minutes later.

Encouraged by this success, the ELPS continued raiding Mauritania: during the next phase, they concentrated their attention upon the railway line linking Zouérate with the port of Nouadhibou and the fortified outposts defending it. On 25 October 1977 they

Ground personnel installing a bank of four Swiss-made, 80mm Oerlikon Sura-FL rockets under the outboard underwing pylon of one of the FAIM's BN-2 Defenders. (via H.B.)

overran one of the mines and took two additional French technicians and 18 Mauritanian maintenance workers as hostages. Although the UN and the Algerian government quickly secured the release of the expatriates, facing a public outcry at home and convinced that the POLISARIO was a 'leftist insurgency', d'Estaing's government in Paris decided to launch a military intervention in Mauritania.[33]

Expeditionary Pioneers

As of mid-1977, the French armed forces were about to finalize a comprehensive reorganization of all of their elements, aimed at developing a significant expeditionary capability for operations well away from Europe. Unknown at that time was the fact that this reorganization moved the French at least ten years ahead of other Western armed forces: while everybody else spent the 1980s preparing for the Third World War in Central Europe – a conflict that never materialised – the French had already developed a powerful expeditionary component capable of launching military interventions all over the world: the sort of conflict that has dominated the operations of all major Western militaries ever since.

One of the most obvious results of this reorganization was the entry into service of the SEPECAT Jaguar A fighter-bomber with nine squadrons of the AdA. Developed in the early 1970s, the Jaguar A was a small, light, simple, rugged, and reliable fighter-bomber, designed to be cheap to acquire and operate, and to facilitate rapid dispersal away from main operating bases and overseas. Contrary to the variants operated by the Royal Air Force (RAF) in the United Kingdom, it was equipped with a much simpler, more reliable, off-the-shelf navigation-attack (nav/attack) system based on a twin gyro platform and Doppler radar originally developed for the Dassault Mirage IVA strategic bomber. Although possessing in-flight refuelling capability, it was much less suited to the high-threat, poor weather conditions over Central Europe, but very easy to deploy and support for overseas operations. By 1976, three squadrons of Fighter Wing 11 (*Escadre de Chasse 11*, EC.11) – EC.1/11 Roussillon, EC.2/11 Vosges, and EC.3/11 Corse – were already operational on the type. While originally tasked with conventional attack and suppression of enemy air defences (SEAD) in Central Europe, they were also assigned a secondary overseas support mission. Correspondingly, their aircraft were all reequipped with laser rangefinders for more accurate conventional weapons delivery, and their crews regularly trained for forward deployments to Senegal (in April 1976), and then the Cote d'Ivoire (in October 1976). Each time, the rapid deployment cell consisted of four fighter-bombers, supported by two Transalls and one Boeing C-135F tanker.

Another new piece of equipment about to enter service with the Aéronavale was the Dassault-Breguet BR.1150 Atlantic Nouvelle Generation. The original variant of this aircraft was operated by French naval aviation and equipped for maritime patrol and anti-submarine warfare. Its production ceased in 1974, but Dassault continued experimental modifications to make the type suitable as an airborne early warning and tactical command post, to control operations by fighter-bombers, to act as a radio-relay, to detect surface targets, and as a platform for electronic intelligence (ELINT). Eventually, Paris placed an order for 42 ATL 2s in 1977, and Atlantics of *21* and *22 Flotilles* (squadrons of the French naval aviation) were made available for overseas operations.

Overall, when Paris issued the order for a military intervention in Mauritania, the AdA was ready: its deployment in that country was to represent the watershed in the use of newly acquired overseas capabilities in the post-colonial era. Not only was a new doctrine put to the test for the first time, but so were a number of brand-new combat and combat-support aircraft.

Operation Lamantin

The intervention in question – codenamed Operation Lamantin – was launched on 26 October 1977, and was run with as low a political profile as possible.[34] The enterprise was run by General of the Air Force (*général d'armée aérienne*) Michel Forget (also a commander of the AdA's Tactical Air Command, the *Force Aérienne Tactique*, FATAC), who had set up his headquarters at the French embassy in Nouakchott, on 2 November 1977. Operation Lamantin began with the deployment of elements of the 9th Marine Infantry Division (9 DIMa) and the 2nd Foreign Legion Parachute Regiment (2e REP) from Toulouse and Tarbes to Ouakam Air Base in Senegal on board 18 Transalls. The AdA then added two C-135F tankers, five Atlantics (from *24 Flotille*), several Douglas DC-8 and Noratlas transports, and two cells with a total of eight Jaguars from EC.3/11, the French Army Light Aviation (*Aviation Légère de l'Armée de Terre*, ALAT) added two Aerospatiale SA.330B Puma helicopters, and Forget had a single C.160 configured as an airborne command post at his disposal. Finally, Dassault Mirage IVA strategic bombers equipped for photo-reconnaissance conducted several high-altitude sorties over Mauritania.[35]

Except for the Mirage IVAs, all of these aircraft were re-deployed to Ouakam Airirfield by 29 October 1977: namely, for reasons related to the history of France and most of the neighbouring countries, Paris deemed it necessary to avoid basing any of its troops directly inside Mauritania. Instead, the initial objective of its forces

A Mirage IV reconnaissance-bomber of the French Air Force, as seen at Yof airfield, outside Dakar, in late 1977 or early 1978. (AdA, via Albert Grandolini)

The first commander of Operation Lamantin, General Forget, together with the commander of the FAIM, Colonel Khader, in front of one of the AdA's C.160 Transalls. (AdA, via Albert Grandolini)

Crucial elements of the French rapid intervention forces – and the 'air policing strategy' – developed during the mid-1970s: a Boeing C-135F tanker, three Jaguar fighter-bombers, and an Atlantic maritime patrol aircraft. (AdA, via Albert Grandolini)

A row of AdA Jaguars, together with three Noratlas transports and a Puma helicopter of the ALAT as seen at Ouakam airport, outside Dakar, in late 1977. (AdA, via Albert Grandolini)

A Puma helicopter of the ALAT, with a team of French forward air controllers, as seen from a Jaguar on a reconnaissance sortie. (AdA, via Albert Grandolini)

was to establish the appropriate infrastructure in Senegal, capable of supporting several cells of Jaguars in combat operations away from local bases, and then to reconnoitre the battlefield in Mauritania. Therefore, only about 60 French military personnel were in the latter country early on: their task was to set up relay stations at five locations, all netted with a special command post established inside the French embassy compound in Nouakchott. Their purpose was to facilitate command and control, intelligence gathering, targeting, and airspace management for the Jaguars and Atlantics. The latter were the first to fly reconnaissance sorties over Mauritania (in addition to tracking the movement of Soviet ships off western Africa).[36]

The French contingent in Dakar was declared ready for mission just around the time the ELPS had restored its forward base in Mali and launched the next series of raids. On 22 November 1977, a column of about 50 insurgent-operated technicals attacked the mine in Touagil. Paris reacted by deploying four additional fighter-bombers to Senegal four days later, thus bringing their total to 12. On 2 December, the insurgents attacked the Mauritanian garrison in Boulanouar, which was protecting the Zouérate-Nouadhibou railway. This time, Forget ordered all of the available AdA combat aircraft into the air over Mauritania: a total of 2 Atlantics, and 8 Jaguars supported by 2 C-135Fs, while he followed on board his C.160 airborne command post. For four hours, the French pilots monitored the insurgents withdrawing towards the north, all the time waiting for the signal from Paris, granting them permission to open fire. Frustrated, and under pressure from the Mauritanians, Forget then ordered a pair of Jaguars – one A, flown by Lieutenant Vergnière, and one E, crewed by 1st Lieutenant Francois and Adjutant Tani – into a 'symbolic attack': they fired their 30mm cannons into the ground in front of the column. Rather uneasy at the situation, Paris subsequently announced that its Jaguars flew an 'air strike against an important POLISARIO fuel and ammunition storage site'. The Mauritanian government was openly bitter and recommended to Forget that if the French came to take photographs, they could also go straight back home.[37]

Jaguars over Zouérate

On 10 December, Atlantics detected an insurgent column of about 40 vehicles heading towards Zouérate. As Moroccan and Mauritanian units moved to counterattack, they requested air support. The column was attacked by FRA F-5s and T-6s. The French joined the pursuit on 12 December. They dispatched a single Atlantic, followed by two Jaguar Es – one piloted by Major Menu with Captain Dehaeze in the rear seat, the other by 1st

Lieutenant Francois and 1st Lieutenant Guerin – supported by a single C-135F. After refuelling in the air over Sant Louis, on the border between Senegal and Mauritania, and then again over Atar, the fighter bombers joined the Atlantic that was tracking a column of about 50 vehicles. Accelerating while diving, the two jaguars descended to about 300 metres altitude (984ft), before strafing the insurgent vehicles with their internal 30mm cannon. The vehicles

A pair of Jaguars from EC.11 in close formation with an Atlantic maritime patrol aircraft of the *Aeronavale* (French naval aviation, or the "*La Royale*" as the *Marine Nationale* is known in France), underway over Mauritania. (AdA, via Albert Grandolini)

A trio of Jaguars escorting a troop-transporting Noratlas of 55 ETOM at very low altitude over the savannah of southern Mauritania. (AdA, via Albert Grandolini)

of receiving an authorisation for air strike a particularly cumbersome affair: a positive reply from Paris arrived only around 15:05 in the afternoon, prompting all the French into a mad dash to their aircraft and a scramble in the hope they might catch the insurgents before they would disappear into the night again. Eventually, four Jaguars were scrambled: the front pair included two As with Major Menu and Capitan Jantet, and the rear two Es, with Lieutenant Hartweck and Adjutant Dechevanne, and 1st Lieutenant Guérin with Adjutant Péron, respectively. Twenty minutes later, two Jaguar As – flown by Captains Dehaeze and Longuet – followed. This time, the fighter bombers found the ELPS column bivouacking in a well-concealed circle among the palms of an oasis east of Tmeimichat, and ready to fight. As the jets approached, they encountered not only fire from multiple 14.5mm ZPU-2 heavy machine guns, but also several SA-7s. Although barely able to see their targets (at least not before they passed directly above them), the French pressed home their attack, and strafed for 15 minutes. Subsequently, all the Jaguars withdrew for an IFR-operation by night and the return back to Dakar. Overall, the French claimed the destruction of two thirds of the vehicles in two days of attacks on this the EPLS column.

quickly dispersed, forcing the pilots to attack them one-by-one. In about 20 minutes of repeated attacks, Menu and Dehaeze claimed the destruction of three Land Rovers, before blowing up the fourth: the vehicle was loaded with fuel drums and ammunition. The first pair was then replaced by the second, piloted by Capitan Jantet with Adjutant Dechevanne, and Lieutenant Harweck with Adjutant Debernardi in the rear cockpit. By the time these two Jaguars ceased their attacks, the French estimated that about a quarter of the column was destroyed. On landing back in Dakar, it turned out that nearly all of the aircraft had been damaged by hits from 7.62mm weapons.

The column was tracked while travelling over 300 kilometres (186 miles) during the night by one of the Atlantics, and thus a decision was taken to attack it again, although it had meanwhile distanced to nearly 1,200 kilometres (745 miles) away from the French base. Once again, contemporary technology made the issue

Jaguar Down

Apparently at least, the French attack left no lasting impressions. On 15 December 1977, another ELPS unit raided the Zouérate-Nouadhibou railway, and Jaguars attacked the withdrawing column. Guided by the BN-2 Defender piloted by Commandant Ould Bah Ould Abdel Kader, they claimed the destruction of 25 vehicles. According to insurgent sources, only a few vehicles were actually hit and most of these carried captured Mauritanian soldiers: 74 out of 82 of these were killed. Late on 17 December 1977, the ELPS raided the Mauritanian garrison and an iron-ore train in Tmeimichat, and Paris promptly ordered an air strike. Before the dawn of 18 December, Forget scrambled a pair each of Jaguar As and Jaguar Es, followed by another two Jaguar As and one Jaguar E. The fighter-bombers caught up with the retreating insurgents early in the morning. The insurgents not only dispersed, but promptly returned fire with their ZPU-2: while their gunners claimed two French fighter-bombers as shot down, they actually hit the Jaguar A A51/11RO, flown by Capitan Jantet, blowing away one of its fuel lines and the radio. As the fumes entered the cockpit, the pilot jettisoned his canopy hood, and – escorted by Jaguar E E31 – made an emergency landing at Nouadibou, in Mauritania.[38]

Meanwhile, another flight of three Jaguars was dispatched to attack the same column again, during the afternoon. This time, the French claimed nearly half of vehicles before returning to Dakar, completely exhausted after eight hours of flying and a total of 40 minutes of fighting. Still, even this proved no deterrence. On the contrary, the ELPS then concentrated about 400 combatants in the Motlani area to unleash an entire series of raids into Mauritania, with the aim of systematically destroying the COMINOR railway. In attempt to cut these off from their supply bases further north-east, between 1 and 8 January 1978, four FAR battalions conducted a sweep operation through northern Mauritania. Described as 'well planned, coordinated and executed', this manoeuvre reportedly resulted in 12 Moroccans and 110-130 ELPS combatants killed. Nevertheless, during this operation the POLISARIO

Jaguar A (A56/11RJ) with one of the C-135F tankers underway over Mauritania: tanker aircraft proved crucial for the French ability to run 'air policing' operations regularly lasting longer than eight hours and ranging as far as 1,300 kilometres away from Dakar. (AdA, via Albert Grandolini)

A view from the position of the boom-operator on board a C-135F tanker of a trio of Jaguars in the process of an in-flight refuelling operation over Mauritania. (AdA, via Albert Grandolini)

claimed not only the downing of another French Jaguar fighter-bomber, but – on 10 January 1978 – its third confirmed kill against a Mauritanian BN-2. The aircraft piloted by Commandant Kader was hit by a single SA-7: this time, Kader managed to remain airborne while his two crewmembers parachuted to safety, but then lost control and crashed. The FAIM thus lost its most experienced pilot.[39]

Two days later, a pair of AdA Jaguars detected and tracked a column of insurgents shortly after they had attacked the Mauritanian outpost in Choum, but received no permission to open fire: Paris was meanwhile not only decreasing its presence in Senegal, but Operation Lamantin was taken over by General Maffre. While this authorised his fighter bombers to deploy not only 250kg bombs but also unguided rockets, the AdA had to reply that its pilots were simply not qualified for the deployment of either. Thus, the

contingent deployed in Dakar spent the next few weeks running extensive exercises against simulated targets in the Mauritanian desert.[40]

Mauritanian Collapse

As far as is known, except for training operations, Jaguars and Atlantics of the AdA flew only a few reconnaissance sorties over Western Sahara for the next month. Upon receiving reports about the diminished activity of the French aircraft, the POLISARIO correctly concluded that the French were becoming preoccupied with the escalating crises in Chad and Zaire, and that the time was opportune to deliver the final coup upon Mauritania.[41]

At dawn of 2 February 1978, the ELPS thus launched a major operation to overrun the Mauritanian garrison in Tichlé. Although Nouakchott subsequently reported this attack as 'repulsed', dozens

A technical of the ELPS set on fire by one of the strafing attacks by French Jaguars in late 1977. (AdA, via Albert Grandolini)

While not damaged by insurgent fire, this Jaguar A (A157/11MQ) made an emergency landing in Dakar, after suffering a technical malfunction. (AdA, via Albert Grandolini)

A Jaguar A (A162/11-EF) low over the suburbs of Dakar. (AdA, via Albert Grandolini)

In order to expose as many as possible of its pilots to combat experience while operating Jaguars, half of such fighter-bombers deployed during Operation Lamantin were two-seater Jaguar Es. The example visible in this photograph is E33/11RC. (AdA, via Albert Grandolini)

of wounded had to be evacuated by FAIM's Defenders.[42]

In late April 1978, a column of up to 100 vehicles drove via Mali to re-attack Zouérate and disrupt mining operations once again. However, the ELPS commanders made a crucial mistake: lacking precise intelligence on French assets deployed in Mauritania, they assumed that the Jaguars and Atlantics had been withdrawn from Dakar. On the contrary: when their columns approached to about 110 kilometres (60 miles) north-west of the target zone, late in the afternoon of 3 May 1978, and to their great surprise, they were detected. The French response was near-instant: in the course of two series of low-level strafing attacks, the fighter-bombers destroyed about a dozen vehicles. The withdrawing survivors were then also counterattacked by units of the Mauritanian Army. The following morning, Captain Champoiseau in a Jaguar A, accompanied by Lieutenant Hartweck flying solo in a Jaguar E, repeated the attack, claiming up to a quarter of the insurgent vehicles. Indeed, the pursuit was subsequently continued all the way through north-western Mali until most of the surviving insurgents were north of the Algerian border. While not keen to report its own losses in this disaster, the ELPS subsequently boasted of shooting down another Jaguar, this time with SA-7s.[43]

Ironically, while a much-publicised success, and although proving the concept of the reorganised French expeditionary capabilities beyond any doubt, ultimately, Operation Lamantin – which was officially ended only in May 1980 – failed to save Mauritania. On the contrary, the government's problems only increased during this period. Earlier attacks by the ELPS had caused heavy losses and threw the Mauritanian military into complete chaos.[44] Moreover,

the military adventures in Western Sahara and the expansion of the armed forces to around 18,000 had gulped at least 60 per cent, perhaps up to 80 per cent of the national budget – while the output of the iron-mines dropped by 12.4 per cent in 1977, and then all but ceased in 1978. Combined with a dramatic fall in the prices of the iron ore on international markets, a drought, and the closure of the Akjout copper mine (where minerals had been exhausted), the effects upon the Mauritanian economy were devastating. Although Saudi Arabia, Kuwait and the United Arab Emirates provided US$400 million in financial support in 1977 and 1978, the draft made the war extremely unpopular among the rank-and-file. Not only was the non-military spending reduced by at least 20 per cent, but also many black Mauritanians – who made up the majority of the lower ranks in the military, yet were often regarded disparagingly by their superiors of Arab and Berber origins – began refusing to take part in a war 'between Arabs', even more so after the government failed to pay most of its officials – and nearly all of its military officers – for six months. Before long, the unrest spread within the armed forces, where there was also constant resentment against the need to rely on French support to defend the country: not a few of the Mauritanian top officers felt directly insulted by this fact.[45]

In April 1979, Lieutenant-Colonel Ahmed Ould Bouceif staged a successful coup in Nouakchott and reconstituted the government of the Military Committee for National Salvation (Comité militaire de salut national). Nominally at least, his intention was to continue Mauritania's involvement in Western Sahara. However, on 27 May 1979, the FAIM DHC-5D registered as 5T-MAY crashed in a sandstorm while underway to Dakar, where Boucief was about to attend a summit of the Economic Community of West Saharan States (ECOWAS). All 12 occupants including the president were killed. This incident was promptly exploited by elements of the armed force to launch a new coup d'etat: on 10 July 1978, Colonel Ould Salek – the Chief of Staff of the armed forces – took power. Salek formed an 18-member Committee for National Recovery, which in turn elected a 16-member cabinet with authorisation to – quickly and almost unconditionally – end the involvement in Western Sahara. Although having to be extremely cautious about the decision due to the presence of up to 10,000 Moroccan troops in the country, the new government in Nouakchott then secretly contacted the POLISARIO with the offer to hand-over the Mauritanian-claimed third of the territory to the insurgency, and that within only seven months. The insurgency signalled its goodwill and, by 12 July 1979, ceased all attacks on Mauritania: combined with offers of aid from Libya, and continuously improving relations with Algeria, these measures coaxed Nouakchott into concluding a peace agreement. The resulting treaty was signed on 5 August 1979 – and was followed by a – polite – Mauritanian request for all Moroccan troops to leave the country. Mauritania pulled out of Western Sahara and ended its commitments there in 1979, then mended relations with its Sahrawi neighbours, and – in 1984 – recognized the SADR.[46]

Chapter 4
A Brutal School

While concentrating upon Mauritania, and eventually forcing the country out of the war in the period 1976-1979, the POLISARIO was much too small, too lightly equipped, and lacking the supplies necessary to run a campaign of similar intensity against Morocco. Therefore, for much of this period it conducted only relatively small operations against the FAR. Even then, the blows that the insurgency delivered upon the Moroccans were painful: they resulted in Rabat launching a major effort to vastly expand its armed forces, bolster its fire power, and – finally – not only reorganise its chain of command, but indeed, to start listening to lower-ranking officers and act according to combat experiences.

Morocco's Shopping Spree

For most of 1976, the ELPS limited its operations against the Moroccans in Western Sahara to occasional raids against the conveyor belt linking Bou Craa with el-Aaiún, and the mining of roads. For its part, the FAR concentrated on securing and fortifying all the major population centres and constructing outposts east of them. Appearing simple on paper, this was anything other than easy in reality. Western Sahara offered no sources for any kind of supplies and thus everything – from water and fuel, to food, spares, and all the other equipment for what was initially about 36,000 Moroccan troops in the territory had to be brought into the country. The distances alone were immense: the road link just from Rabat to el-Aaiún was at least 1,164km (723 miles) long at the time; from el-Aaiún to Samara another 218km (134 miles); from el-Aaiún to Farsia more than 300km (186 miles); to Guelta Zemmour 257km (160 miles), and to Dakhla 533km (331 miles) – all of this along mere desert tracks and inhospitable terrain with next to no water or fuel-sources. Most of this mammoth task was undertaken by ship to the ports of el-Aaiún (re-named Laayoune by the Moroccans), Cabo Bojador (Boujdojur) and Vila Cisneros (Dakhla). However, once there, everything had to be distributed to diverse garrisons by truck or aircraft. The FAR thus first had to organize a massive logistical infrastructure, capable of supporting all of its units over huge distances. This issue grew even more important when the first few clashes with the insurgents revealed the block-obsolescence of even the basic firearms with which the mass of the Moroccan infantry was equipped: as of 1975, these still consisted of old Mauser Modell 98 carbines, MAS.36/51 bolt-action rifles, and MAS 49/56 semi-automatic rifles: the number of old, Swiss-made MG.30,

French AA.52 and Belgian FM BAR machine guns was also limited. Unsurprisingly, in 1976, Rabat rushed to re-equip all of its infantry with Belgian-made FN FAL and German-made Heckler & Koch G3 assault rifles, as well as FN MAG machine guns. Similarly, old variants of Land Rover were replaced by Spanish-made Land Rover Santanas, which had two fuel tanks and thus significantly better autonomy.[1]

This was only the beginning: such acquisitions were run parallel to extensive purchases of heavy weaponry. With the help of Saudi financing, in 1976 Morocco placed an order for Eland 90 Mk.7 (an advanced variant of the AML-90) armoured cars in South Africa, and then for about 100 Ratel-20 and Ratel-90 APCs in 1978. Meanwhile, in 1977, Rabat requested deliveries of more advanced Northrop F-5E Tiger II fighter-bombers, Fairchild OV-10 Bronco COIN aircraft, and Bell AH-1 Cobra attack helicopters from the USA. Because earlier US-Moroccan agreements stipulated deliveries of US-made armament on condition of these being used for internal security and in self-defence only, and because Washington did recognize Moroccan administrative control over Western Sahara *but not* its sovereignty over the same, while Morocco made use of US-supplied arms at war in that territory, the administration of the US president Jimmy Carter turned down all of such demands.[2] Instead, it delivered 37 launchers and 504 Chaparral SAMs (between January and May 1978), Vulcan air defence systems, six OV-10As, and – perhaps more importantly for the FAR's engagement in Western Sahara – 54 M48A3 and 54 M48A5 MBTs.[3]

In 1978, Rabat placed an order for 108-111 (sources differ) SK-105 Kürassier light tanks (equipped with a 105mm high-velocity rifled gun) in Austria with the aim of replacing old and worn-out AMX-13s and EBR.75s. Interestingly, instead of transport by ship, the majority of such vehicles for the FAR were brought to Western Sahara by civilian-operated, truck-towed tilt-trailers, down the coastal road from Sidi Ifni.[4]

Even more significant – and certainly more expensive – was the acquisition of diverse aircraft and helicopters. As mentioned in *Volume 1*, and in Chapter 2, Morocco already had 25 Mirage F.1CH on order since December 1975. With the USA refusing to deliver F-5Es, Rabat turned to Paris, where the government – because of its economic interests and traditional military ties – had taken an openly pro-Moroccan stand on the Western Sahara issue. Therefore, on 23 March 1977 the French and the Moroccan representatives

The sixth and seventh (out of 29 produced, serials 126 to 155) Mirage F.1CHs manufactured for Morocco seen at Dassault's plant in Bordeaux, before delivery. The tail of the second aircraft is just visible behind that of serial 132. (Dassault, via Albert Grandolini)

A pre-delivery view of the right-hand side Mirage F.1EH serial number 167 (one of 14 produced, serials 156 to 169) providing a nice view of the camouflage pattern applied on that side of the aircraft: this was the same for all the F.1CHs and F.1EHs. (Dassault, via Albert Grandolini)

One of only six Mirage F.1EH-200s (serials 170-175) manufactured for Morocco. Notable is the usual 1,300-litre RP.35 drop-tank under the centreline. (Dassault, via Albert Grandolni)

BF radar-warning receivers (RWRs) already installed on earlier F.1CHs, but had also received Tractor ALE-40 chaff and flare dispensers (installed in the underside of their rear fuselages) made to deploy cartridges with decoys for infra-red and radar-guided air-to-air and surface-to-air missiles. Curiously, while wired to carry Thompson-CSF CT-51J Caiman pods for electronic countermeasures, such systems seem to have never been delivered to Morocco. Similarly, while Colonel Kabbaj is known to have enquired about a possible acquisition of Baz-AR anti-radar missiles, originally developed for Iraq, none were purchased because of their excessive price. Instead, the first Mirage F.1CHs reached Morocco in 1978 and entered service with the newly-established Lion Squadron (*Escadron Assad*) while still armed with obsolete – and nearly useless – Matra 530F air-to-air missiles. At least from the Moroccan point of view, more was not necessary: the FRA deployed them foremost as fighter bombers, equipped with US-made bombs like M117 (375kg/700lbs), Mk.82 (250kg/500lbs), and Mk.84 (500kg/1000lbs).[6]

Also with Saudi financial backing, and in order to better prepare its future pilots for flying Mirages, in 1978, Rabat ordered 24 Dassault-Dornier Alpha Jet H twin-engined training-jets and light strikers in France. These eventually entered service with the Training Centre for Combat Pilots (*Centre d'Instruction Pilotes de Combat*, CIPC) – and were used for advanced training and ground attack.[7]

Fire Birds of Allah

At least as important was the major expansion of the FRA's helicopter fleet. As mentioned above, Rabat placed an order for 40 SA.330 Pumas, and these became available by 1975. However, early experiences from Western Sahara had already highlighted the lack of a cannon-armed helicopter. Correspondingly, the technicians of the AMG modified a SA.330B to carry one 7.62mm AA.52 machine gun in the nose, and a 12.7mm Browning M2 machine gun in a side door. However, the performance of such a heavily-loaded helicopter suffered significantly. Therefore, the FRA pushed for the acquisition of SA.342 Gazelle helicopters. The first six 20mm

signed the contract for Project Safran-2, stipulating deliveries of five additional Mirage F.1CHs (scheduled for the period between July and December 1979), 14 advanced Mirage F.1EHs (deliveries between December 1979 and July 1982), and 6 Mirage F.1EHs equipped for in-flight refuelling (IFR).[5]

While the Mirage F.1CH was originally little more than a high-altitude interceptor with the capability to deploy free-fall bombs for ground-attack, the Mirage F.1EH was a significantly upgraded, multi-role variant. It not only included the improved Cyrano IVEH Ramadan radar with moving-target-indicator (making it capable of detecting low-flying targets), but also the Sagem ULISS 43 inertial nav/attack platform that – coupled with a number of other navigational aids – enabled automatic deployment of air-to-ground weaponry against pre-selected geographic coordinates. For self-defence purposes, F.1EHs were equipped with the same cannon-armed SA.342K arrived in 1976, followed by six SA.342Ls equipped with HOT (high-subsonic, optical, remote-guided, tube-launched/*Haut subsonique Optiquement Téléguidé Tiré d'un Tube*) anti-tank guided missiles (ATGMs). In service with the newly-established Anti-Tank Squadron (*Escadron Anti-Char*), the fast, small, and quite silent, HOT-armed Gazelles proved capable of engaging targets the size of a Land Rover over a range of 2,000-3,000 metres. Quickly recognizing this new threat, the insurgents dubbed them the 'Fire Birds of Allah'. Eventually, Gazelles were to prove to be the FRA's 'weapon of choice' for most action in the Western Sahara, and in 1981 Rabat placed another order for 24 examples, including 12 SA.342Ls, 12 SA.342Ks, and 200 HOT ATGMs.[8]

Other than selling fighter-bombers, advanced jet trainers, and helicopters, the French maintained minimal presence in Morocco: when the 1st Parachute Battalion was expanded into four units of that size, in 1977-1978, its new members were trained by French advisors at Ben Guérir. However, except for having their pilots trained on Mirages, Alpha Jets, Pumas and Gazelles in France, the Moroccans generally ran their operations entirely on their own.[9]

Overall, between 1975 and 1979, the FAR was expanded in size by at least 50 per cent and had up to 60 per cent of its battalions deployed in Western Sahara – where most of these remain at the time of writing (for an order of battle of the FAR since 1980, see Table 4). Moreover, the defence budget was quadrupled by 1979 – and this at a time when the prices of phosphate rock experienced a major downfall and recovered only slowly. The effects upon the Moroccan economy were unavoidable: the growth rate collapsed from 8.5 per cent in 1976, to 1.3 per cent in 1977. Despite continuous and significant financial aid from the oil-rich countries of the Persian Gulf, Rabat was thus paying a deft price for its designs in Western Sahara – and it did much of that on credit: its foreign debt quadrupled, reaching US$1.6 billion in 1980.[10]

Quiet Before the Storm

While the above 'shopping list' of the Moroccan military in the late 1970s might sound imposing, the reality in Western Sahara at the time looked significantly different. Although primarily consisting of a huge desert, the local terrain offered near endless opportunities for guerrilla activities – including plenty of cover and good positions

for small, well-concealed bases. Moreover, especially the older of the ELPS' combatants knew how to avoid enemy air power by operating at night – and had since the colonial period, when the French and then the Spaniards were practicing their so-called 'air policing'. Making excellent use of their intimate knowledge of the terrain, they took advantage of the vast amount of available space – but also their enemy's limited resources and unfamiliarity with the environment. Starting from February 1976, the insurgents set up their first ambushes for Moroccan supply convoys. These were small operations, including groups of up to 20 combatants in 4-5 Land Rovers, which usually mined the most frequented roads, like those connecting el-Aaiún with Samara and Bou Craa.

The FAR troops frequently called for air support, but the ELPS was already reasonably well-equipped with Soviet-made 12.7mm heavy machine guns installed on its technicals. This is how the FRA suffered its first two combat losses – a pair of T-6Gs shot down on 28 February 1976, while attempting to support one of the ambushed supply convoys and then pursue the assailants (for a complete list of aircraft and helicopters known to have been shot down, damaged, or claimed as such in 1975-1991, see Table

A total of 18 SA.342Ls constituted the Anti-Tank Squadron of the FRA, one of the most combat-effective units during the war in Western Sahara. Thanks to their HOT ATGMs (this photograph shows a helicopter equipped with stubs and rails upon which tubes containing missiles were installed), the Gazelle could engage car-sized targets from a range well outside most of the heavy machine guns and light anti-aircraft artillery pieces operated by the insurgents. (Albert Grandolini Collection)

Also acquired by Morocco in the late 1970s were three Dornier Do.28 Skyservant light transport and utility aircraft. The type was greatly appreciated by Moroccan crews for its excellent short take-off and landing capabilities, but foremost used for flying maritime patrols. Notable on this photograph is the construction number (4336) applied on the fin of this example, together with its registration, CAN-NP. (Albert Grandolini Collection)

Wreckage of one of two of FRA T-6Gs claimed shot down by the ELPS in February 1976. (Albert Grandolini Collection)

7). Contrary to the POLISARIO's claim, however, the loss of the C-130H on 4 December 1976 was not caused by the insurgents: the transport crashed on take-off from el-Aaiún because the flight-engineer suddenly cut one of the engines by mistake, killing all four crewmembers.[11]

Convoy Ahoy!

While the year 1976 remained a relatively quiet one in Western Sahara, in early 1977 the ELPS began directing an ever-increasing number of its raids against the Moroccan supply convoys. With these initially consisting of soft-skin vehicles – like the US-made M35-series – escorted by Land Rover-mounted infantry, and the Moroccans lacking even mine-detecting equipment, they were easy

pickings. Indeed, before long, the ELPS felt emboldened to not only ambush, but also loot the convoys. In turn, because of the huge distances, and the complex and cumbersome chain of command of the FAR, the Moroccans were almost always slow in reacting: usually, it took hours for any of their garrisons to be granted the permission to move out of their bases and then actually do so. The air force acted slightly better in this regard, but on 25 February 1977 suffered its next loss to the insurgent-operated SA-7s when an F-5A was shot down outside Cap Bojador and the pilot captured.[12]

By July, the ELPS felt free enough to also start raiding diverse Moroccan military outposts. On 24 August, it overran a small FAR unit in the Litcima area, and two F-5As were scrambled from el-Aaiún in response. Once again, the fighter-bombers were ambushed by the insurgents: Captaine Ali Othman was shot down by SA-7s and captured. Not only was every such loss a painful blow for the FRA – which as of 1977 still had only 100 pilots, of which only 45 were qualified to fly jets – but Othman was to experience a particularly sad fate: he was to spend the following 26 years in one of the POLISARIO's prisons outside Tindouf.[13]

Motorised battalions of the Moroccan Army subsequently ran several search-and-destroy operations, and even forced the ELPS out of Tifariti once again, but never managed to pin down and destroy any enemy units. On the contrary, by 1978, the FAR found no other solution but to move its supplies only in large convoys, and then protect these with large units – usually the 6° RIM. While grossly ineffective when measured in terms of fuel spent, they proved the only way of providing vulnerable transports with sufficient protection. Nevertheless, efforts related to convoy-escort resulted in the gradual development of the FAR's capability to run joint-arms operations, because headquarters of such units as the 6° RIM had a forward air controller (FAC) attached: early on, these were specially selected army officers equipped with a suitable UHF-radio, and trained to guide pilots either into attacks on selected objects, or on specific quadrants of the map. Moreover, convoys were supported by AB.205 helicopters, armed with pods for 76mm unguided rockets.[14]

Nothing but Trouble

The ELPS returned to Western Sahara in full force in early-mid 1978: by then, the Moroccans began work on repairing the conveyor belt from Bou Craa to el-Aaiún: this was damaged again in a raid on 2 June 1978. As the insurgents attempted to withdraw towards the east, however, they were pursued by Moroccan aircraft. Once again, a quick ambush was set up and one of the involved F-5As received a hit from a heavy machine gun that caused it to crash while attempting an emergency landing at el-Aaiún. Three days later, another F-5A was hit by at least one SA-7 while attacking an ELPS unit in the Oum Dreyga area, about

A typical supply convoy of the FAR, consisting of a large number of M813 trucks of US origin, and diverse supply vehicles. This one was photographed while underway protected by Task Force Ouhoud. (Albert Grandolini Collection)

Another view of the 'escort element' of a supply convoy, this time showing UNIMOGs and Land Rovers of the 6°RIM, FAR. (via E.C.)

A still from a video showing a Moroccan AB.205, armed with two rocket pods, in the process of landing near one of the supply convoys. (via Tom Cooper)

300km south of el-Aaiún: once again, the pilot attempted to nurse his badly damaged aircraft back to base, but eventually lost control.[15]

During the following months, the insurgency re-directed its attention towards a new appearance on the battlefield: in 1978, the FAR began recruiting Sahrawis and establishing auxiliary military units staffed by them, the so-called 'Méharis'. The first of these was a reinforced company of about 300, commanded by Moroccan officers and NCOs, and including a mortar section, and about 80 vehicles (M151 MUTT jeeps, Kaiser trucks, a few AML-90s and Panhard M3 APCs, Land Rovers and UNIMOG trucks equipped with 12.7mm Browning M2 heavy machine guns, 106mm recoilless rifles, and a few 14.5mm ZPU-2 heavy machine guns). At least four further such units – though each only about 100 strong – emerged over the next 18 months: they became known as the Green March Commandos (*Commando de la Marche Verte*, CMVs), to which sequential numerical designations were added, 1st, 2nd, 3rd, 4th and 5th. Colloquially known as 'stations' in the local military jargon, their task was to patrol the desert, search for and attack or ambush the widely dispersed ELPS at every opportunity.[16]

While certainly a sound idea – because the Méharis also possessed a good knowledge of the local terrain – the original 1° CMV was quite short-lived: as it operated by daylight and in good weather only, the ELPS found it relatively easy to set up an ambush in the Sidi Amara area, in the valley of the River Dra'a, on 27 August 1978, and almost completely destroy the unit.

Free from the new threat, and thanks to their network of forward supply bases, the insurgents remained in the area for a while longer, and on 10 September 1978 also shot down a Moroccan F-5A outside Samara, capturing its pilot.

As soon as it became clear that Mauritania was well on the way to abandoning its designs for Western Sahara, in August 1978, the ELPS re-directed its attention once again, and began launching raids into southern Morocco. By December, the FRA was forced to fly continuous combat air patrols over that country – primarily by

Tantan-based CM.170s. The first air strikes on insurgent columns were reported on the 12th of the same month, against insurgent units active in the Msied area (called 'Lem Ziyed' by the Sahrawis), in south-eastern Morocco, about 200 kilometres south/south-east of Tantan.[17]

Operation Houari Boumedienne

All of this was only the beginning, because the success of the raid on Tantan led the ELPS to the idea for Operation Houari Boumedienne – named after the Algerian president, who provided so much support for the Sahrawis and the POLISARIO before his death on 27 December 1978. This offensive was designed as a general, systematic, and near-simultaneous attack on multiple positions and economic targets in Western Sahara and Morocco. The primary target was the town of Tantan, an important logistical hub on the road from Agadir to el-Aaiún with an airfield, but also a place populated predominantly by ethnic Sahrawis.

As usual, the first objective was the conveyor belt of Bou Craa: this was heavily damaged on 4 January 1979. On 16 January, the ELPS simultaneously raided Tantan and Msied. The attack on Tantan was particularly heavy and might have included up to 2,000 insurgents. They overran the local airfield and claimed the destruction of four helicopters and one F-5A, before reaching the local prison to free 118 inmates, and then continuing to demolish most of the military installations, the local fuel depot and the electric powerplant. Moreover, they felt free enough to remain in the area and in the course of a follow-up action claimed to have shot down two additional F-5As over southern Morocco, on 28 January and 10 February 1979, respectively. While SA-7s were probably responsible for most such successes, it was during this operation that the ELPS began deploying ZPU-2 and then ZPU-4 14.5mm heavy machine guns: thanks to their high cyclic rate of fire, they proved vastly superior to nearly everything in the Moroccan arsenals. Unsurprisingly, the related statement issued by the POLISARIO cited the FAR's casualty figures from these two operations alone as 600 dead, 250 wounded, and 51 taken prisoner. Four armoured vehicles and 60 Land Rovers were reported as captured intact, while 7 tanks and 95 trucks were destroyed.[18]

On 10 February 1979, the ELPS launched a series of raids on the principal population centres in northern Western Sahara, and late that month captured Tifariti in a battle in which an entire battalion of the FAR was destroyed. Quickly converting the oasis into a forward supply base, it then set up a series of ambushes of military convoys moving from Tantan via Tarfaya to el-Aaiún. The severity of the situation reached a level where all the road traffic from Morocco to Western Sahara had to be stopped, and the FAR units further south had to be re-supplied by sea and from the air, while all units were ordered to cluster into major population centres and give up trying to venture outside. For the next few months, the insurgents were thus left to roam freely anywhere between Assa in the north and Bir Ghandouz in the south.[19]

Technology to the Rescue

The catastrophes in Tantan and Tifariti set the alarm bells ringing not only in Rabat, but even in Washington. Having just experienced the fall of Shah Reza Pahlavi of Iran and feeling it had not done enough to support its Moroccan ally, the Carter Administration rushed to approve two major arms deals. The first, signed in May 1979, approved the sale of ground sensor systems made by Northrop Page Communication worth US$200 million, and was supposed to enable the FAR to detect approaching insurgents in time. The

Officers, pilots and ground personnel of *Escadron Borak*, FAR, with two of their F-5As, on the tarmac of el-Aaiún AB in the late 1970s. Notable are additional VHF aerials on the spine of both jets in the rear, and the code 'F' atop of the fin of the example in the rear – indicating it as one of ex-Jordanian aircraft. (via E.C.)

One of Moroccan F-5A, seen loaded with 50kg bombs and ready for another sortie, on the apron of el-Aaiún AB. Intensive operations have caused massive wear on the camouflage pattern of the aircraft. (N.B. Collection)

Early during their combat operations against the Sahrawi insurgents, FRA's Mirage F.1s were frequently equipped with Matra 155 or Matra F4 pods for 68mm unguided rockets. The use of these, and of their internal DEFA 553 cannons forced their pilots to expose themselves to the full spectrum of weapons operated by the insurgents, resulting in several losses.

Not all the insurgent raids were entirely successful: this collection of two captured Toyota Land Cruisers (both mounting heavy machine guns) and two Land Rovers was put on display by the Moroccans after the ELPS' defeat at Bou Craa in November 1979. (N.B. Collection)

second, signed in October 1979 and financed by Saudi Arabia, was worth US$230 million and included 16 Northrop F-5E and 4 F-5F Tiger II fighter jets, and 6 Fairchild OV-10 Bronco COIN-aircraft.[20]

As described in *Volume 1*, Morocco originally acquired 23 Northrop F-5As, 3 F-5Bs and two RF-5A Freedom Fighters. This fleet saw significant attrition due to the coup of 1972, at least one collision and then the war in Western Sahara. It seems it survived into the 1980s only thanks to a donation of several F-5As from Jordan (not from Iran, as frequently reported) sometime after that country was granted permission to acquire Northrop F-5E Tiger IIs, in 1977. At least one F-5A originally manufactured and delivered to Jordan is known to have ended its days in Morocco: this was the example with the serial number 70-1381.

Deliveries of Tiger IIs to Morocco were undertaken between June 1981 and January 1983 and were run by Fenix Aircraft Delivery Inc. – a private company, rather than by the US armed forces, or by means of airlift. Fenix is known to have outbid not only Northrop, but also the USAF to win the delivery contract. The aircraft were flown on the North Atlantic ferry route via Canada, Greenland, Iceland, and the United Kingdom, stopping both at military and civilian airfields along the way to refuel.[21]

Perhaps more important was the fact that the catastrophe at Tantan prompted even King Hassan II to admit there was more than a 'security crisis in the South', and authorise a series of reforms of the FAR that was long-overdue. Correspondingly, three new military districts were established and headquartered in Guelim, Tantan, and el-Aaiún. Moreover, the FAR rushed new equipment acquired earlier to the units deployed in the Western Sahara: this is how 1°GEB, deployed in Samara, became the first unit to be re-equipped with US-made M48A5 MBTs and M113 APCs, 20mm M163 anti-aircraft guns, and Austrian-made SK-105s. In comparison, the last unit to operate T-54s and OT-62s, the 3°GEB, was meanwhile withdrawn to Lebouriat (called 'Ibourate' by the Sahrawis), and ordered to wait for its turn, just like the – meanwhile de-facto besieged – garrison in Zag.

The FAR's Task Forces[22]

Instead of reinforcing units, and in an attempt to regain the initiative, the General Command FAR used its new equipment to re-equip other units, which were then grouped into three brigade-sized formations: officially designated 'joint tactical groups' (*groupe tactique inter-armes*, GTIA), these consisted of a miscellany of battalions and companies of tanks, APCs, artillery, and motorised infantry. By the summer of 1979, three GTIAs came into being: Ouhoud, Arrak and Zellaka.

Established in 1977, Ouhoud was the first of the FAR's task forces. Originally home-based in Taza, it consisted of the three-battalion strong 7° BIM, equipped with US-made M113 APCs, supported by M163 Vulcan six-barrel, 20mm anti-aircraft guns, and

M577s (command vehicles on the cassis of the M113 APC). These were reinforced by the 7° GEB equipped with SK-105s, and a RAG equipped with French-made 155mm AMX F3 self-propelled howitzers, and then two battalions of mechanised infantry mounted in M113 APCs. Meanwhile reorganized as the 7° BRIMeca, the unit was then re-deployed to Tantan, and – in October 1979 – reinforced through the addition of the 8° RIM. Task Force Ouhoud's vehicles were easily recognized by the application of two vertical white lines on their front.

After the initial success of the Ouhoud GTIA, in December 1979 the FAR followed with the establishment of its second task force: the Zellaka GTIA. Initially home-based in Tantan, this consisted of the 8° MIR (equipped with French-made VAB wheeled-APCs), a GEB each of SK-105s and AML-90s, and a RAG equipped with AMX F3 self-propelled howitzers. Task Force Zellaka's vehicles were marked with a big white 'Z' applied on the fronts and sides of its vehicles.

The third GTIA was dubbed the Arrak: this was centred on the 10° MIR (equipped with Ratel-20 and Ratel-90s), reinforced by GEBs equipped with SK-105s and AML-90s, a RAG of AMX F-3s. The vehicles assigned to this task force wore a big white 'X' applied on the front and the rear of their hulls.

Windscreen Vipers

After withdrawing to the Tindouf area for rest and reorganisation in late spring, the ELPS was back in southern Morocco during the early summer of 1979 – meanwhile reinforced through the acquisition of Toyota 4WDs (which began replacing the venerable Land Rovers), and BM-21 multiple rocket launch systems (MRLS). In July, it raided Lebouirat. Nominally at least, the attack was 'beaten back' by veteran Moroccan troops, but the garrison commander's requests for help were never answered by the General

Insurgent raids into southern Morocco prompted the FRA into making extensive use of its Fouga CM.170 Magister jet trainers. Armed with two internal machine guns and unguided rockets (installed underwing), these flew intensive combat air patrols over southern Morocco, and at least one is known to have been shot down by the insurgents. (Photo by Ivo Sturzenegger)

A pre-delivery photograph of an F-5E Tiger II manufactured for Morocco. Notable is the absence of an IFR-probe, the RWR-housings and the VHF-antenna on the aircraft's spine: all of these were attached only after their delivery in June 1981 – January 1983 (the RWR-housings on the FRA's F-5s were white on their installation, starting in 1982, until repainted in black, in 1999). (Albert Grandolini Collection)

An SK-105 Kürassier of the 7°GEB, assigned to Task Force Ouhoud: notable is the standardised identification insignia for vehicles of this GTIA, consisting of two vertical white lines applied down the front of its turret and the hull. (N.B. Collection)

Command in Rabat: the latter refused to believe his reports. Instead, the General Command ordered Task Force Ouhoud, commanded by Colonel Haik, to drive out of its main base in Tantan and sweep the desert all the way to Dakhla (operations Ouhoud and Qadr).

A column of M113 APCs, M163 Vulcan anti-aircraft cannons, and M577 command vehicles of Task Force Ouhoud on the advance through southern Morocco or northern Western Sahara. (N.B. Collection)

A column of Task Force Arrak (recognizable by the big white 'X' on the front), consisting of M113s and Land Rovers, underway in northern Western Sahara in late 1978. (via E.C.)

A VAB BCI Toucan of Task Force Zellaka (as indicated by the white Z applied on the driver's doors). Notable is the camouflage consisting of the vehicle's original green overall, crudely oversprayed with dark sand colour. (N.B. Collection)

Simultaneously, Task Force Zellaka (commanded by Major Abrouk) was to relieve the garrison of Zag before continuing into the Dra'a Valley towards the ELPS forward bases in the Ouarkziz Mountains (Operation Iman). Finally, Task Force Arrak (commanded by Colonel Ben Othman but still in the process of being established) was to act as a reserve.[23]

The mission of Task Force Ouhoud began well: on 11 August

1979, it overran a small ELPS unit outside Bir Inzarane – a village only a few kilometres outside Tantan, controlled by the 1°BIS. In addition to destroying and capturing about a dozen Land Rovers, the Moroccans found a sizeable stock of RPG-7Vs with thermobaric warheads: much to their dismay, the FAR thus found out that the insurgents were operating some of the most-advanced Soviet-made infantry weapons, while they were still lacking all sorts of equipment and supplies. However, the ELPS was meanwhile on the move, too: not only was the movement of such massive formations as Task Force Ouhoud easy to detect and avoid (so much so, the Moroccan troops sarcastically dubbed them the 'windscreen vipers'), but its smaller and lighter units were also travelling much faster. After distracting its enemy's attention by raiding the Mauritanian and the FAR garrisons in Dakhla, on 10 August, it returned to attack the weak 3°GEB in Lebouirat late on 24 August 1979. Assaulting simultaneously from three directions, it quickly overpowered the defenders and drove straight for the main base. Amid the ensuing chaos and panic, the commander of the garrison fled and the resistance collapsed: 811 troops were killed and 92–111 were captured – together with extensive loot including 37 T-54s and 13 OT-62 APCs (most were non-operational and actually in storage), 12 AML-90s and Eland-90s, 21 Land Rovers and 4–6 trucks. Worse yet: when Task Force Zellaka moved out of Zag in an attempt to relieve the garrison in Lebouirat, it was ambushed and partially destroyed: the village and the ruined FAR base nearby thus remained under the POLISARIO's control for nearly a year. Ultimately, the FAR was forced to re-route the huge Task Force Ouhoud from its march in the direction of Dakhla in order to secure the Ouarkziz Mountains, while re-deploying Arrak – which lost three SK-105s and several AMLs while capturing one T-55 and several Toyotas in the Ras al-Khanfra area – further south, to block the ELPS' access to the road from Tantan to el-Aaiun.[24]

Raid on Samara

While driven out of the Ouarkziz Mountains, the insurgents were back in force only a month later. On 30 September 1979, one group raided Guelb Ben Rzouk, a station on the border between Algeria and Morocco. When the FAR reacted by re-routing Task Force Ouhoud in this direction, the ELPS quickly withdrew to Algeria, before regrouping and then launching a major assault on Samara, the Sahrawi holy town, on 5 October 1979. Attacking from three sides, they overran the outposts and reached the area known to the locals as Rbayb, which was then quickly converted into a major supply dump and base for its BM-21s. From there, they penetrated the defensive perimeter, drove into the town to kill the garrison-commander and 120 of his troops, and free about 700 Sahrawi prisoners from the local jail. However, most of the garrison – centred

One of the insurgent-operated Land Rovers captured by Task Force Ouhoud at Bir Anzarane. Notable is the Browning M2 heavy machine gun. (via E.C.)

A Czechoslovak-made OT-62 APC of the FAR knocked out by the insurgents outside Lebouirat. The Moroccans stress that all of the 37 T-54s and 13 OT-62s lost in this attack had been non-operational for months before. (Albert Grandolini Collection)

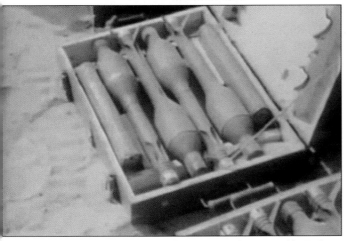

What the Moroccans mis-identified as RPG-7V rounds captured by Task Force Ouhoud at Bir Anzarane, in August 1979, were rounds for Yugloslav-made M57 anti-tank rocket launcher. (via E.C.)

on the 6°RIM reinforced by the 1°GAR and the 1°GEB – held out and withstood a 24-hour pummelling and substantial hand-to-hand fighting. Indeed, they were reinforced with the help of helicopters during the night from 5 to 6 October. The next morning, the General Command in Rabat ordered the FRA's brand-new Mirage F.1CHs into combat. Forward deployed at el-Aaiún, and guided by the FACs, these flew a series of devastating air strikes on the Rbayb area, deploying Mk.82 bombs first, before returning to strafe with 30mm DEFA automatic guns. Ultimately, one of the bombs blew up the main ELPS ammunition dump. This, and the fact that the insurgents subsequently withdrew from Samara, enabled Rabat to claim that this attack was repulsed with the insurgents losing 50 vehicles and 330 killed, subsequently increased by 200 additional vehicles and 735 'dead mercenaries' during pursuit operations. However, Western observers described the battle as a 'rout', while the POLISARIO reported only minimal losses: indeed, on their way back to their bases in Algeria, on 14 October 1979 the insurgents raided Mahbas. Abandoned by its civil population already back in 1975, the place was defended by a battalion of about 780 officers and other ranks. Isolated, the FAR unit stood no chance: about 1,200 insurgents overran and dispersed the garrison in the course of a 24-hour battle, and then also ambushed and forced the relief troops to withdraw. Before withdrawing, the ELPS completely demolished all the military installations: even the official Moroccan military reports admitted that more than 20 per cent of the personnel of the garrison had fallen, and that the proportion of those wounded was even higher.[25]

Failed Raid on Bou Craa

Falling back upon their 'success' in Samara, the FAR attempted to continue Operation Ouhoud in early October 1979. However, the ELPS would not let it do so: in a matter of one week, it raided not only Zag, but also

One of 3°GEB's T-54s knocked out during the ELPS-raid on Lebouirat in August 1979. (Albert Grandolini Collection)

A still from a video showing an insurgent Land Rover, heavily loaded with a ZU-23 heavy machine gun. (via E.C.)

A Land Rover of the 6°RIM, FAR, mounting a 106mm recoilless rifle, underway in north-eastern Western Sahara, in late 1979. (via E.C.)

Akka, Tata, the oasis of M'hamid (the site where Mohammed V first announced his country's aspirations for Spanish Sahara), Lemsert, Tata, Bir Anzahran, and Tantan again, causing heavy losses and additional damage as it went. Just to dot the i, and proving that they had suffered – relatively – light losses in Samara, the insurgents next concentrated about 600 combatants to raid the Bou Craa mine, on 5 November 1979. The crucial mine was protected by the 3,000-strong 4° RIM of the FAR, which put up fierce resistance. While withdrawing from a battle that lasted five hours, some of the insurgents found their way blocked by the nearby 'river' created by torrential rains of the previous day, which converted a normally dry landscape into a muddy quagmire: several reportedly drowned, a few others were killed, and ten taken prisoner.[26]

Two weeks later, during a 'routine' ground attack on an ELPS column underway in the Zag area, in southern Morocco, the FRA lost its first Mirage F.1CH – and then to the first of the 'heavy' SAMs deployed by the insurgents: the aircraft flown by Ahmed el-Fane was shot down by an SA-9 over Abtih, and its pilot killed.[27]

Overall, no matter how downplayed by official Rabat, the reality was that there was not only a war raging in Western Sahara, but in much of the southern Morocco too, and that, under pressure at multiple points, the FAR was unable to defend everywhere at the same time. Indeed, the ELPS was quick in deploying its BM-21s to successively rocket nearly all of the FAR outposts protecting el-Aaiún on 6 December 1979, and to shoot down another Mirage F.1CH, the pilot of which was captured. On the same day, the insurgents re-raided Zag too: when Task Force Zellaka attempted to intervene, it was ambushed and forced to retreat. The POLISARIO subsequently claimed to have killed 329 enemy troops in these two operations alone – which Rabat flatly denied.[28]

Chapter 5
The POLISARIO's Pyrrhic Victory

Through 1980, the ELPS continued saturating the Moroccan armed forces with a series of raids against widely dispersed targets all the way from southern Morocco to northern Mauritania. Debilitated by its complex and cumbersome chain of command and logistics, the FAR nearly always reacted much too late – usually only responding hours after an attack: the insurgent raiding parties thus continued delivering murderous blows, while escaping unscathed. The effect was unavoidable: not only had Morocco lost the initiative in the war, but it was well on the way to losing it, and no turnaround was in sight: many units were tied down defending all the important positions over a frontline longer than 2,500 kilometres (1,553 miles), the FAR was suffering crippling losses, while its best units were running all over an empty desert. Unsurprisingly, the morale within the armed forces was in tatters, in turn prompting dramatic desertion rates within the newly-established CMVs.[1]

The Mess of 1980
On 25 January 1980, the insurgents again raided Akka, a small oasis town just across the border from Algeria, and then went all the way to attack Tarfaya near the coast. Having thus forced the Moroccans to bolster the defences of their own property, in February the ELPS drove all the way to attack the garrison of Cape Bojador, leading to a two-day pitched battle, in the course of which its SA-7s shot down

an F-5A and a Mirage F.1CH. The FAR reacted with one of its rare counteroffensives into the Ouarkziz Mountains, but in March 1980 one of its task forces was ambushed there, and the ELPS captured six Eland-90 Mk.7 armoured cars of South African origin.[2]

The Moroccans then deployed Task Force Ouhoud into a deep sweep of north-western Sahara, aiming to cut off the forward-deployed insurgent units from their bases in Tindouf, but also to destroy any forward supply bases they could find. Supported by F-5s, Mirages, and helicopters forward deployed at el-Aaiún, Bou Craa and Samara, the unit moved out in a large formation from the area between Bir Anzaran and el-A'argub. Nothing happened for at least a week, until at least two insurgent columns – reportedly a total of 370 vehicles, including a few T-55 tanks – were discovered on 7 May 1980, and Colonel Haik ordered a pincer attack. According to Moroccan sources, in the course of the next eight hours, Task Force Ouhoud killed 450 insurgents and destroyed 162 of their vehicles, while losing 36 killed and several dozen wounded. Moreover, the F-5s then attacked a column of 32 vehicles 'fleeing to the east' and destroyed 29 of these. After replenishing, the task force launched an assault on the next insurgent stronghold, Abtih. According to the Moroccan version, the oasis was subjected to a pincer attack and quickly overrun on 23 May: the FAR claimed the destruction of 45 vehicles and another 150 dead insurgents. When the ELPS

By 1980, the POLISARIO was well on the way to winning the war in Western Sahara: dozens of raids against southern Morocco, and Moroccan garrisons in Western Sahara, resulted in the capture of a huge volume of loot, which the insurgents proudly put on display for foreign visitors. This photograph shows diverse artillery pieces, recoilless rifles and mortars, and a row of about 20 AML-90/Eland-90 armoured cars. (Albert Grandolini Collection)

A column of ELPS Land Rovers, underway for another raid into southern Morocco or northern Western Sahara, in 1980. (Albert Grandolini)

attempted to counterattack, four days later, the Moroccans repelled their assault, killing 176 and destroying another 29 vehicles.[3]

However, there is a big question mark over such Moroccan claims: the simple matter of fact is that as of that time in the war, the ELPS never attempted to directly challenge the vastly superior FAR: whenever confronted by such massive units as Task Force Ouhoud – all of which were easy to detect and track in the otherwise 'empty' desert – it would withdraw, change its primary area of operation and seek to raid poorly defended targets instead.

Indeed, the fact that the POLISARIO did not suffer any major blows from the windscreen vipers became obvious at least on 21 June 1980, when multiple insurgent columns – reportedly: more than 500 vehicles in total – raided 4°GIM's positions in the Guelta Zemmour area. Certainly enough, the FAR claimed to have destroyed 53 vehicles and killed 'more than 300 mercenaries', while admitting a loss of 16 killed and 52 wounded. Moreover, FRA F-5As then destroyed another 60 vehicles while pursuing 'those that fled'. However, just eight days later, the ELPS assaulted and overran the garrison of Akka, before pushing all the way to the local administrative capital Tata and causing even more damage. Frustrated, the Moroccans recalled GTIA Ouhoud back to the Zag area, while the FRA was ordered to bomb any 'suspected sites of insurgent activity' that the intelligence services could find in south-eastern Morocco

and north-eastern Western Sahara. Moreover, on 29 July 1980, the Mirages even flew an air strike against Boulanour in Mauritania. Overall, there was no denial of the fact that by early 1981, Morocco's grip on Western Sahara was limited to two enclaves: the area between el-Aaiún and Samara in the north and the other around the port of Dakhla in the south. Correspondingly, the FAR took care to re-settle and concentrate what was left of the native Sahrawi population in the areas of Jacinta, Samara, and Guelta Zemmour, all of which were heavily fortified, thus making them – at least nominally – inaccessible to the POLISARIO. It was in the light of this situation that the ELPS for the first time reported an engagement with Moroccan forces involved in the construction of a large 'earthwork defence system', and knocking out several 'earthmoving machines', that were digging a 'double-walled trench'.[4]

This was the first indication that Morocco had switched to an entirely defensive strategy: one centred around the FAR's effort to control the insurgency, rather than defeat it – through a concentration on previous gains, clearing land, and holding it with well-defended barriers. In this fashion, the war became much more affordable for Rabat, while also allowing for the gradual establishment of a functional civilian administration in the most important parts of Western Sahara.

Morocco's Great Wall

With FAR's poor showing against the insurgents slowly crystallizing into a major problem for the throne – as a direct threat from the war-weary armed forces – King Hassan II authorized a major change in the strategy of the Moroccan military operations. Starting in late 1980, the FAR was to concentrate on the construction of an earthen wall, some three to five metres high, protected by barbed wire and minefields, supported by fortified observation posts every two to three kilometres. This wall was to serve as a 'trip-wire': deeper behind it the FAR was to consolidate its major units within bases constructed every 20-30 kilometres from where these could react to any insurgent attack.[5]

Contrary to what might be expected, the berm – to become known as the 'Moroccan Great Wall' over time – was not constructed directly on the border between Algeria and Mauritania. The first portion only protected a triangular-shaped region in the far north-west corner of the territory, including the capital of el-Aaiún, the

A section of the 'Morocan Great Wall', together with one of the observation posts – effectively a fire-base, occupied by a company of infantry, supported by heavy machine guns and mortars. (via E.C.)

Another section of the Moroccan berm: notable is the relatively big base sprawled atop a dominating peak in the foreground, including multiple firing positions for tanks and other armoured vehicles. Such fortifications were to prove of crucial importance later on, when the ELPS was forced to realize that it couldn't elevate the guns of its Soviet-made tanks high enough to directly target the Moroccans. (via E.C.)

phosphate mines of Bou Craa and the holy town of Samara, the so-called 'useful parts' of Western Sahara. It consisted of not only one, but two berms running parallel to each other, and was constructed on numerous hilltops and ridges, so as to have command of the highest ground possible, wherever possible. Roughly 3m (7ft) tall and 8m (25ft) thick, the wall extended for about 450 kilometres from east to west, and was dotted – at intervals of about every one or two kilometres – by bunkers constructed atop elevated sand embankments, each of which protected its neighbours with overlapping fields of fire. Every bunker was protected by mines and French-built radar sensors capable of detecting vehicle movement up to 40 kilometres away. Topped with barbed wire, the rest of the berm was heavily mined on the insurgent side and monitored by sophisticated electronic sensors. Deeper behind the berm, at much greater intervals, the FAR's engineers constructed a number of small forts that served as bases for mechanized units and artillery, ready to provide back-up support for the defenders of the berm.

While some have dismissed this massive construction as 'Hassan's folly', the use of barrier defences in COIN warfare has a long history.

A Moroccan 90mm M59 Scorpion self-propelled anti-tank gun of the FAR in a firing position on an unknown section of the berm. (Albert Grandolini Collection)

An interesting 'technical', consisting of a US-made M813 truck, with a Soviet-made 23mm ZU-23 anti-aircraft cannon, in a firing position along the Moroccan berm. Although nominally acquired for air defence purposes, the ZU-23's high cyclic rate (up to 2,000 rounds per minute), and the heavy punch it could deliver over a range of 2.5km (1.5 miles) made it a fearsome weapon in ground fighting too. (N.B. Collection)

The Italians used them during their conquest of Libya in the 1910s and 1920s, the French in Algeria in the late 1950s, too. Usually, they proved highly effective, and thus it was unsurprising when at least a few foreign military observers concluded that their appearance would be disastrous for the POLISARIO. However, at least initially, the Moroccans and their foreign advisors experienced a number of issues with the sophisticated electronic equipment including ground surveillance radars and infra-red sensors provided by the USA and France to support the monitoring operations along the berm. These tended to fail in the searing heat and the frequent sandstorms, but there were issues also due to insufficiencies in the technology, an insufficient number of devices available, and poor training of their operators. Correspondingly, they frequently failed to detect insurgent movement. Before long, the ELPS learned how to avoid these early installations: its combatants would often dig up mines and re-position them on the Moroccan side of the berm. Furthermore, early on, Moroccan fortifications proved vulnerable to bombardment: troops protecting the berm could not withdraw or launch a counterattack without leaving portions of the berm undefended. In other cases, the ELPS would attack at different places at the same time, forcing the FAR to divert its rapid-reaction forces, and then launch the actual attack inside Western Sahara.

Fatal Mistake

While the Moroccans were busy building their great wall, as early 1981 the POLISARIO was preoccupied with an entirely different issue: that of making a mistake of strategic proportions. Always sensitive about the levels of international support it was receiving, the leadership of the insurgency noticed a

Region	Units	Notes
Table 4: FAR Order of Battle in Western Sahara and Southern Morocco, since 1979-1980		
Region	Units	Notes
Place d'armes Guelim	2° BSS	
	BA-FRA	
	1° BM	meanwhile withdrawn from Western Sahara
	3° BSMAT	
	3° BSMUN	
	4° BG	
	PC/GMM	
Place d'armes Tantan	BA-annexe FRA	
	6° GAR	
	8° BIM	
Place d'armes Laayoune	4° Ba-FRA	
	1° BSS	
	4° BSMAT	
	2° BG	
	7° GTr	
	3° BISMAR	
	2° BSI	
	3° HPM	
	4° BT	
	4° BP	meanwhile withdrawn from Western Sahara
	4° GLS	meanwhile withdrawn from Western Sahara
	5° BM	meanwhile withdrawn from Western Sahara
	8° GEB	
	PC/GMM	
	34° GMM	
Place d'armes Dakhla	3° BSS	
	BA-FRA	
	3° BN	
	2° BISMAR	
	5° BISMAT	
	4° GFT	
	4° HPM	
	5° BSI	
	PC/GMM	
Secteur Oued Draa (S. O. D.)		
Sous-Secteur Akka	17° BIS	
	37° BIS	
	71° BIS	
	14° GMM	
Sous-Secteur Toizgui	41° BIS	
	52° BIS	
	62° BIS	
	1° CMV	
	2° CMV	
	33° GMM	
	3° GLS	meanwhile withdrawn from Western Sahara
Sous-Secteur Farcia	8° BRIMoto	
	10° GEB	
	1° GAR	
	14° BIS	
	48° BIS	
	57° BIS	
	66° BIS	
Secteur Saquia el-Hamra (S. S. H.)		
Sous-Secteur Haouza	10° BRIMoto	
	3° GAR	
	9° GAR	
	69° BIS	
	70° BIS	
	72° BIS	
	3° CMV	
	5° CMV	
	17° GMM	
Sous-Secteur Samara	BA-annexe FRA	
	6° RIM	
	1° GEB	
	4° GAR	
	16° BIS	
	58° BIS	
	64° BIS	
	3° BP	meanwhile withdrawn from Western Sahara
	5° GLS	meanwhile withdrawn from Western Sahara
Sous-Secteur Amgala	28° BIS	
	29° BIS	
	42° BIS	
	59° BIS	
Sous-Secteur Guelta	1° RIM	
	5° GAR	
	18° BIS	
	19° BIS	
	51° BIS	

Continued on page 52

Continued from page 51

	61° BIS	
	11° GMM	
	31° GMM	
Secteur Oued ed-Dahab (S. O. ED.)		
Sous-Secteur Oum Dreiga	3° RIM	
	7° GEB	
	11° GAR	
	30° BIS	
	47° BIS	
	50° BIS	
Sous-Secteur Beggari	4° RIM	
	12° GAR	
	35° BIS	
	63° BIS	
	67° BIS	
	4° CMV	
Sous-Secteur Aouserd	11° BRIMoto	
	11° GEB	
	10° GAR	
	1° BIS	
	36° BIS	
	68° BIS	
Sous-Secteur Tichla	12° BRIMoto	
	8° GAR	
	44° BIS	
	45° BIS	
	55° BIS	
	60° BIS	
Sous-secteur Bir Gandouz	53° BIS	
	54° BIS	
	56° BIS	

'slight decrease' in the tempo at which the SADR was recognized by foreign governments. Therefore, a decision was taken to unleash the ELPS into a major offensive aimed at attracting world-wide attention again. However, preparations for this operation were undertaken under increasingly negative circumstances. The POLISARIO's aim of securing the existence of the SADR and its international recognition forced the ELPS to operate in a way it was not suited for: instead of continuing the strategy of its highly-successful raids, it had to switch to operations in ever larger formations supported by heavy weapons systems. As time was to show, not only did this make the movement hopelessly overdependent on foreign support: despite initial success, the insurgency actually never managed to adapt itself to fight under such circumstances. Instead, it was to

expose itself to the vastly superior firepower of the FAR.

The writing was on the wall, however, because by mid-1981 there was a growing crisis between the POLISARIO and Algiers, as the new Algerian president began showing impatience with the prolonged hostilities and a greater eagerness to have the dispute settled. A high-ranking POLISARIO official averred around that time that Algeria no longer supported the war with any enthusiasm, that it was looking for ways to extricate itself from its relationship with the insurgency, and that it was prepared to seek a political solution at any price. Worse yet – at least from the standpoint of the insurgent leaders – around the same time even the Libyan leader Muammar el-Qaddafi had promised King Hassan II that he would curb arms supplies to the POLISARIO in exchange for normalised relations with Rabat and Hassan's assurance that Morocco would assent to Qaddafi's nomination as chairman of the OAU in 1982.[6]

The Last Big Libyan Shipment

Certainly enough, before this agreement came into effect, the Libyans hastened delivery of another large arms shipment for the ELPS via Algeria. Contrary to earlier times, this predominantly consisted of heavy arms – including T-54/55 MBTs and BMP-1 IFVs, but also Soviet-made self-propelled surface-to-air missiles (SAMs). The ELPS had operated a few SA-9s – short-range, infra-red homing SAMs installed on the chassis of the Soviet-made BRDM-2 armoured reconnaissance car – provided by Libya since around 1979 but used them only to protect its camps in the Tindouf area. Some of their crews were trained in Cuba, and others in Czechoslovakia. Additional SA-9s arrived with the last big Libyan arms shipment in 1981. However, the same shipment then also included a full battery of SA-6s and at least one P-15 early warning radar. It remains unclear who exactly provided the latter two systems: while the Moroccans – in general – blame the Algerians, Algerian, Sahrawi, and better-informed Moroccan sources point to either Cuba or Libya. Indeed, even Sahrawi sources – grudgingly – confirm that the first SA-6s to reach ELPS were at least maintained, if not operated, by Cuban and Syrian personnel, instead of by hurriedly trained ELPS personnel. While currently there is no way to cross-examine such reports, and they thus might be considered as disputable by many, there is no doubt about the fact that the availability of these systems enabled the insurgents to achieve a major surprise: indeed, their appearance was to cause a big shock for the Moroccans, and – at least temporarily – 'seal the airspace over the battlefield' for the FRA.[7]

After studying its options, the ELPS decided to target the oasis and town of Guelta Zemmour. For this operation, it concentrated nearly all of its forces, including units from what were now its 1st, 2nd, 3rd, and 4th Military Regions (for the composition of the ELPS as of mid-1981, see Table 5). While the majority of the force consisted

Table 5: ELPS Order of Battle, mid-1981		
Military Region	**Area of Operations**	**Notes**
1st	Ued, Tukat, Lehseyat, al-Farcia, Kara, Echederia	
2nd	Ratmia, Lemgasem, Samara	
3rd	Oued Qsat, al-Fauar	
4th	Amgal, Budreiga	
5th	Al-Mesmar (Zmul Niran)	Including 6th Battalion (SA-6, SA-9) and 7th Battalion (RM-70)

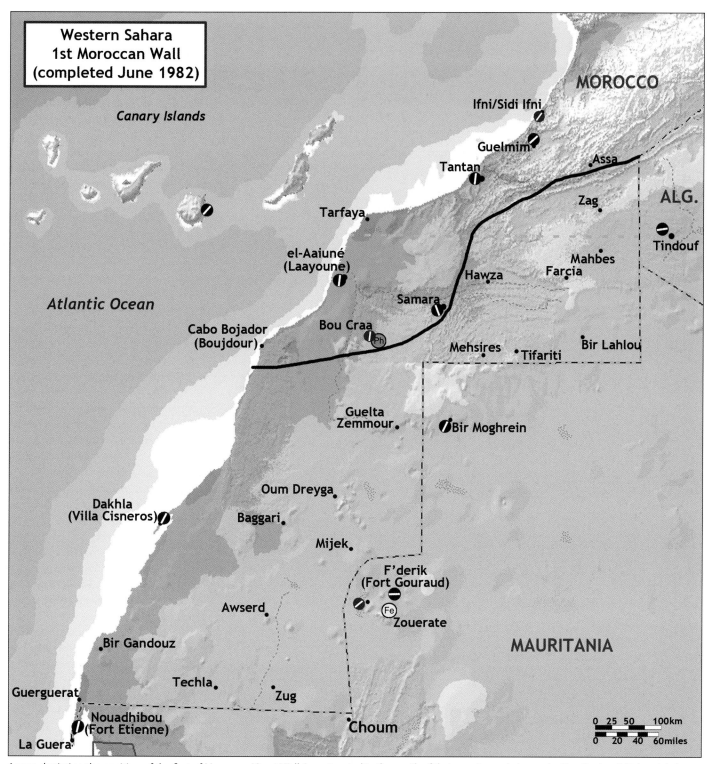

**Western Sahara
1st Moroccan Wall
(completed June 1982)**

Canary Islands

Atlantic Ocean

MOROCCO

Ifni/Sidi Ifni

Guelmim

Tantan

Assa

Zag

ALG.

Tarfaya

Tindouf

el-Aaiuné
(Laayoune)

Mahbes

Farcia

Hawza

Samara

Cabo Bojador
(Boujdour)

Bou Craa

Mehsires

Tifariti

Bir Lahlou

Guelta
Zemmour

Bir Moghrein

Oum Dreyga

Dakhla
(Villa Cisneros)

Baggari

Mijek

F'derik
(Fort Gouraud)

Awserd

Zouerate

MAURITANIA

Bir Gandouz

Techla

Zug

Guerguerat

Nouadhibou
(Fort Etienne)

Choum

La Guera

0 25 50   100km

0   20   40   60miles

A map depicting the position of the first of Moroccan 'Great Walls' constructed in the south of that country and also protecting the 'useful triangle' of Western Sahara, including the mine of Bou Craa, el-Aaiún and the holy town of Samara. (Map by Tom Cooper)

of lightly armed insurgents mounted in Land Rovers and Toyotas, the 5th Military Region provided not only an 'infantry company', but also an entire air defence battalion and an artillery battalion. For the first time ever, this concentration of forces received support of the ELPS' mechanised battalion, equipped with 10 T-54 and T-55 MBTs, 20 BMP-1 IFVs, and 30 AML-90/Eland-90 armoured cars (captured from the FAR and nick-named 'rattlesnakes' by the insurgents).[8]

El-Keichafa
While defended by the reinforced 4°RIM (comprising three infantry battalions with supporting artillery) the garrison of Guelta Zemmour

was isolated and thus in a vulnerable position – especially if left without air support. Certainly enough, the Moroccans had converted the entire area of the oasis and its outreaches into a true fortress, protected by an elaborate system of berms, ditches and minefields. Moreover, they were supplied with enough ammunition, food and water for up to 12 months of intensive combat. However, even once reconnaissance by FRA RF-5As detected signs of an impending attack – such as different ELPS units vacating their forward bases – in early October 1981, the commander of the garrison of Guelta Zemmour failed to put his troops on alert.

The plan for the ELPS attack envisaged an early deployment of the SA-6 in order to knock out the FRA's C-130H used as

The transporter-erector-launcher for an EPLS SA-6, fully loaded with three missiles, as seen in a parade after the war. Notable is the camouflage pattern consisting of dark sand and an almost black-green colour. (POLISARIO release)

An SA-9 system operated by the ELPS, seen after the war. (Albert Grandolini Collection)

Crewmembers of two insurgent technicals that met in the desert: notable is the Toyota in the rear, mounting a ZU-23 anti-aircraft gun. (Albert Grandolini Collection)

airborne command and control post – known as el-Keichafa ('the explorer') amongst the insurgents. The usual versions of the Battle of Guelta Zemmour point out that the C-130 forward deployed at el-Aaiún was equipped with a side-borne looking radar (SLAR), capable of detecting and tracking the movement of ground vehicles out to about 50-60 kilometres range (31-37 miles). Actually, as of 1981, the FRA did not operate any such Hercules – yet: SLARs equipped with radars code-named Nadir in Morocco were installed in two C-130s (one of which was subsequently almost always deployed at el-Aaiún) at Mojave, in the USA, only a year later. As of October 1981, the Moroccan C-130 crews were still running little more than 'vertical reconnaissance' missions, using hand-held binoculars to find and track insurgent movements.[9]

According to the plan, once the el-Keichafa was down, the ground assault was to be undertaken in the form of a pincer attack from two directions, supported by two diversionary attacks. Units of the 2nd and the 4th MRs were to advance from Cheljet Elban towards the Spanish fort, from the south, while the 3rd MR attacked from Ued Timuchat, uphill towards the citadel of Guelta Zemmour from south-east. Meanwhile, 1st MR was to launch a diversionary attack on Udeyat Tius in the West, and intercept any reinforcements deployed from Bou Craa or el-Aaiún, while a company of the 5th MR was entrusted with setting up an ambush at Samara, north of Guelta Zemmour, and taking care of logistics.[10]

Several days before the start of this offensive the 6th Battalion of the ELPS deployed its SA-6s by night close to the combat zone, and then camouflaged their vehicles as a Bedouin camp. Other involved units deployed to their starting positions during the nights between 8 and 10 October. The 'D-Day' for this attack was set for 12 October 1981, but this had to be postponed for 24 hours, as the work on removing mines along approaches to specific objectives proved more difficult than expected.[11]

First Battle of Guelta Zemmour

At 05:00 early on 13 October, the SA-6 system was powered up and almost instantly detected the C-130 high in the skies above Guelta. The lumbering transport was underway at an altitude of 5,486m (18,000ft) when a single SA-6 was fired. This scored a direct hit in clear sight of thousands of combatants from both sides. The Hercules turned into a blazing torch while plummeting towards the ground, electrifying all the insurgents that could see it: the el-Keichafa was down.[12]

The FRA reacted around 11:00 in the morning, in the form of one RF-5A, one F-5A and a single Mirage F.1 that flew reconnaissance. However, their approach was detected by the ELPS' P-19 and the Freedom Fighter was chopped out of the skies from a range of nearly 25 kilometres (15.5 miles). The pilot was captured alive, while

In addition to US-made M117, Mk.81 and Mk.82 bombs, the FRA's F-5As frequently deployed US-made LAU-3 pods for 19 68mm unguided rockets in Western Sahara. (Albert Grandolini Collection)

Starting in 1980, the FRA's principal means of reconnaissance became Mirage F.1CHs equipped with the COR-2 pod, in the configuration shown in this photograph taken at el-Aaiún AB. While a Mirage F.1 underway on a reconnaissance mission over Guelta Zemmour on the morning of 13 October 1981 came away, the F-5A escorting it was shot down. (Albert Grandolini Collection)

the other two fighters rapidly disengaged. With the Moroccan air force out of the way, the minesweepers intensified their work. Nevertheless, they were not ready by the scheduled time for the attack, at 14:01, and thus the ELPS' mechanized formation was forced to deploy through a minefield. In order to cover this manoeuvre, the insurgent battalion equipped with Czechoslovakian-made RM-70 multiple rocket launchers plastered all major Moroccan positions. From the Moroccan point of view, the situation initially appeared to be developing in a satisfactory fashion. The garrison was taken by surprise, but its artillery went into action and, seemingly, kept the insurgents at bay for hours. Even once the ELPS did launch its assault, heavy volumes of fire from positions of the 2°GAR and the 4°BIS forced the units of the 3rd Military Region to attack west from their intended aim. Eventually, they ended right next to the units of the 2nd Military Region, underneath the Spanish fort. However, this apparent success cost the Moroccans a number of outposts, their battalion commander and nearly all of their anti-tank ammunition.[13]

At 16:00, the ELPS unleashed a major attack by units of the 2nd and 3rd Military Regions at Bleibat Alfemman – a major FAR fortification about five kilometres outside Guelta. Occupied by

most of the Moroccan artillery and protected by the 1st battalion of the 4°RIM, this position held out for several hours – primarily because many of the insurgents were distracted by the capture of plentiful supplies of fresh meat left behind by the Moroccans in the positions that they had already captured. However, as the battle continued into the evening, the Moroccans were forced to re-asses their position. At 03:00 in the morning of the next day, 14 October 1981, the FAR attempted to infiltrate reinforcements on foot. After two hours of intense fighting, this attempt was repelled. Supposedly running short on ammunition, the Moroccan artillery was then ordered to withdraw. Lieutenant Gaima, a young officer that took over the command of the 1/4°RIM, ordered his anti-tank company into a counterattack to cover this manoeuvre. By knocking out a few of the insurgents' vehicles, this effort managed to temporarily stop the onslaught.[14]

At 06:00 in the morning, the ELPS resumed its attack on Bleibat Alfemman. Initially, the Moroccans held their position, but then a tank shell smashed Lieutenant Gaima's position, killing him and several others on the spot. By 09:00, the Moroccan defences collapsed and all resistance ceased, turning Guelta Zemmour into one of the worst defeats that the FAR had experienced in this war.

ELPS insurgents guarding Moroccan troops captured during the battle for Guelta Zemmour. (via Adrien Fontanellaz)

The 6th Battalion of the ELPS then added salt to the injury: around 11:00, its P-19 early warning radar detected an incoming air raid and sounded the alarm. With SA-9s meanwhile deployed around Guelta Zemmour towards the north and west, this unit was in the best position to intercept. The lead Mirage F.1 was shot down by SA-9s and its pilot captured alive. The rest of the Moroccan formation aborted its mission.[15]

Moroccan Desert Fox

The long-expected FAR counterattack developed only during the afternoon when the 6°BIS advanced from the Bou Craa area. Commanded by Colonel al-Ghaydami, this seasoned unit advanced very quickly because the ELPS had issued an order for all of its units to withdraw. With all the prisoners and civilians of Guelta liberated, and a group of foreign journalists brought in to verify the magnitude and scope of this success, there was no point in exposing their forces to superior Moroccan firepower. Knowing they lacked the capability to seize and hold this location, and that they could not defeat any of the major FAR units, and also aware of the fact that they merely needed to discredit Moroccan claims about Western Sahara, the POLISARIO remained loyal to its general strategy. Furthermore, the insurgent leadership wanted to let the other FAR units see the results of the catastrophe that befell the garrison of Guelta Zemmour'.[16]

Correspondingly, all the insurgents had vacated the combat zone by the morning of 15 October and – indeed – almost immediately after reaching Guelta, even al-Ghaydami decided to retreat. On the way back in the northern direction, his column drove into an ambush on the morning of 16 October. The insurgents first hit the Moroccans with a volley of ATGMs, and then with RM-70s. Al-Ghaydami quickly re-directed his unit in a western direction: while this helped his unit avoid most of the fire, it did leave behind about a dozen knocked out vehicles, which were quickly collected by the insurgents. Certainly enough, the ELPS attempted to set up another ambush for the 6°BIS further west, but around noon al-Ghaydami changed the route of his withdrawal again and

disappeared in a north-western direction instead. Something similar happened during the early hours of 17 October 1981 at Cheljet Elban: this time, al-Ghaydami turned in a southern direction and directed his column to el-Feidha and then to Zberia, about 50 kilometres away, thus evading another ambush entirely.[17]

Far-Reaching Consequences

While the fighting on the ground ceased once the 6°BIS disappeared from the battlefield, that in the air only intensified, as the FRA was unleashed to target convoys of withdrawing insurgents – including those underway inside Mauritania. A series of air strikes was reported on 20 October, including the deployment of CBUs. The 6th Battalion of the ELPS remained at Um Ghreid, near Guelta, to cover this withdrawal. Its gunners claimed several unconfirmed kills over the next few days and, on 24 October 1981, shot down a SA.330B Puma helicopter of the FRA, killing all 12 on board. The FRA also flew demonstrative operations along the border with Algeria, as recalled by a retired officer of the QJJ:

> After Guelta, Mirages or F-5s – for us, it was impossible to tell – would frequently approach our border over the Hammaguir area, then suddenly turn away while dropping chaff and flares. They did so again and again. We did not understand why: perhaps they were attempting to provoke a reaction from our air defences? Certainly enough, we had no SAM-sites deployed along that part of the border.[18]

Overall, in the course of this battle the POLISARIO claimed to have destroyed or captured a total of 48 Land Rovers, 16 large trucks and 40 UNIMOGs, 7 fuel transports, 1 VLRA, 15 different artillery pieces, 12 mortars, 6 ZU-23s and 17 12.7mm machine guns in Guelta Zemmour. Also captured were 204 Moroccan soldiers and two pilots. Furthermore, it claimed the destruction of up to eight aircraft and helicopters: while none of these were ever officially confirmed by Rabat, unofficial Moroccan sources confirmed the loss of five.[19]

Chapter 6
Stalemate

The rout of the Moroccan garrison and the loss of five aircraft at Guelta Zemmour had far-reaching consequences for both of the parties involved in Western Sahara. Immediately afterwards, the ELPS stopped much of its activity in an attempt to enable the POLISARIO's political leadership to shift its focus to the political arena and capitalise on the seating of a SADR delegation at the OAU summit, held in February 1982. However, while the insurgency requested that Tripoli help bolster and expand its air defence capabilities, because of the same summit and its agreements with Morocco, Libya stopped all further arms shipments. It was only in March 1982 that these resumed – and then on a much smaller scale than before: the next significant shipment thus arrived in Algeria only in August 1982, in the form of 16 T-55 MBTs and three MAZ-537 heavy-lift transporter-trailers. As usual, all the equipment was transported by rail form Oran to Bechar, and then by truck to Tindouf.[1]

Rabat reacted too. The FAR was ordered to withdraw all of its isolated garrisons to behind its 450-kilometre long defensive berm. By November 1981, the only Moroccan units remaining outside the north-western corner of Western Sahara were those inside the perimeter of Dakhla. For all practical purposes, the POLISARIO was now in effective control of at least two thirds of its homeland.

Reagan's Support

However, and much to POLISARIO's dismay, the attack on Guelta Zemmour substantially strengthened US support for the Moroccans. Namely, the administration of the new US president, Ronald Reagan, tended to monitor the war in Western Sahara entirely through the prism of the Cold War and the confrontation with Libya.[2] Correspondingly, during the first week in office, in late January 1981, Reagan approved the controversial sale of 108 M60 MBTs to Morocco. The US Ambassador to Rabat, Reed, went on the record to tell King Hassan II to, 'count on us; we are with you… it is obvious that the next pressure point for the Soviets is going to be the Kingdom of Morocco, situated strategically as it is on the Straits of Gibraltar.'[3] A year later, in May 1982, the Reagan Administration announced its decision to increase the value of foreign military sales (FMS) credits to Morocco from US$34 million to US$100 million annually.[4] Morally and ideologically, the US decisions could not be more wrong, because the POLISARIO had always proved extremely reluctant in establishing a direct link to Moscow, and generally never adopted any kind of 'leftist' agendas. The reason was obvious: the insurgents not only feared that this would jeopardise their standing in much of the West, but also that this might put their all-important relations with Algiers at risk, which meanwhile insisted on avoidance of internationalising the dispute over Western Sahara. Correspondingly, the POLISARIO actually turned down various Soviet offers, while Moscow then signed a 30-year economic aid agreement worth US$2 billion as well as a major fishing agreement with Morocco and, together with Czechoslovakia and Poland, signed major deals for the acquisition of phosphate rock – while the USA was meanwhile on the path to becoming the major importer of Algerian oil and gas.[5]

Nevertheless, the Reagan Administration continued its politics. In November 1981, it granted permission for the supply of cluster bomb units (CBUs) to the FRA – which the Moroccans had been requesting for years. Eventually, by 1995, the US transferred to Morocco 2,994 CBU-52, 1,752 CBU-58, 748 CBU-71, and 850 Rockeye CBUs. Furthermore, the White House took care to deliver 381 AGM-65B Maverick electro-optically guided, air-to-ground missiles together with the second batch of F-5Es scheduled to arrive in Morocco by early 1983.[6]

The SA-6 Problem

However, advanced armament could never help solve the FRA's problems. Namely, the Moroccans were already receiving plenty of modern arms, and increasing amounts of intelligence from the USA and France, yet repeatedly proved unable to make use of these. The problem was not only limited to the incompetent generals in Rabat: in the case of their air force, it was the low number of available pilots, and their poor tactical training. At the time of the battle of Guelta Zemmour, the FRA had only eight F-5A/Bs left in operational condition, and only 12 pilots qualified to fly them. Because most of the fast-jet pilots were meanwhile re-qualified to fly Mirages, the condition of their brand-new F-5E unit was even poorer: there were only six pilots qualified to fly 13 available aircraft. Correspondingly, when the US Assistant Secretary of Defense for International Security Affairs, Francis J West, visited Rabat in November 1981, he offered a team of 20 US Army instructors to train the Moroccans in commando-style tactics against the POLISARIO's SA-6s. The American advisors are known to have been deployed to work with troops of 1st Parachute Brigade, and then diverse other units, but the effects of their instruction remain largely unclear: as far as is known, they intended to use combined operations including air strikes by fighter aircraft and special operations forces inserted with the help of helicopters to target insurgent SA-6s.[7]

The next US attempt to help find a solution to the SA-6 problem was undertaken by the USAF. Knowing that Moroccan pilots had received no instruction on how to defeat this threat during their training in the USA, and that FRA F-5s lacked the radar warning receivers (RWRs) that would warn their fliers that their aircraft had been acquired by a radar, the USAF deployed a three-man training team to Meknes AB. During their 60-day long stay, the Americans concluded that the Moroccans were excellent students, willing to take risks, and had a great potential to improve, but had little knowledge about high-speed, low-altitude work. Correspondingly, the USAF team worked intensively on training them to fly their aircraft to their operational limits.[8]

Probably at the suggestion of the advisors in question, Washington next offered to furnish Morocco with 10 ALQ-119 ECM-pods and 10 ALE-38 chaff and flare dispensers in the form of a non-renewable, 180-day lease at a cost of between US$20 and 40 million, payable in cash, was a far less attractive solution. Chronically short of money, the Moroccans could neither afford this offer, nor did they consider it seriously. For similar – cost-related – reasons, Rabat also dropped Colonel Kabbaj's idea to buy Baz-AR anti-radar missiles manufactured for Iraq, from France. Instead, in the course of a meeting with the US Ambassador to Morocco on 20 January 1982, Kabbaj officially requested assistance in countering the SA-6s in the form of satellite intelligence. Washington reacted positively and ordered the National Reconnaissance Authority (NRA) to locate and track ELPS's SAMs, and to start providing satellite photographs to the FRA. Furthermore, the Reagan Administration approved the sale of General Instrument Corporation ULR-666 radar-warning receivers (RWRs) to Morocco, while additional help in the search for ELPS forward bases was then also provided by the French foreign intelligence service – Directorate-General for External Security (*Direction Générale de la Sécurité Extérieure*, DGSE).[9]

The Americans worked quickly: the first satellite photographs of the ELPS SA-6s at the Ain el-Ben Camp were provided to Morocco by February 1982: by early March of the same year, the NRA and the CIA also detected the presence of at least one SA-9 TEL about 1,000 metres outside the Ain el-Bel Camps 3 and 5 – both some 135 kilometres (84 miles) east of Samara.[10]

Moreover, the USA then granted permission for deliveries of Northrop AN/AAQ-8 infra-red countermeasures systems to the FRA: this was a pod containing electronically modulated and fully automatic systems and laser warning receivers designed to protect aircraft from heat-seeking missiles. While of no use against SA-6s, it at least increased the survivability of those F-5Es carrying it against the SA-7s and SA-9s.[11]

SEAD, Moroccan-Style

Meanwhile, the Moroccans found out that the Italian company Elettronica was manufacturing ELT-555 pods for active electronic countermeasures (ECM or jammer pods). These were available in two versions:

- one with a transmitter comprising a travelling-wave-tube (TWT), and a traditional sectorial antenna, capable of simultaneously jamming two continuous wave emissions and two pulsed missions on low duty; and
- one capable of simultaneously jamming four emissions, regardless the duty.

Concluding that these would be 'cost-effective' systems capable of disturbing the work of radars in the pulse- and continuous-wave mode (and the mixed mode, too), and would perfectly match the fire-control radar of the SA-6, the Moroccans decided to acquire ELT-555s. According to unofficial Moroccan sources, although made in Italy, the FRA bought about a dozen such pods 'via another country', and the first arrived in 1983.[12]

However, the FRA had to fight without any kind of electronic warfare support. To survive such operations, its pilots sought for a way to deliver their bombs in a fashion that would expose them to weapons systems like SA-6 and SA-9 for the shortest possible period of time. One of the solutions was the so-called 'loft' or 'toss-bombing': a method of bomb-delivery in which the attacking aircraft would approach its target at a low altitude (between 100 and 200ft or 31-61m), before entering a full-power climb, releasing its bombs while still climbing, and then quickly returning back to low altitude. When applying this tactic – based on the experience that older Soviet-made SAM-systems had a major problem with tracking aircraft that made sharp turns (so-called 'breaks') in the vertical and horizontal axis – the attacking aircraft need not actually overfly its target: depending on the weight of bombs, it could release these from several kilometres away before quickly returning to a low-altitude flight, outside the 'no-escape' zone of such weapons as the SA-6 and SA-9, but also SA-7 MANPADs and ZU-23 automatic guns. The FRA is known to have flown its first air strike against ELPS SA-6s in this fashion sometime in early January 1982, when a pair of Mirage F.1EHs targeted the system detected outside the Ain el-Bel Camp 2. Their bombs missed however: the loft/toss-

A Mirage F.1 with an ELT-555 pod installed in its usual position – the left outboard underwing pylon. (N.B. Collection)

bombing required extremely precise navigation – not only during the approach phase: once such an attack was initiated, the pilot had to fly the climb portion of manoeuvre in a very exact fashion because even the slightest deviation in speed, g-force, and angle could result in the bombs missing their target by several kilometres.[13]

In early March 1982, at least six Mirage F.1CH/EH flew an air strike on the ELPS forward base in Raudat el-Hach, known to have been protected by a single SA-9 and seven ZU-23. After approaching at a very low altitude, the jets deployed 24 bombs in a loft/toss-bombing attack to hit the target zone – yet failed to cause any kind of damage.[14]

The FRA attempted to solve the problem by using CBUs instead of general-purpose bombs: later the same month, three Mirages led a pair of two F-5As into an attack on an area of 'suspected POLISARIO activity' outside Bou Craa, in which US-made CBU-58s were deployed for the first time. The planning for this operation was for Mirage F.1EHs to use their advanced nav/attack systems to lead the F-5As to a pre-determined point: once there, all five aircraft were to loft their bombs into an area about two by one kilometres in size. However, no pre- or post-strike reconnaissance was flown for this air strike and thus its results remained unknown: actually,

Insurgents inspecting an unexploded parachute-retarded Mk.82 or Mk.83 bomb left behind by the FRA. The fact that many of the bombs armed with conventional fuses failed to detonate was not missed by the Moroccans and they soon began deploying weapons with so-called Daizy Cutter extensions instead. (Albert Grandolini Collection)

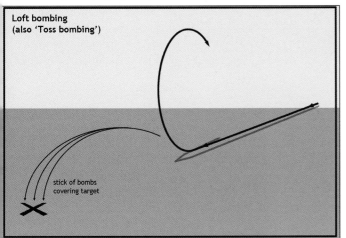

A diagram depicting toss/loft-bombing tactics. Using this method, the aircraft can release its bombs during a climb towards the target – without actually overflying the latter. (Diagram by Tom Cooper)

The empty casings of CBU-58 and CBU-71s deployed by the FRA and collected by the insurgents. (Albert Grandolini Collection)

all such early efforts proved to be a waste of time and resources, but they were also a good indicator of just how overcautious the FRA became because of the SA-6s.[15]

Improved Reconnaissance

Determined to solve the problem, the FRA continued its search for a solution, nevertheless. After the next few air strikes, it discovered a major issue with bomb fusses: those in widespread use on the US-made Mk.80-series bombs detonated only on impact with the ground. The soft sand of Western Sahara tended not only to dampen the force of their explosion, thus minimising blast effects, but actually caused many of the bombs to fail to detonate altogether. This prompted the FRA to start using so-called Daisy Cutters: extensions which caused the fuse to activate early, thus detonating the bomb about one metre above the ground surface. When even these proved insufficient, the solution was finally found in South Africa in the form of AB400 electronic proximity fuses, dubbed 'Jupiter'. Adaptable to all types of weapons from the Mk.80-series, the Jupiters proved not only much superior in their reliability: they could be set to detonate bombs at diverse altitudes up to 15 metres above the ground surface. Thanks to them, the FRA finally found its weapons of choice for striking not only ELPS SA-6s and SA-9s, but all sorts of other ground targets too.[16]

The next issue was not only that of finding a solution for the early detection of insurgent SAM-systems, but indeed for tracking the movement of these. As well as taking care to equip two of its C-130s with SLARs, in 1982 the FRA concluded that it required a better combination of optical and electronic reconnaissance. Together with its Mirage F.1CHs and F.1EHs, the Moroccans had already obtained French-made COR-2 reconnaissance pods, equipped with KA83/85 cameras, and locally designated ATAK. The COR-2 could be used by F.1CHs, but proved much more effective when deployed by F.1EHs, because it could be linked-up with their INS nav/attack system and thus resulted in reconnaissance photographs with precise geographic coordinates – which made the job of photo-analysts much easier. To enable not only its ground crews, but also pilots to better concentrate on their reconnaissance tasks, over the following years the FRA went as far as to establish three units specialised in reconnaissance tasks.

Several Mirage F.1EH and F.1EH-200s were grouped into the *Escadron Iguider*; similarly, the available two RF-5As and several F-5Bs were grouped into the newly-established *Escadron Erige*. Both units had the reconnaissance and gathering of electronic intelligence as their primary task. The crews of the *Escadron Iguider* worked hand-in-hand with engineers of Aéro Maroc Industrie (AMIN) – established at Casablanca International in October 1981 – and a group of French technicians to develop the Hares photo-reconnaissance pod. Based on the French-made 1,300-litre RP.35 drop tank, the front and centre section of this contained a gyro-stabilised long-range oblique photography (LOROP) Itek Corporation KA-85A camera with auto-focus, capable of taking photographs from high altitudes and stand-off ranges; the rear part of the pod contained sensors capable

A rare photograph of a Mirage F.1CH from around 1982 with its typical combat configuration: this included two Mk.82 bombs equipped with Daisy Cutter extenders on inboard underwing pylons, one with a Jupiter fuse on the right outboard underwing pylon (left side of the photo), and an ELT-555 ECM-pod on the left outboard underwing pylon. (via E.C.)

An FRA Mirage F.1EH-200 as seen during the flight-testing of the Hares pod with a LOROP camera. (via E.C.)

A close-up view of the Mirage F.1EH-200 serial 171, with an AMIN Hares pod under the centreline. (N.B. Collection)

Finally, the FRA replaced the BF radar warning receiver (RWR) on its Mirage F.1s with the more advanced, US-made AN/ALR-66 – which was subsequently installed on all of its F-5Es, and the F-5Bs operated by the *Escadron Erige*, too.

Hunter-Killer Tactics

The availability of Hares-equipped F.1EHs in turn gave birth to the idea to combine them with bomb-equipped Mirages, thus leading to the emergence of so-called 'hunter-killer teams': these usually consisted of a reconnaissance aircraft, which flew high and sought for enemy ground forces and SAMs, followed by the low-flying Mirage (or two), which would then attack coordinates provided by the first jet. Led by Commandant Houari, the first such sortie was attempted on 27 September 1982, when – for testing purposes – the Moroccans attacked a pair of ELPS-operated T-55 MBTs accompanied by a large truck and several supply vehicles. Houari managed to pin-point the target and forward the coordinates to his wingman, Mohammed Hadri, who used one Mk.82 bomb with a Daisy Cutter fuse-extender to precisely destroy one and damage the other T-55. Hadri then returned to deliver the second strike, and hit the second tank, but was then shot down by SA-9s, forced to eject and captured by the insurgents. Despite this failure, the hunter-killer tactics with help of the Hares pod proved highly successful, and eventually became the principal way in which the FRA's Mirages operated over Western Sahara.[18]

Finally, in order to ease the transfer of FRA fighters from their distant bases in central Morocco (especially so the Sidi Slimane-based Mirages), Colonel Kabbaj requested the delivery of tanker aircraft from the USA. The FRA had already operated two suitably equipped Lockheed KC-130H Hercules transports. They proved satisfactory in terms of range and fuel-carrying capability, but were also much too slow, making IFR-operations on long transfer flights to Western Sahara troublesome

of detecting and tracking the work of radar systems operated by the EPLS. The third unit was even more specialised: the *Escadron de ECM/ELINT* was equipped with two heavily-modified Dassault Falcon 20 business-jets, outfitted to monitor, track and record electronic emissions emitted by ELPS-operated radars and provide stand-off electronic countermeasures-support for fighter-bombers in the combat zone.[17]

for pilots of single-seat jets. Correspondingly, as the FRA began to receive its first 10 F-5Es and 4 F-5Fs, between January and August 1981, Kabbaj entered negotiations with Washington for the acquisition of two Boeing KC-135E tankers. When these proved too expensive, in 1982 he acquired the last Boeing 707-320C airliner ever manufactured instead, and two Beech 1080 IFR-pods: with some assistance from the USA, the AMIN then converted the aircraft into a B707-3W6C tanker at home, in Morocco. To test the installation (which proved 35% cheaper than a KC-135E), the AMIN also installed a US-made IFR-probe on one of the FRA's F-5Bs: after successful testing, additional equipment was acquired from the USA and then a similar modification applied to all 10 F-5Es from the first batch, while the remaining six aircraft were all equipped with similar installations before their delivery in January 1983. Morocco thus obtained a force-multiplier, capable of significantly extending the reach of its F-5- and Mirage-fighter bombers.[19]

One of the F-5Bs assigned to the Escuadron Erige. Notable are large housings for the AN/ALR-66 RWRs installed on the forward fuselage and near the top of the fin. (N.B. Collection)

This post-war photograph shows one of the F-5Es assigned to the Escadron Erige, equipped with the AAQ-8 IR-countermeasures pod (left side of the photograph), and an ELT-555 ECM-pod. (N.B. Collection)

Rift within the OAU

While the FAR initially proved unable to use all the foreign aid it began receiving, it was obvious that the immense volumes of Saudi money, US, French, Israeli, and South African instruction and advanced equipment

Two Moroccan C-130Hs (registrations CN-AOP and CN-AOQ) were modified to serve as radar surveillance aircraft in 1982. For this purpose, each of them received a large pod (similar to those installed on Grumman OV-1 Mohawk aircraft of the 1960s-1970s) on each side of the fuselage: each of these contained the SLAR code-named Nadir in Morocco. (Photo by Bob Shake via Milipix/Martin Hornliman Collection)

would have their desired effects in turning the war against the POLISARIO – at least in the long term. Foremost, the major effect of all the foreign support was to make the war and occupation of Western Sahara affordable for Rabat – even if it was obvious that the conflict was not winnable by military means. In order to buy time until his forces would receive all the new equipment and train on it, King Hassan II launched a diplomatic offensive. During the OAU summit in Addis Ababa, in Ethiopia, in February 1982, he announced that he would allow an OAU-organized referendum on independence and offered a truce with the POLISARIO. Although this offer was issued at the same time as the SADR's representation was admitted to the OAU, combined with Moroccan complaints that the insurgency was 'blatantly violating cease-fires', it not only caused deep divisions all over Africa, but also cost the POLISARIO dearly in terms of international support. While 26 African countries

The crew of one of the two FRA C-130Hs modified through the addition of a SLAR: this photograph is interesting because it shows an installation of the radar-pod on the left side of the fuselage – in addition to the one on the right side. The aircraft thus had two such pods and could provide 360-degrees coverage, or constant coverage, regardless of what direction was it flying in. (N.B. Collection.)

Table 6: FRA Order of Battle, 1985-1988

HQ	Base	Squadron	Aircraft Type & Notes
BA-FRA 1	Rabat/Sale	*Escadre d'Hélicoptère*	AB.205A, AB.206A, SA.330, SA.342, CH-47C
		Ecole de Spécialisation Hélicoptères	AB.205A, AB.206A, SA.342
		Escadron de Liaison & VIP	King Air 100/200/300, Falcon 50, Gulfstream II/III, Boeing 707-
BA-FRA 2	Meknes/Bassatine	*Escadron Chahine*	F-5E/F
		Escadron Borak	F-5A/B/E/F
		Escadron Erige	F-5E/F & RF-5A; reconnaissance unit
		CIPC/*Ecole de chasse*	Alpha Jet; fighter weapons school
		Escadron Anti-Char	SA.342
BA-FRA 3	Kenitra	*Escadron de Transport*	C-130H, KC-130H
		Escadron de Ravitaiment	Boeing 707
		Escadron de ECM/ELINT	Falcon 20ECM
		Patrouille maritime	Do.28D2, OV-10A
BA-FRA 4	Laayoune	no permanently assigned units	detachments of up to eight F-5A/RF-5A, F-5E and/or Mirage F.1s; up to four C-130s and diverse helicopters
BA-FRA 5	Sidi Slimane	*Escadron Atlas*	Mirage F.1CH; interceptor and fighter-bomber unit
		Escadron Assad	Mirage F.1CH/EH; interceptor and fighter-bomber unit
		Escadron Iguider	Mirage F.1CH/EH with COR-2, ATAK and Hares; reconnaissance unit
BA-FRA 6	Ben Guerir	*no permanently deployed units*	
Air Force Academy	Marrakesh	*Ecole de Pilotage*	AS.202, T-34C, CM.170
	Meknes/Bassantine	*CiPC Escadron d'Entrainement Avancé*	Alpha Jet
		CIPC Escadron de Instruction Sol	CM.170, replaced by Alpha Jet

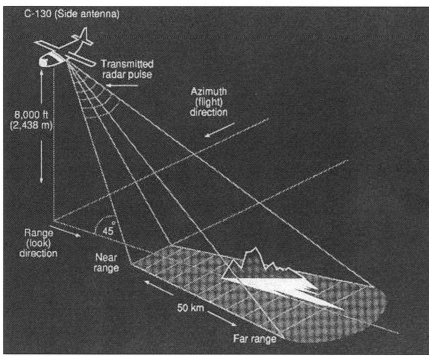

Description of the function and approximate range of the SLARs installed on the two Moroccan C-130Hs. (via N.B. & E.C.)

– and over 40 other nations world-wide – recognized the SADR and thus the POLISARIO-run government in exile, 19 delegations walked out in protest over the appearance of the SADR-delegation. Furthermore, in an attempt to lessen tensions, not only Algeria,

but even Libya insisted that the ELPS refrain from further significant military action in order to give OAU efforts to arrange a cease-fire and referendum a better chance of success.[20]

The synergy of all this manoeuvring was that the insurgency restrained itself from attacks on Moroccan forces in Western Sahara for most of 1982. This in turn enabled the Moroccans to intensify their construction efforts on the 'great wall', entirely undisturbed: by the end of the year, they started work on its second section, running about 50-100 kilometres (31-62 miles) south of the first one. While completed only in 1984, there was soon no doubt that the berm worked: it minimalized Moroccan troop and material losses, while giving the FAR a desperately needed morale boost. At the same time, it demoralized the ELPS because the insurgents had to tolerate its construction: even if their foreign backers would have permitted them to attack, they would first have to concentrate on overcoming the berm, instead of continuing their spectacular raids against targets behind it. Overall, the Moroccan great wall resulted in the de-facto stalemate of the rest of this war.

The Square of Death and an Insurgent Radar Station
Despite the cease-fire and negotiations, the FRA continued flying sporadic SEAD strikes, all the time improving the combination

of its intelligence-gathering methods and attack tactics. For example, a formation of Moroccan fighter-bombers targeted the SAMs protecting the Bir Lehmar camp in January 1983. However, the operations of SLAR-equipped C-130Hs and Mirage F.1EQs equipped with Hares pods meanwhile resulted in a surprising realisation: the fact that it was de-facto impossible to find and destroy the ELPS SA-6s. The reason was not only that the system was highly mobile, or that the Sahrawis frequently moved their SAMs, but the way the entire system was designed, built and operated. In service in the USSR since 1967, the 2K12E Kvadrat (Square) was the export variant of a system the name of which was derived from the most common arrangement pattern for its typical battery: in this, the 1801 fire-control radar (ASCC/NATO-codename 'Straight Flush') was positioned in the centre, surrounded

The sole Boeing 707-320C (registration CN-ANR) acquired by the FRA in 1981 and converted into a tanker by the AMIN. (Tom Cooper Collection)

A right-hand view of the same aircraft after its conversion. Notable is the Beech 1080 IFR-pod installed under the wingtip. (Albert Grandolini Collection)

by four 2P25 transporter-erector-launchers (TELs) deployed in a square around it.[21] Each of the TELs carried three 3M9E, two-stage, solid-fuel, ramjet-powered missiles weighting 630kg (1,388lbs), with radio-command guidance in the first phase of flight, semi-active, continuous-wave terminal homing, and with an effective engagement range of between 6 and 22 kilometres (3.7-13.7 miles). Each SA-6-battery was supported by its own, organic early warning radar, usually a P-18 or one of the systems from the P-15/P-19 series, and all of its elements were very easy to deploy: the unit could go into action within 20 minutes of halting. However, deploying a SAM-site and making it work together with early warning radars was a different story – because the radar picture collected by the early warning radar had to be provided to the command post of the unit. This was done with the help of cables, the positioning of which was a major issue: even if the early warning radar was deployed close to the SAM-site, it could take about two hours to link it up with the command post and the Straight Flush. Indeed, as not only the Moroccan reconnaissance, but also the recollections of the Algerian eyewitnesses showed, because the P-15/P-19 was a piece of equipment considered particularly sensitive, none was ever deployed inside Western Sahara. On the contrary, the primary radar site of the ELPS used a P-15/P-19 radar provided by Libya and positioned at the Oued Tatrat Camp No.1, near Tindouf, in Algeria.[22]

For obvious reasons, this site was outside the reach of the FRA – unless Rabat was looking to provoke a major war against the big neighbour, which it was not. Therefore, the most that the Moroccans could do in terms of SEAD was to try locating and destroying one of the Straight Flush radars. This, however, proved next to impossible: the Sahrawis were activating their 1801s only for

extremely short periods of time, when these were supporting the actual fire action of their SAM-sites. Thus, for 99 per cent of the time, even the FRA's SLAR-equipped C-130s and Hares-equipped F.1EHs proved entirely useless against ELPS SA-6s.

Unsurprisingly, the Moroccans bitterly complained about the Algerians, and suspected not only the latter to be actually operating the ELPS' SAMs, but also that the insurgent air defences were integrated with those of the Algerian armed forces. However, several interviews with officers of the ANP revealed an entirely different situation. One of them explained:

I know that views in the USA and Europe are different, strongly coloured by the Moroccan points of view. Accordingly, relations between Algeria and POLISARIO should have been a true love story. However, in reality there was next to no relationship between our militaries. We never even came to the idea to ask them about experiences with their T-54/55 tanks, BMP-1s or other stuff we have in common. ...My first and only contact with the ELPS was when my team was sent to Tindouf to help them repair their P-15/19 radar deployed there. At the time, the Sahrawis still depended on our help to maintain such radars, so they sent a corresponding call up the chain of command, and we received the order to help them. Even then, that order was strict in dictating us to use only spare parts from their, not from our own logistic system.

Another stated categorically:

Yes, sure, the Moroccans are convinced that the Sahrawis received their radar and targeting information from our services. But, that's

A formation of Mirage F.1EHs during an IFR-exercise in 1985. Notable are IFR-probes installed on the nearest three aircraft, identifying them as F.1EH-200s, and the COR-2 pod under the centreline of the second aircraft. (Albert Grandolini Collection)

While still predominantly depending on its technicals mounting ZPU-2s – like the one visible in this still from a video from March 1985 – and ZU 23s, starting in late 1981 the ELPS decided to adopt more conventional methods of combat instead. (via Tom Cooper)

A BMP-1 of the ELPS seen after the war. While the appearance of insurgent units – foremost the 6th Battalion – equipped with such heavy weapons might appear spectacular, it was also to prove a fatal mistake for the POLISARIO's designs. (POLISARIO release)

ELPS Conventional Forces

The appearance of SA-6s in the ELPS arsenal was actually no exception: rather a logical consequence of all the support provided to the POLISARIO by Libya. Even if temporarily stopped, and then resumed for a short while in summer 1982, this reached such proportions that the ELPS – which meanwhile grew to an estimated 8,000-10,000 combatants and support personnel – obtained an impressive arsenal of heavy equipment. Alone it's holdings of main battle tanks and diverse other armoured vehicles – many of these actually captured from the Moroccans during earlier battles – equalled about 70 per cent of the entire FAR inventory.

Indeed, for a while at least, the numbers were a major problem for the ELPS as the insurgency proved ill-prepared for larger, conventional operations that became necessary in order to breach the Moroccan berm. Base camps in the Tindouf area supported only small-unit infantry operations; combined arms training – including armour and field artillery – was run only at Oudiane Lemkhaf and took time. Furthermore, the small overall size of the insurgent force made it highly sensitive to casualties: the ELPS could not afford to lose any of its best-trained men. So far in the war, it had to – and was able to – avoid operating in massed formations because of the greater chances of detection and of Moroccan air power, even in cases where it was obvious that larger formations were necessary to achieve at least marginal military and political success. However, by 1983, there was no way around attacking one of the major Moroccan fortifications, regardless of the hazards that such an operation represented – especially for slow-moving armour. In order to obtain the capability necessary in order to operate as a conventional military force, the ELPS spent much of 1983 training intensively, and went into action again only once it became clear that Morocco would hold no referendum. As time was to show, this was

wrong: the ELPS has had its own Batalion de Reconnaissance et de Transmission, and this was never linked to our air defence system.

Algerian Air Defences

As pointed out already several times, many of the Moroccan accounts of the Western Saharan War stress the deployment of Algerian-supplied and operated SAM-systems as early as 1976. The actual situation was entirely different: the growth of Algerian air defences during this period was curtailed by a shortage of experienced personnel and, time and again, not only by shortages of spares for the equipment acquired from the USSR, but indeed a lack of suitable equipment.

Algeria imported only enough equipment for two battalions of SA-75M Dvina (ASCC/NATO-codename SA-2 Guideline) systems with 48 missiles in 1967. However, preoccupied with working up an expeditionary force that would be deployed to Egypt in the case of the next war with Israel, the Algerian Air Force (*al-Quwwat al-Ja'wiya al-Jaza'eriya*, QJJ) de-facto ignored the necessity of developing air defences for its own homeland. Indeed, by 1975 both of the SA-2 systems were in poor condition: most of the time they were deployed in the Oran area, and only rarely trained, their personnel were in urgent need of re-qualification on their equipment. Eventually, any related designs were abandoned: both systems were withdrawn from service and their equipment positioned as decoys in the Tindouf area.[24]

Launching a new attempt, in 1979 Algiers placed the first in a series of orders that resulted in deliveries of 4 S-125M and 8 S-125M1A Pechora (ASCC/NATO-codename 'SA-3 Goa') systems, together with 455 V-601PD missiles, in the 1982-1987 period. Egyptian experiences from the wars of 1967 and 1973, and the slow growth of the ground-based air defence elements led the Algerians to the conclusion that an independent and specialized service was necessary to operate the complex equipment needed to establish an integrated air defence network over the huge country. Thus, as soon as enough personnel became available following training in the Soviet Union, all the available early warning radars – including a number of Soviet-made P-14s, P-18s and P-19s, P-37s and P-40s, height-finders such as the PRV-16 and PRV-17, and US-made TPS-70/78/103 systems – and SA-3s were organized into the Territorial Air Defence (*Défense Aérienne du Territoire*, DDAT) as a separate independent branch of the military in 1985. Originally commanded by Major-General Laoudi Achour (who remained in charge until 2005), the 10,000-15,000-strong DDAT was also separated from the mobile air defence units of the army, which operated its own air defence branch in the form of the Surface-to-Air Missile Regiment (*Régiment de Missiles Sol-Air*, RMSA), equipped with SA-6s and SA-8s.[25] Contrary to the air defence services of Egypt, Iraq and Syria for example, the DDT

was quite a unique service, well ahead of its time by composition, equipment and purpose. It became responsible for the constant control of all Algerian airspace but was actively involved in protection of only a few small parts of it. Its well-developed, fully integrated and automatized network of early warning radars (locally designated the *Couverture radar atuomatisée*, CRA) was designed to provide timely warning and then support operations of the QJJ's interceptors and the army's air defences. For this purpose, the DDAT deployed three layers of radar sites, including 'primary' and 'secondary', fixed radar sites, and so-called 'gap-fillers': mobile radars that could be re-deployed to cover specific areas as necessary. In 1986, the DDAT was re-designated as the Territorial Air Defence Command (*Commandement de la Défense Aérienne du Territoire*, CFDAT). By that time, each of its 12 SA-3 batteries (four each of these were operated by three *Groupement des Moyens Anti-Aérien*) was reinforced through the addition of its own battery of 23mm ZU-23 AAA. However, none was ever deployed in Western Sahara: a single brigade with four batteries first arrived in the Tindouf area only in 1986. While its early warning radars could see deep inside Moroccan airspace, the effective range of their missiles was still within the Algerian borders. The other Algerian DDAT/CFDAT SAM-sites were used to protect specially designed 'destruction zones' around installations of strategic importance in northern Algeria. Unsurprisingly, all available Algerian sources have categorically denied even a chance of cooperation between their air defence branch and the ELPS. Indeed, one of them explained:

> We could have easily taken a much more active role in that war, but we did not. For example, we had most of Morocco under our radar coverage already then. Correspondingly, it would have been easy for us to provide the ELPS with our radar picture in order to prevent them from being attacked by Moroccan fighter-bombers. Our artillery could have provided them with support too. However, we never did that. They did ask us to do so, but we turned [them] down and replied, "You have your own radars, use them". … our role was that of providing our territory as a sanctuary, our diplomacy in support of the SADR, and our military provided technical help – maintenance and repair – for some of their equipment. Such methods were far more discrete: we could run such operations without anybody ever finding out about them.[26]

Obviously, all of this took place only well after even the First Battle of Guelta Zemmour.

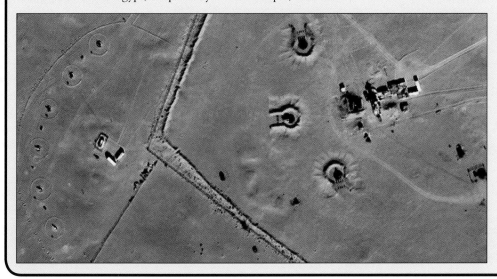

SA-3 site of the 3rd Battalion, 13th Air Defence Brigade of the DDAT/CFDAT, deployed for the defence of Tindouf AB. (Courtesy Google Earth)

not the least to its advantage.

Small scale raids were still undertaken, but rather sporadically. In July 1983, insurgents raided Msied in southern Morocco again, provoking an engagement that was to last for nearly a month. The fighting in this area was foremost characterised by the intensive deployment of RM-70 MRLS in hit-and-run style raids. While the insurgents subsequently managed to withdraw without suffering unnecessary losses despite large volumes of FAR counter-battery fire, this operation had a major negative effect in so far that Algiers – keen to improve its commercial ties with the USA – strictly forbade any kind of further attacks into Morocco. From that time onwards, the insurgency's freedom of operations was severely curtailed by factors outside its influence.[23]

Power Demonstration

As described earlier, enmities between Algeria and Morocco were almost 'traditional': no matter what was happening on the diplomatic scene, and despite friendship treaties, because of Western Sahara, and the Algerians letting the POLISARIO use their soil as a base for operations against the FAR, each side regarded the other with distrust. As the FRA gradually improved its tactics and flew ever more intensive air strikes on the identified and suspected ELPS forward positions, and then bombed ever closer to the Algerian border, the commanders of the QJJ and DDAT units deployed in the Tindouf area designed a plan to suppress Moroccan activity. Accordingly, a pair of MiG-17 was to scramble and drag Moroccan fighter-bombers in front of a pair of MiG-21s. However, as soon as the FAR detected a renewed deployment of MiG-21s at Tindouf, it stopped flying close to the border. A retired QJJ officer recalled:

We have played interesting "mind games" with the Moroccans, time and again, often for little other reason but to test our men and material. In one case, in November 1986, the Moroccans and the US Air Force ran a large-scale exercise, and the fighters of the FAR flew very close to our borders, often in provocative manner: they flew simulated air strikes against potential targets in an area that was exceptionally difficult (not to say "impossible") to defend for us. They never entered our airspace, but it became very frustrating for our radar operators to see them that close to the border but be unable to do anything against this. Therefore, we deployed a single MiG-25 from Ain Oussera AB to Tindouf – at low level and by night, so that the Moroccans would not notice its arrival. Then we prepared a small show. The next day, we saw the Moroccans and Americans running their exercise. We knew they would have to land to refuel and de-brief, as usual. Then, once they landed, we scrambled our MiG.

Now, the runway at Tindouf is pointing directly in the direction of the border to Morocco. Because of this, all our aircraft – except for MiG-21s – had to turn very sharply shortly after taking off, so not to violate the foreign airspace. In turn, because of the local terrain, the Moroccans were able to monitor our operations: they would detect and track our fighters as soon as these became airborne. Of course, our jets always turned away. However, on that day, our MiG-25 did not: it continued straight ahead, accelerating and climbing in the process. It continued climbing and flying ever faster as it flew out – over all of Morocco and over the Atlantic Ocean, then turned around and came back.

There was no reaction to our power demonstration. The FAR did not scramble a single interceptor and did not activate even one of its air defence sites. Subsequently, the Moroccan flying along our border became "much more diplomatic". We had delivered the message.[27]

Two of the USAF McDonnell-Douglas KC-10A Extender tankers that participated in the African Eagle exercise with the FRA in November 1986. (US DoD, via Albert Grandolini)

An FRA Mirage F.1EH-200 seen during a joint exercise with the French Air Force in September 1986. Advanced training in France and at home, and joint exercises with US forces in Morocco, not only improved the skills of Moroccan pilots, but emboldened them into power demonstrations vis-à-vis Algeria. The latter, in turn, 'hit back' in its own fashion. (Photo by Jean-Francois Lipka)

The Beginning of the End: Raid on Zimoul el-Niran

While securing its position on the international scene, and vis-à-vis the reinforced FAR and the FRA, as of 1983 Algiers was still ready to permit the ELPS to run offensive operations into Western Sahara. In October of that year, when the weather was most suitable for such an enterprise, the insurgents concentrated five mechanized and two armoured battalions – about 2,000 combatants supported with about 50 MBTs and IFVs, and a large number of RM-70s, protected by SA-6s and SA-9s – for an attack on Zimoul el-Niran, about 140 kilometres west of Tindouf. The assault on Zimoul el-Niran began at 06:00 on 13 October 1983 with a massive barrage from RM-70s. Forewarned by

US intelligence – which found out that the insurgents had vacated at least nine camps in north-eastern Sahara and re-deployed a concentration of up to 14 MBTs and BTR-60 armoured personnel carriers, and 20 trucks to an area between 30 and 45 kilometres south and south-east of Samara – the FAR was ready for this attack.[28] The Moroccans absorbed the first blow and then reacted according to a well prepared plan: strong mechanized reinforcements were rapidly deployed from Zag and provided with plentiful support from FRA F-5s and Mirage F.1s. Whether due to the massive use of electronic countermeasures, or effective SEAD operations, this time ELPS SA-6s proved entirely ineffective: they failed to shoot down even one of the involved fighter bombers.[29]

Indeed, in a matter of only a few hours, it became obvious that not only the ELPS' tactics but also its firepower were inadequate, to say the least, and that even such a large concentration of its forces was no match for the much better equipped Moroccans. Exposed to the withering fire of the FAR, the insurgents were left without a choice but to rapidly withdraw east, leaving numerous destroyed vehicles behind. Emboldened by this success, in November 1983, the FAR departed from its long-standing strategy of maintaining a strictly defensive posture and made a brief excursion outside the berm: with support from the FRA, it overran at least one major forward insurgent base. Although the ELPS SA-6s managed to ambush at least one Moroccan fighter-bomber formation, and to knock down another Mirage F.1, this was a significant morale booster for all of the Moroccan armed forces.[30]

Indeed, a development of this kind was of immense importance for Rabat, too: dissent caused by a worsening economic situation had caused public unrest in 1980, when riots erupted in Casablanca, that were suppressed only after the security authorities killed 637 civilians. By 1982, the country's position had deteriorated sharply in the wake of drought-induced grain imports and substantial depreciation of the national currency, the dirham, against the dollar, caused by decreased demands for phosphates – which in turn was a result of the economic slowdown in developed countries. Unsurprisingly, every new battle that ended with only minimal loss was now considered a major success.

Operation Grand Maghreb

Through all of this time, the combat engineers of the Moroccan military – the unsung heroes of this war – continued patiently working to expand their berm, often under fire. By May 1984, they had constructed a new berm from the Samara area almost to the Algerian border, and thus cutting off al-Farcia and Mahbas from the reach of the insurgency.

In October 1984, the ELPS launched its Great Maghreb Offensive against the berm under construction south of Sa'ac, between Dakhla and Argub. However, one of its mechanized columns tripped off sensors and radar alarms while approaching the wall and was then caught in a crossfire that left scores of insurgents dead and more than two dozen of their vehicles destroyed or captured. With this it became clear that the war had converted from one of rapid manoeuvre into a costly battle of attrition – which the ELPS could never afford: unsurprisingly, after this experience the insurgents kept their distance, limiting their activity to occasional harassment with shellfire.[31]

Libyan Withdrawal

Elsewhere in 1984, Rabat scored a major coup when it signed the Treaty of Oujda with Libya, in which Tripoli agreed not to challenge Morocco's claim on Western Sahara, and to impose a self-declared

An M113 of Task Force Zellaka, mounting a ZPU-2 machine gun, seen in its firing-position along the 'great wall'. (via Tom Cooper)

The crew of another Moroccan M113 – this time one equipped with the launcher for a BGM-71 TOW ATGM – seen in its firing position. The TOW proved highly successful in operations along the Moroccan Great Wall, prompting the FRA to attempt installing the system on its SA.342 Gazelle helicopters too. (via Tom Cooper)

embargo on arms to the ELPS. Although King Hassan revoked this treaty by August 1986, Libya never renewed its military support to the insurgency – at least not to the levels of the 1979-1982 period. The Libyan withdrawal hit the POLISARIO particularly hard, because Tripoli was not only the source of most of its equipment and training, but also as much as 80 per cent of its financial assistance.[32]

The Libyan withdrawal left the insurgency in a state of shock: the Moroccans were thus largely left unmolested while completing the next branch of the wall – from the Samara area to Guelta Zemmour, via Oum Dreyga and Baggari to Imlily on the Atlantic coast – by September 1985. This section of the berm made an exception from the rule in that it penetrated about eight kilometres deep into Mauritanian territory: at earlier times, and whenever possible, the berm was not constructed directly along the border because the FAR wanted to have small pockets of territory free for engaging the ELPS without violating international borders and thus the sovereignty of other countries. This exception was motivated by the attempt to – at least in theory – cut off the insurgent bases in Algeria from southern regions of Western Sahara. Nevertheless, because Mauritania continued tolerating insurgent operations on its soil, this had only a minimal effect.[33]

Searching to hit areas not yet protected by the berm, the ELPS outflanked the FAR by driving into Morocco before turning south to attack. This manoeuvre resulted in a major clash that raged on 12 and 13 January 1985, north of the Tenuchad River, only 15km (9.3 miles) from the Moroccan border and about 110km (68 miles) from the Algerian border. What exactly happened when – reportedly – three motorized battalions and one armoured battalion of the FAR ran into at least one major ELPS unit, around 16:00 in the afternoon, remains unclear. The POLISARIO claimed that its ambush mauled the Moroccans, who left behind 311 killed and

A Ratel-90 of the 10°MIR (Task Force Arrak), in a firing position along the great berm. (Albert Grandolini Collection)

250 injured troops, while losing six T-55s, two light armoured and six other vehicles. Moreover, Algerian and insurgent sources have provided firm evidence that one FRA F-5E was shot down by SA-7s right over Mahbes while on a CAS mission. Rabat responded with a claim that 66 insurgents were killed, and several tanks destroyed before the ELPS withdrew beyond the Algerian border. In a separate report, the POLISARIO then announced another major clash in the area east of Sakiet el-Hamra and south of Dakhla, in the course of which it shot down two Mirages, killed 25 and injured 48 Moroccan troops. Interestingly, Morocco subsequently confirmed the loss of one Mirage and corresponding casualty figures.[34]

Algerian Restrictions

A major crisis in the international oil and gas markets in late 1986 forced Algeria to cut state spending across the board. Unsurprisingly, the aid it provided to the POLISARIO was significantly reduced, too. Moreover, President Bendjedid revised the official position

of his government to that of a face-saving formula, including a semi-independent Western Saharan state under a Moroccan flag. Indeed, he went as far as to publicly announce his preparedness to accept less than total independence and a strict limit on EPLS military activity. Certainly enough, the insurgents had stockpiled enough arms and ammunition for protracted combat by this time, but combat attrition meanwhile resulted in a quantitative and qualitative decline of their total force: the number of active fighters decreased to about 3,000, greatly limiting their options. While at earlier times the ELPS was able to at least temporarily place its provisional capital in Hawzah, meanwhile it could not even run offensive operations inside Western Sahara anymore. Combined with the effect of the Moroccan 'great wall', financial problems caused by the Libyan withdrawal and the decrease in Algerian support resulted in major morale problems and then a rift within the insurgency. Internal strife resulted in several high-profile defections. Unsurprisingly, although launching attacks upon Guelta Zemmour, al-Farcia, Hawzah and Jdriya in 1986, POLISARIO's leader Mohammed Abdelaziz had to admit that the victory by arms was, 'more difficult [than before], if not impossible'.[35]

The Algerians meanwhile demonstratively kept their distance, as described by one of their retired officers:

After another of their raids on Guelta Zemmour, in 1986, several ELPS columns were withdrawing towards our border. The Mirages pursued, and two of them violated our airspace, prompting the QJJ to scramble a pair of MiG-21s from Tindouf AB. Before the MiGs were in a position to open fire, the Moroccans flew into the range of the nearby SA-3 SAM-site, and the ground control thus ordered our interceptor pilots to stay away, so to avoid a possible fratricide engagement. The SAM-site then acquired and locked-on one of the Mirages but did not open fire. This forced the acquired Moroccan into a series of hard manoeuvres: for almost a minute, our crew watched the "air show" on their TV-system, as the pilot flew one hard manoeuvre after the other, all the time trying to evade. He did not activate his ECM-systems. After getting tired of this, he finally rolled

At the climax of the war in Western Sahara, when the ELPS began deploying SA-6 SAMs, the FRA was forced to reorganise its F-5-force: both of RF-5As (including this example photographed at el-Aaiún AB) and several F-5Bs were groupped into the Escadron Erige, a dedicated reconnaissance asset, trained to search and track the insurgent-operated SAM-systems. (N.B. Collection)

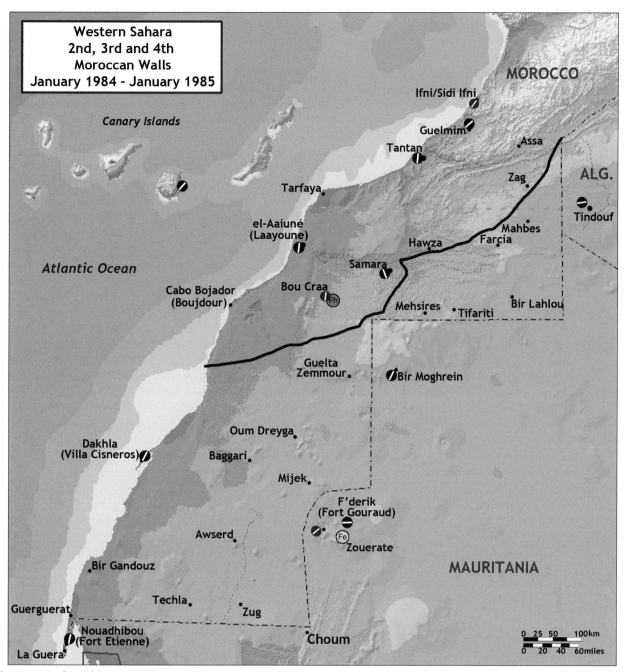

A map depicting the flow of the 2nd, 3rd and 4th Moroccan walls, constructed in the period January 1984 – January 1985. With this the FAR for the first time secured its control of parts of Western Sahara outside the 'useful triangle'. (Map by Tom Cooper)

out and distanced towards the west. After this incident, our government issued a diplomatic protest, but nothing happened, because neither side was keen to provoke a war.[36]

Battle of Farcia

In early 1987, the ELPS mobilised more than one hundred MBTs and APCs and deployed a force protected by SA-6s against the Mahbas-Farcia region again. The insurgents picked out two small garrisons on the berm manned by only 80 and 50 troops: these were approached by two mechanized battalions by night on 4 February and then assaulted simultaneously, fixing the Moroccans until they came under the assault of the ELPS tank battalion. However, contrary to earlier times when they continuously displayed superior tactical skills, the insurgent deployment of armour proved rather orthodox: single MBTs led columns of BMP-1s, which brought the infantry to the combat zone, but then stopped and remained in the rear, leaving tanks and infantry alone. Moreover, the Sahrawis began losing heart in the face of superior Moroccan firepower: as

soon as one of the M48s knocked out the lead T-55, the rest of the ELPS turned around and fled. It was only when a rapid-reaction force of the FAR attempted to counterattack the following morning that the insurgents fought with greater effectiveness: they set up another ambush, destroyed two dozen vehicles and killed up to 200 Moroccans. This in turn enabled them to deploy their third unit – responsible for logistical support – to evacuate all the captured material, all the prisoners, and all of their own casualties to the rear before they withdrew from the battlefield. The magnitude of this defeat was such that King Hassan II solicited a report from the general in charge of his 'southern province' the same evening.[37]

However, this was to remain the only major clash for most of the year and the FAR was thus free to complete the construction of its sixth berm, roughly from Baggari to Awsard and Techla, in April 1987. Certainly enough, the FAR was forced to recruit between 10,000 and 15,000 additional troops, and create a host of new units, including a mechanized regiment, one airborne battalion, six infantry battalions, two artillery groups, a sapper battalion, and a transportation battalion – to man this section alone. However, Rabat could meanwhile afford such a massive effort – foremost thanks financial support from Saudi Arabia, Kuwait and the UAE. Moreover, with the completion of the sixth berm, the entire defence complex from the Moroccan border in the north to the coast of the Atlantic Ocean in the south was nearly 2,500km (1,553 miles) long and became not only the largest functional military barrier in the world, but also provided Rabat with nearly absolute control over 80 per cent of Western Sahara. The mass of the Moroccan forces was thus safe from the insurgent raids that had regularly caught it by surprise at earlier times. Finally, from the safety of its bases, the FAR and the FRA were able to launch their own strikes upon selected insurgent bases at will. For example, on the basis of satellite intelligence provided by Washington, at an unknown date in 1987, FRA Mirage F.1EHs supported by both Boeing 707 tankers, attacked the same ELPS supply depot in north-western Mali that had been bombed by F-5As ten years earlier.[38]

The ELPS did come back to attempt another attack against the berm in the Mahbas-Farcia region: on 13 October 1987, it used an engineering vehicle based on the hull of a T-34 to breach the berm, while T-55s and BMP-1s waited in the rear and attempted to provide fire support. However, Moroccan M48s were positioned high atop a nearby hill: while having an excellent command of the terrain in front and below them, they were so high that the insurgent tankers couldn't hit them because of the low maximum elevation of their guns. Thus, as soon as the FAR tanks knocked out the engineering vehicle, the ELPS was forced to withdraw. With this it became obvious that the POLISARIO was unable to take control of any part of the Western Sahara west of the great wall: it not only lacked manpower but began showing deficiencies in skills and equipment necessary for sustained combat operations. The berm robbed the insurgency of their highly mobile tactics and forced them to adopt ever more sophisticated weaponry in order to counter sophisticated weaponry already mastered by the Moroccans.

The ELPS engineering vehicle based on a T-34 chassis, captured by the FAR during the fighting in the Mahbas-Farcia area, in October 1987. (Albert Grandolini Collection)

Moroccan prisoners of war in one of the notorious camps of the ELPS: most of these were actually constructed by the prisoners, who were forced to work and survive under catastrophic conditions. (Albert Grandolini Collection)

Regardless of how much it tried, the ELPS could not follow in fashion, and thus became ineffective on the battlefield. The result was that the reminder of 1987 was characterised by the lowest level of military activity in eleven years of this war. For some time at least, the POLISARIO did consider regaining the military initiative by adopting more aggressive tactics – including increased use of armour and even terrorism against Moroccan interests elsewhere: however, the Algerian president Bendjedid meanwhile exercised strict control over the insurgency and would not let it realise any of these.

Second Battle of Guelta Zemmour

In January 1989, the UN mediated the first-ever meeting between King Hassan II and POLISARIO's representatives. This was followed by Spanish permission for the insurgency to open an office in Madrid, in exchange for a promise to stop military actions. However, the apparent rapprochement soon proved to be another of Hassan's feints: in May, Rabat ratified the Treaty of Ifrane from 1972, thus officially ending its border dispute with Algeria, while in September 1989, the Moroccan monarch announced that there was no need for further talks with the POLISARIO. Left without a choice, but in a need to remain committed to the penetration of the berm, in early October 1989 the ELPS thus staged a new major attack on Guelta Zemmour. Once again, the insurgents concentrated all of their major units, including those equipped with T-54/55 MBTs and BMP-1 IFVs, and nearly all of their artillery. However, the FAR was ready this time: Guelta Zemmour was protected by the entire 1°RIM, reinforced by the 5°GAR, 18°, 19°, 51° and 61° BIS, and two artillery groups. Moreover, as soon as the insurgents began approaching, the FRA began flying hunter-killer operations against its SA-6s, followed by air strikes on the enemy armour. The Moroccan advantage in firepower became obvious almost as soon as this battle began: when Mirages knocked out the ELPS's SA-6s, the HOT-equipped Gazelles were free to hit MBTs and IFV from stand-off distances. In only two days of fighting – on 6 and 7 October 1989 the SA.342s claimed 18 Sahrawi tanks knocked out by ATGMs, all of these well away from the defence perimeter of Guelta Zemmour. The ELPS did – repeatedly – try to set up ambushes for the Gazelles, primarily with the help of ZSU-23-4 Shilka self-propelled, radar-directed 23mm anti-aircraft guns. However, these remained unsuccessful. Ultimately, although causing substantial FAR casualties in the course of their diversionary attacks on the Hawza section of the Moroccan Great Wall, and in Amgala, the insurgents had to call off further attacks when it became clear they could not reach even their minimal objectives: the Second Battle of Guelta Zemmour ended with their clear-cut defeat.[39]

Operation Rattle and the Cease Fire

Despite the failure of negotiations in 1989, the UN continued efforts to effect negotiations and even a return of the Sahrawi refugees from the camps in the Tindouf area. Therefore, multiple non-governmental organisations launched projects aimed to reconstruct the infrastructure damaged by the war and clear millions of mines in the eastern Western Sahara, especially in the Tifariti area. In June 1990, the UN published its peace plan that envisaged a referendum on the future of Western Sahara. This received support from France before further negotiations lost momentum because of the Kuwait Crisis, which erupted in August of the same year, and which Morocco skilfully exploited for gaining further sympathies and support from abroad by deploying its troops on the side of the US-led coalition that then fought against Iraq.

In April 1991, the UN General Assembly approved the UN

POLISARIO's Naval Operations

The least-known aspect of the POLISARIO's – and thus the ELPS' – combat activities is the fact that during the late 1970s and early 1980s the insurgency operated a small naval force, equipped with speedboats and deployed these in harassing attacks on the Moroccan Navy along the coast of Western Sahara. Next to no details are known in this regard. Slightly more is known about the ELPS harassing operations against foreign fishery vessels though. On 28 November 1978, the Spanish trawler *Cruz del Mar* was attacked, and five of the crew killed. From that date onwards, the F-5As of the EdA flew regular combat air patrols along the coast of Western Sahara, their pilots ready to strafe any boats used by the insurgents with their 20mm cannons – and that despite the constant SA-7 threat. Nevertheless, the ELPS then attacked the trawler *Mency de Abona* in October 1980. During the same period, the Spanish Air Force also flew patrols to monitor the activity of Soviet 'trawlers' – actually electronic intelligence-gatherers that frequently sailed close to the coast of the Canary Islands.

On other occasions, their RF-5As took photographs of Soviet merchants hauling heavy arms – including fast missile craft – to Angola.

In 1982, the Spaniards disbanded the 464th Squadron of the EdA, and replaced it with the re-established 462nd Squadron, equipped with 22 Mirage F.1EEs and 2 F.1EBs. These jets continued flying combat air patrols along the coast of Western Sahara. It remains unclear how much deterrent they actually exercised because Sahrawi and Moroccan sources released next to no details. The last known ELPS attack on Spanish fishery vessels took place in June and September 1986, when the trawlers *Andes* and *Puenta Canario* came under attack, respectively, and no fewer than ten seamen were killed. Additional attacks may have hit Portuguese vessels, but next to no details are known about them. POLISARIO's naval operations eventually came to an end due to the construction of the sixth and final section of the Moroccan Great Wall, which closed the coast of southern Western Sahara to the insurgency.

One of six OV-10As delivered to Morocco together with the F-5E/Fs, starting in 1981. According to unofficial sources, the fleet saw relatively little action against the ELPS in north-eastern Morocco but was utilised to fly combat air patrols along the coast of Western Sahara. (Albert Grandolini Collection)

A Moroccan OV-10A in a turn, showing its armament to advantage. The latter included LAU-3/M260 (19-round) and LAU-59/Mk.66 Hydra (7-round) pods for 2.75in (68mm) unguided rockets, and a pod for a 20mm gun and ammunition under the centreline. (Albert Grandolini Collection)

The wreckage of an FRA OV-10A shot down by the ELPS near Dakhla on 13 January 1985. The aircraft was either underway for another patrol along the coast or involved in operations against one of the final insurgent raids in Western Sahara. Another OV-10A was shot down by the insurgents later the same year, but in the Samara area. (via E.C.)

An ELPS BMP-1 knocked out during the Second Battle of Guelta Zemmour. (via Tom Cooper)

A view of the rear hull of one of the insurgent T-55s knocked out during the Second Battle of Guelta Zemmour, showing the hull registration (262512) and an unidentified insignia. (via Tom Cooper)

A row of ELPS SA-9s. The weapon continued scoring sporadic kills against FRA aircraft well into the 1980s, although its effectiveness was greatly diminished by improved tactics and countermeasure systems of the Moroccans. (Albert Grandolini Collection)

Replaced in their attack role with SA.342 Gazelles by 1980, FRA's AB.205As were primarily used as utility helicopters for the rest of the war. This example was photographed while delivering supplies to one of the Moroccan outposts. (Albert Grandolini Collection)

Secretary-General's plan for a referendum in Western Sahara and established the United Nation's Mission for the Organisation of a Referendum on Western Sahara (*Mission des nations unies pour l'Organisation d'un Référendum au Sahara Occidental*, MINURSO). However, Morocco then launched a series of air strikes and ground offensives on the population centres held by the ELPS: on 4 August 1991, FRA fighter-bombers simultaneously flew air strikes on Tifariti, Mehsiers and Mijek. Although the insurgent-operated SA-9s shot down one of the involved F-5Es, and the ELPS captured its pilot, heavy damage was caused, especially to recently reconstructed civilian infrastructure, and dozens of civilians were killed. Moreover, large areas around all three oases were effectively mined by unexploded bomblets sown by CBUs deployed by the FRA fighter-bombers.[40] On 22 August, the FRA flew another wave of airstrikes that, according to the POLISARIO, targeted water wells. Three days later, insurgents reported that Moroccan ground forces had reached the oasis of Bir Lehlou, the POLISARIO's provisional capital, killing at least 20 people and causing hundreds of civilians to flee. Whether because it was taken by surprise, or because it lacked the capability to oppose this attack, the ELPS offered no resistance, officially explaining this as being out of respect for the UN peace plan. Concerned that the conflict was likely to continue escalating, UN Secretary-General Javier Pérez de Cuéllar then single-handedly announced a cease-fire: the POLISARIO accepted promptly, while the Moroccans began withdrawing their troops on 27 August 1991. De Cuéllar's cease-fire was effective from 6 September 1991, and respected by both sides, thus bringing the military phase of the war in Western Sahara to its end.

Cost of the War

The cease-fire of 1991 left Morocco in control of over 80 per cent – the 'useful part' – of the disputed territory, and the POLISARIO in rather shaky control of the rest. Although Rabat was supposed to reduce its forces from 130,000 to 65,000, and let in a UN peacekeeping force, it never did so: supported by Saudi Arabia, Kuwait, the UAE, and the West, and benefitting from improved relations with Algeria and Libya, King Hassan was able to act from a position of strength, and was in no need to make any concessions.

The human cost of the war from 1975 until 1991 is only roughly known. While the war in Western Sahara is often described as a 'clean' conflict in terms of the suffering of civilians, and no figures were ever published by any of the involved parties, there is little doubt that several thousands of civilians were killed. When Moroccan King Mohammed VI – who took over following the death of Hassan II in 1999 – established a reconciliation committee in 2004 to shed light on the issue of forced disappearance and arbitrary detentions of the Sahrawis from the period from 1956 until 1999, this reported its findings on 742 persons. However, Rabat never published the list of their names and the fate of about 500 further Sahrawis remains unclear.[41]

Official Moroccan military casualties remain unknown (and are often the cause of fierce online debates); those of Mauritania are usually assessed at about 2,000 soldiers killed, while a prominent defector from the POLISARIO claimed as many as 3,000 deaths amongst the insurgents. Dependable figures are available only for the number of Moroccan military officers and other ranks captured by the ELPS: correspondingly, between 2,155 and 2,300 of these were held in POW camps outside Tindouf, where they were subjected to regular torture and forced labour under catastrophic

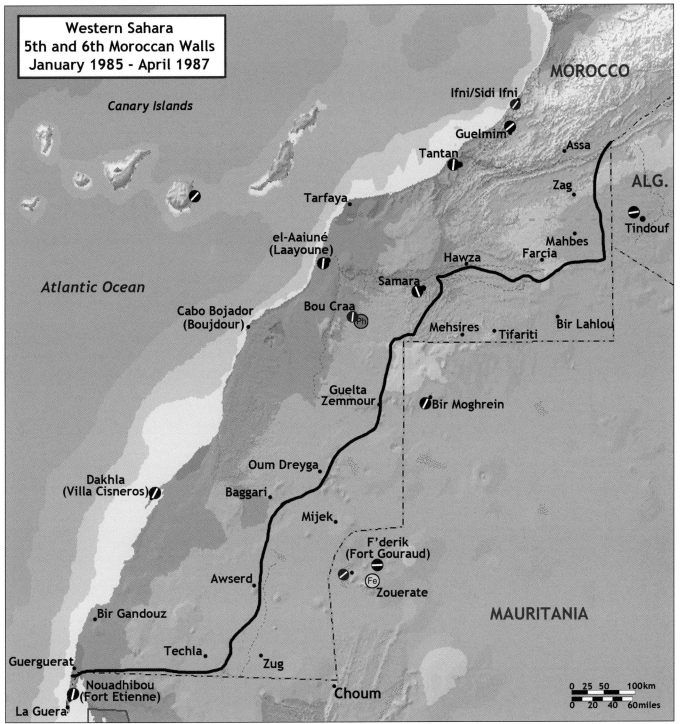

**Western Sahara
5th and 6th Moroccan Walls
January 1985 - April 1987**

Canary Islands

Atlantic Ocean

MOROCCO

Ifni/Sidi Ifni

Guelmim

Assa

Tantan

ALG.

Zag

Tarfaya

Tindouf

el-Aaiuné
(Laayoune)

Mahbes

Farçia

Hawza

Samara

Cabo Bojador
(Boujdour)

Bou Craa

Mehsires

Tifariti

Bir Lahlou

Guelta
Zemmour

Bir Moghrein

Oum Dreyga

Dakhla
(Villa Cisneros)

Baggari

Mijek

F'derik
(Fort Gouraud)

Awserd

Zouerate

MAURITANIA

Bir Gandouz

Techla

Zug

Guerguerat

Nouadhibou
(Fort Etienne)

Choum

La Guera

0 25 50   100km
0 20 40   60miles

A map depicting the line of the Moroccan wall once its 5th and 6th sections were completed, in the period January 1985 – April 1987. With this, the FAR secured its control over 80 per cent of Western Sahara, which it maintains at the time of writing. (Map by Tom Cooper)

conditions. Because the government in Rabat refused to recognize the POLISARIO and negotiate with it, negotiations for their release were particularly problematic: it took extensive efforts by multiple diplomats from the USA and Argentina to repatriate all of them, in the period 2003-2005. For similar reasons, there was a major issue regarding the return of a mere 20 insurgents captured alive by the FAR during the war. Known aircraft losses caused and suffered by all parties in this conflict are listed in Table 7 on page 74.[42]

Post Scriptum
Despite often very high tensions, threats of the resumption of hostilities, countless complaints and outright violations, the cease-fire between Morocco and the POLISARIO continues to hold at the time of writing. With the military aspects of this war being the

primary focus of this project, all the diplomatic, legal and human-rights related aspects, the intifadas of the Sahrawis in 1999 and 2005, and the effects of the so-called 'Arab Spring', in 2011-2012, are outside its scope. It is sufficient to observe that even after nearly two decades of related attempts, Morocco continues to reject any notion of independence or even of autonomy for Western Sahara and shows no signs in related negotiations. Just the attempts to re-energise the idea of a referendum from the year 1991 have frustrated something like a dozen prominent intermediaries – because each side is stubborn in interpreting census figures and the role of Moroccan settlers in Western Sahara in its own way. For all practical purposes, and even if the cease-fire of 1991 is still respected, the war in Western Sahara is thus still going on.

Table 7: Known Claims and Confirmed Aircraft Losses over Western Sahara, 1975-1991[43]

Date	Type	Crew	Remarks
1-7 January 1976	**C-119G**	**unknown**	**crashed in Western Sahara, circumstances unknown**
1-7 January 1976	helicopter	unknown	claimed shot down, circumstances unknown
21 January 1976	**F-5A**	**Ahmed Ben Boubker**	**97099; shot down by SA-7 near Ain Bentili; pilot MIA**
21 January 1976	F-5A		claimed shot down by SA-7 near Dakhla; pilot reportedly POW
28 February 1976	**T-6G**	**Bourzaine/Kecem**	**shot down by small arms fire between Tantan and Tarfaya; pilot POW, technician KIA**
28 February 1976	**T-6G**	**Sellouni**	**shot down by small arms fire near Samara; pilot KIA**
4 December 1976	**C-130H**	**-**	**4537/CNA-OB; crashed on take-off from el-Aaiún; crew KIA**
17 December 1976	**CM.170**	**Mohammed Bettich**	**shot down by small arms fire near Hagunia; pilot POW**
18 December 1976	Jaguar A		damaged by ZPU-2; recovered safely at Dakar IAP
29 December 1976	**BN-2**	**Ould Heyine**	**787/5T-MAR; shot down by SA-7 near Bir Moghrein; crew of three killed**
21 January 1977	BN-2	-	765/5T-MAT claimed shot down
25 February 1977	**F-5A**	**Ahmed Brahim Allai**	**shot down by SA-7 near Bojador; pilot POW**
?? March 1977	**CM.170**	**Mohammad Zarwani**	**shot down; pilot fate unknown**
16 July 1977	**BN-2**	**Abdel Kader**	**shot down by SA-7; pilot and co-pilot OK, observer killed**
?? July 1977	**F-5A**	**Driss Bahji**	**crashed on take-off from Samara; pilot died three days later**
24 August 1977	**F-5A**	**Ali Athman**	**shot down by SA-7 near Liteima, el-Aaiún; pilot POW**
18 December 1977	Jaguar A	Jantet	A51/11RO; claimed shot down over Mauritania; made emergency landing at Nouadibou and was subsequently repaired
18 December 1977	Jaguar A		claimed shot down over Mauritania
8 January 1978	Jaguar A		claimed shot down over Mauritania
10 January 1978	**BN-2**	**Abdel Kader**	**shot down by SA-7; pilot killed, two of the crew captured**
14 January 1978	**Broussard**	**Boukhima Habib; Ahmed Amellal**	**119; shot down by small arms fire; crew fate unclear**
28 February 1978	F-5A		claimed shot down in Touagil area
3 May 1978	Jaguar A		claimed shot down by SA-7 over Mauritania
2 June 1978	**F-5A**		**shot down by 12.7mm DShK near Sken, crashed near el-Aaiún; pilot KIA**
5 June 1978	**F-5A**	**Mohammed Belkadi**	**hit by SA-7 near Oum Dreyga, crashed short of el-Aaiún; pilot killed**
10 September 1978	**F-5A**	**Ali Najab Abdel Salam**	**shot down by SA-7 near Khreibichate, Samara; pilot POW**
?? October 1978	**F-5A**		**97177; shot down near Jebel Ouarkiss; pilot fate unknown**
?? November 1978	F-5A		claimed shot down
16 January 1979	F-5A		claimed destroyed at Tantan
16 January 1979	Helicopter		claimed destroyed at Tantan
17 January 1979	Helicopter		claimed destroyed at Tantan
17 January 1979	Helicopter		claimed destroyed at Tantan
17 January 1979	Helicopter		claimed destroyed at Tantan
28 January 1979	F-5A		claimed shot down near Tantan
10 February 1979	**F-5A**		**69120; shot down, pilot recovered**
19 November 1979	**Mirage F.1CH**	**Ahmed el-Fane**	**shot down by SA-9 near Abatih; pilot KIA**
19 November 1979	Mirage F.1CH		claimed shot down by SA-7 near Zag
6 December 1979	**Mirage F.1CH**	**Mahjoub Ma'atawi el-Arbi**	**shot down by SA-7 near Zag; pilot POW but died in captivity**
13 February 1980	**F-5A**	**Habib Boucherif**	**shot down by SA-7 near Bojador; pilot POW**
14 February 1980	**Mirage F.1CH**	**Salek**	**shot down by SA-7 near Bojador; pilot KIA**
27 February 1980	**Mirage F.1CH**	**Hassan el-Nazi**	**shot down by SA-? Near Rous Lakhyalat; pilot POW**

17 September 1980	Mirage F.1EH	Mohammad Dahhou	shot down during a CAS sortie; pilot killed
27 December 1980	F-5A	El-Nazi Hassan	shot down by SA-7 near Rous Lakhyalat; pilot POW
5 April 1981	Mirage F.1CH	Ahmed el-Kili	shot down by SA-7 near Guelta Zemmour; pilot KIA
12 October 1981	C-130H	Amin + 4 others	4717/CNA-OH; shot down by SA-6 near Guelta Zemour; crew KIA
12 October 1981	F-5A	Hassan Boughenou	shot down by SA-6 near Guelta Zemmour; pilot captured
13 October 1981	Mirage F.1CH	Driss el-Yazami	shot down by SA-9 near Guelta Zemmour; pilot captured
13 October 1981	Mirage F.1CH	Ben Jeddi Boujemma	shot down by SA-9 Near Guelta Zemmour; fate unknown
23 October 1981	SA.330B	El-A'adel/Madih	shot down by SA-9 near Guelta Zemmour; crew of three and nine passengers KIA
9 August 1982	Mirage F.1		claimed shot down; pilot reported as POW
27 September 1982	Mirage F.1EH	Mohammed Hadri	shot down by SA-9 near Hawza while on reconnaissance mission; pilot POW
11 October 1982	Mirage F.1	Hamri	shot down by SA-7 or SA-9; pilot fate unknown
12 January 1985	F-5E		shot down by SA-6 near Mahbas; pilot KIA
13 January 1985	OV-10A	Oudghiri/Rabhi	shot down near Dakhla, crew fate unknown
21 January 1985	Piper		shot down by small arms fire after take-off from Dakhla; two on board killed (claimed as OV-10)
24 February 1985	Do.228		D-IGVN; shot down by SA-7 near Dakhla; three on board killed
?? ?? 1985	OV-10A		shot down near Samara; crew fate unknown
3 April 1986	C.160		AdA transport narrowly missed by what was assessed as 'POLISARIO-operated SA-9 SAM' while underway about 20 kilometres off the coast of the Western Sahara
16 March 1987	Mirage F.1		shot down; pilot fate unknown
26 April 1987	F-5E		9193?; shot down in Guelta Zemmour area; pilot fate unknown
21 August 1987	F-5E		claimed shot down, circumstances unclear
25 August 1988	Mirage F.1	Tazerny	shot down; pilot POW
8 December 1988	DC-7		N284; shot down by SA-9 near Bir Moghrein; five on board killed
8 December 1988	DC-7		damaged by SA-9 near Bir Moghrein; landed safely at Sidi Ifni
4 August 1991	F-5E	Youssef al-Megzari	91921, shot down by SA-? near Tifariti; pilot POW

Bibliography

Many of the materials presented in this book were obtained in the course of research for the book series Arab MiGs, which reconstructs the history of Arab air forces at war with Israel in the 1955-1973 period. Additional information was acquired during interviews with participants and eyewitnesses mentioned in the acknowledgements and elsewhere, primarily in Algeria and Morocco, but also in France and the USA. Sadly, concerns for their security and that of their families have prevented most of them from speaking openly, and thus they have been mentioned only by their initials. Their contributions have enabled the authors to cross-examine the following publications (as well as those mentioned in footnotes) that were consulted in preparation of this book:

Aguirre, J. R. D., *El Oscuro Pasado del Desierto: Approximación a la Historia del Sáhara* (Madrid: Casa de África, 2004: ISBN 84-95498-64-2).

Alaoui, H., *Guerre secrète au Sahara occidental* (Paris: Encre d'Orient, 2010).

Alvarez, J. E., Bowen, W. H., *A Military History of Modern Spain: From the Napoleonic Era to the International War on Terror* (Praeger Security International, 2007; ISBN 978-0-27599-3573).

Barbier, M., *Le conflit du Sahara occidental* (Paris: L'Harmattan, 1982; ISBN 978-2-29627-877-6).

Bárbulo, T., *La historia prohibida del Sáhara Espanol* (Barcelona: Desino, 2002).

Bévillard, A. (General), *La saga du Transport Aérien Militaire Français, Tome 1: de Kolwezi à Mazar-e-Sharif et de Port au Prince à Dumont- d'Urville* (Sceaux: L'esprit du Livre Edition, 2007).

Bhutani, S., 'Conflict in Western Sahara', *Strategic Analysis, Volume 2/Issue 7*, 1978, pp. 251-256.

Brent, W., *African Air Forces* (Freeworld Publications, 1999).

Casas De La Vega, R., *La ultima guerra de Africa, campana de Ifini-Sahara* (Madrid: Ministerio de Defensa, 2008).

Catala, M., La France, *l'Espagne et l'indépendance du Maroc 1951-1958*, (Paris: Rivage des Xantons, 2015; ISBN 978-2-84654-366-8).

Collectif, *Chronique du Charles de Gaulle; L'apogée d'un siècle d'aéronautique navale* (Chroniques Them, 2002; ISBN 978-2205053234).

Collectif, *Le Jaguar dans ses Missions de Guerre Electronique* (Paris: Lavauzelle/ Association Guerrelec, 2007).

Cooper, T. & Nicolle, D., *Arab MiGs, Volume 1: Mikoyan i Gurevich MiG-15 and MiG-17 in Service with Air Forces of Algeria, Egypt, Iraq, Morocco and Syria* (Houston: Harpia Publishing, 2009, ISBN 978-0-9825539-2-3).

Cooper, T., Nicolle, D., with Nordeen, L., Salti, P., and Smisek, M., *Arab MiGs, Volume 4: Attrition War, 1967-1973* (Houston: Harpia Publishing, 2013, ISBN 978-0-9854554-1-5).

Cooper, T., Weinert, P., Hinz, F.& Lepko, M., *African MiGs, MiGs and Sukhois in Service in Sub-Saharan Africa, Volume 1: Angola to Ivory Coast* (Houston: Harpia Publishing, 2010, ISBN 978-0-9825539-5-4).

Crosnier, A., *l'armée de l'Air en Afrique du Nord, Maroc-Algérie-Tunisie, 1940-1967, Tome 1* (Paris: Histoire & Collection, 2015, ISBN 978-2-35250-420-7).

Crosnier, A., *l'armée de l'Air en Afrique du Nord, Maroc-Algérie-Tunisie, 1940-1967, Tome 2* (Paris: Histoire & Collection, 2015, ISBN 978-2-35250-421-4).

Cruz, G. A., 'Homegrown Pedros: Spanish-Built Heinkel He 111s, Part 1', *Air Enthusiast No. 90* (November/December 2000).

Cruz, G. A., 'Homegrown Pedros: Spanish-Built Heinkel He 111s, Part 2', *Air Enthusiast No. 91* (January/February 2001).

Daguzan, Jean François, *Le dernier rempart? Forces armées et politiques de défense au Maghreb* (Paris: Edition Publisud, 1998, ISBN 2-86600-819-7).

Dean, D. J., *The Air Force Role in Low-Intensity Conflict* (Maxwell AFB: Air University Press, October 1986, ISBN 1-58566-014-0).

Flintham, V., *Air Wars and Aircraft: A Detailed Record of Air Combat 1945 to the Present* (London: Arms and Armour Press, 1989, ISBN 0-85368-779-X).

Forget, M., *Nos forces aériennes en OPEX, un demi-siècle d'interventions extérieures* (Paris, Economica, 2013)

François Pernot & Marie-Catherine Villatoux, 'l'Aéronautique Militaire au Maroc avant 1914', *Revue Historique des Armées Troupes colonials, Troupes de marine* No.1/2000.

Fricker, J., 'Lockheed F-104 Starfighter', *Wings of Fame; The Journal of Classic Combat Aircraft, Volume 2* (Aerospace Publishing, 1996).

Fuente Cobo, I., Marino Menendez, F., *El Conflicto Del Sahara Occidental* (Madrid: Ministerio de Defensa, 2005).

Gomá Orduna, J., *Historia de la aeronáutica Espanola* (Madrid: Prensa Espanola, 1950).

Green, W. & Fricker, J., *The Air Forces of the World: Their History, Development, and Present Strength* (London: MacDonald, 1958).

Hagedorn, D. & Hellström, L., *Foreign Invaders: The Douglas Invader in Foreign Military and US Clandestine Service* (Leicester: Midland Publishing Ltd., 1994; ISBN 1-85780-013-3).

Hodges, T., *Origine et enjeux d'une guerre du désert* (Paris: L'harmattant, 1982, ISBN 2-85802-7641).

Holeindre, R., 'Les Nouveaux Renard du Desert', *Paris Match*, (September 1979), pp. 82-85, 96.

Hollwell, T., *Allah's Garden: A True Story* (Urbana: Tales Press, 2009; ISBN 978-09641423-9-8).

Hughes, S. O., *Morocco Under King Hassan* (Ithaca Press, 1999, ISBN 978-0863723124).

Husson, J. P., 'L'Armee de Liberation Populaire Sahraouie: Le bras armé du Front Polisario', *Raids No.173*, (October 2000).

Johnsen, F. A., *Northrop F-5/F-20/T-38* (North Branch: Speciality Press Publishers and Wholesalers, 2006, ISBN 978-1-58007-094-2).

Keagan, J., *World Armies* (Facts on File Inc., 1979; ISBN: 978-0871964076).

Kissling, H. J., Spuler, B., Barbour, N., Trimingham, J. S., Bagley, F. R. C., Braun, H., Hartel, H., *The Last Great Muslim Empires, Part II* (Brill: Leiden, 1969).

Lake, J., *Northrop F-5*, *World Air Power Journal*, Volume 25/Summer 1996 (ISSN: 0959-7050).

Liébert, M. & Buyck, S., *Le Mirage F1 et les Mirage de seconde generation à voilure en fleche, Vol.2:* Les Mirage F1 deserie, Un avion aux multiples facettes (Outreau: Éditions Lela Presse, 2007, ISBN 2-914017-41-3).

Lorell, MarkA., *Airpower in Peripheral Conflict: The French Experience in Africa* (Santa Monica: RAND, 1989, ISBN 0-8330-0937-0).

Louit, Michel-Ivan, *Ecouvillon? Discrète opération de maintien de l'ordre franco-espagnole, Sahara occidental 1957-1958* (Paris: Marsouins et Méharistes, 2009).

Lovelace, Douglas C., *War and Insurgency in the Western Sahara* (Carlisle Barracks: US Army War College Press, 2013, ISBN 1-58487-569).

Mergui, R., 'La grande riposte', *Jeune Afrique No. 985*, November 1979.

Ministerio de Defensa, *Ala 46, 50 anos de historia, 1965-2015* (Madrid: Ministerio de Defensa, 2015).

Miske, A., *Front Polisario, l'âme d'un peuple* (Paris: Rupture, 1978).

Mokhtar, G., *General History of Africa II: Ancient Civilizations of Africa* (London: Heinemann Educational Books Ltd., 1981; ISBN 0-435-94805-9).

Nicolle, D., Cooper, T., & Air Vice Marshal Gabr Ali Gabr, *Wings over Sinai. The Egyptian Air Force During the Sinai War, 1956* (Solihull: Helion & Co. 2017; ISBN 978-1-911096-61-0).

Ougartchinska, R., & Priore, R., *Pour la Peau de Kadhafi: Guerres, Secrets, et Mensonges, (1969-2011)* (Paris: Fayard, 2013).

Pivka, Otto v., *Armies of the Middle East* (Leicester: Book Club Associates/ Patrick Stephens Ltd., 1979).

Sahara Info: Bulletin de l'Association des Amis de la Republique Arabe Saharaouie Démocratique (volumes as quoted), sahara-info.org

Said, H. M., *La batalla de Guelta Zemmour, 13 y 14 de octubre de 1981* (online publication posted at arso.org, on 2 February 2012).

Sales Lluch, J. M., *Alas sobre el desierto: La aviacion militar espanola durante el conflicto del Sahara, 1975* (Galland Books, 2013; ISBN 978-8415043560).

Scutts, J., *Northrop F-5/F-20* (Runnymede: Ian Allan Ltd., 1986; ISBN 0-7110-1576-7).

Staface, C., *Arab Air Forces* (Carolton: Squadron/Signal Publications Inc., 1994, ISBN 0-89747-326-4).

Thomas, M., *The French Empire between the Wars: Imperialism, Politics and Society* (Manchester, Manchester University Press, 2005; ISBN 0-7190-6518-6).

Vézin, A., *Jaguar: le félin en action* (Boulogne-Billancourt: ETAI Editions, 2008).

Western Sahara Resource Watch, *P for Plunder: Morocco's Exports of Phosphates from occupied Western Sahara, 2016* <https://wsrw.org/a105x4159> (accessed 10 October 2019).

Willis, D. (editor), *Aerospace Encyclopaedia of World Air Forces* (London: Aerospace Publishing Ltd., 1999, ISBN 1-86184-045-4).

World Defence Almanac, *Military Technology* magazine volumes 1/91, 1/93, 1/95, 1/97, 1/98 & 1/03.

Yara, Ali Omar, *L'insurrection Sahraouie, de la guerre à l'état 1973-2003* (Paris: l'Harmattan, 2017, ISBN 2-7475-4656-X).

Zunes, S., & Munday, J., *Western Sahara: War, Nationalism and Conflict Irresolution* (Syracuse: Syracuse University Press, 2010, ISBN 978-0-8156-3219-1).

Various volumes of *el-Djeich* Magazine (the official publication of the Algerian Ministry of Defence), *Air Fan, le Fana de l'Aviation, Aviation Magazine Internationale, Air et Cosmos, Icare, Revue Historique des Armées* and *Raids* (France), *Raids* (France), *Revista de Aeronautica y Astronautica, Aeroplano, Revista de Historia Aeronautica* (Spain), and personal notes of both authors based on other daily and weekly printed publications.

Africa@War Series

Cooper, T., Grandolini, A., and Delalande, A., *Libyan Air Wars, Part 1* (Solihull: Helion & Co Ltd., 2014, ISBN 978-1909982-39-0).

Cooper, T., Grandolini, A. and Delalande, A., *Libyan Air Wars, Part 2* (Solihull: Helion & Co Ltd, 2016, ISBN 978-1-910294-53-6).

Cooper, T., Grandolini, A., and Delalande, A., *Libyan Air Wars, Part 3* (Solihull: Helion & Co Ltd, 2016, ISBN 978-1-910294-54-3).

Cooper, T. & Grandolini, A., *Showdown in Western Sahara Volume 1: Air Warfare over the last African Colony, 1945-1975* (Warwick: Helion & Co., 2018; ISBN 978-1-912390-35-9).

Kowalczuk, D., *Kolwezi 1978, Operations 'Leopard' and 'Red Bean', French and Belgian Intervention in Zaire* (Warwick: Helion & Co. Ltd., 2018; ISBN 978-1-912390-59-5).

Middle East@War Series

Cooper, T. & Sipos, M., *Iraqi Mirages: The Dassault Mirage Family in Service with the Iraqi Air Force, 1981-1988* (Warwick: Helion & Co. Ltd., 2019; ISBN 978-1-912390-31-1).

Cooper, T., *MiG-23 Flogger in the Middle East: Mikoyan i Gurevich MiG-23 in Service in Algeria, Egypt, Iraq, Libya and Syria, 1973-2018* (Warwick: Helion & Co. Ltd., 2018; ISBN 978-1-912390-32-8).

Cooper, T., *Moscow's Game of Poker: Russian Military Intervention in Syria, 2015-2017* (Warwick: Helion & Co. Ltd., 2018; ISBN 978-1-912390-37-3).

Notes

Page 1

1   While theoretically considered equivalent to an NCO-rank in the USA or Great Britain, the French rank of adjutant actually falls between officer and NCO ranks, and is considered the lowest officer rank, though also the highest NCO rank.

Chapter 1

1   CIA, *Viability and Orientation of a Western Saharan State*, PA81-10069, March 1981, CIA Freedom of Information Act Electronic Reading Room (henceforth CIA/FOIA/ERR). According to the census of 1974, the Tekna tribe made about 31 per cent of the Sahrawi population, the Reguibat about 28 per cent, and the Delim 15.5 per cent (for details, see Barbier, p. 17).

2   Unless stated otherwise, this sub-chapter is based on Aguirre, *El Oscuro Pasado del Desierto* (details in Bibliography).

3   For details, *Volume 1*, pp. 15-29.

4   Ibid, pp. 51-59.

5   CIA, *Viability and Orientation of a Western Saharan State*, PA81-10069, March 1981, CIA/FOIA/ERR. Notable is that, according to the same document, the Spanish military originally recommended the construction of a railroad line, because it considered other solutions to be 'too vulnerable'.

5   CIA, 'The role of Morocco and Spanish Sahara in the World Phosphate Rock Market', 6 November 1974, CIA/FOIA/ERR; Western Sahara Resource Watch, *P for Plunder*, p. 8; Dean, p. 30; Aidan Lewis, 'Morocco's fish fight: High Stakes over Western Sahara', BBC, 15 December 2011; Sarah Zhang, 'The World's Largest Conveyor Belt System can be seen from Space', 24 April 2014, gizmodo.com. Notably, Spain sold its 35 per cent share of the Bou Craa mine in 2002.

7   Another matter to play an important issue in more recent times are the rich fishing grounds off the Atlantic coast. While not a major economic factor in the 1970s or 1980s, they did become one following a fishing agreement between Morocco and the European Union of 2006. While of poor value for money and environmentally damaging – and illegal because the UN does not recognize Morocco's claims of sovereignty over the territory – this agreement de-facto legitimised Morocco's occupation and firmly established its position with Brussels, in exchange for up to 70 per cent of the EU's fleet capacity operating in the waters of Western Sahara.

8   Established in the 1930s, the *Tropas Nómjadas* was an auxiliary regiment of the Spanish Colonial Army composed of Sahrawi tribesmen. Commanded by Spanish officers and equipped with small arms it was usually responsible for the protection of various outposts and – mounted on camels – patrolling the hinterland.

9   Full details of arms deals between Czechoslovakia and Morocco are to follow in a future volume of the Europe@War series, currently being prepared by Martin Smisek.

10 Detail of FAR T-54s as provided by E. C., interview, August 2019.

Chapter 2

1   CIA, *Morocco: National Intelligence Survey*, March 1973, CIA/FOIA/ERR. Notably, the use of military abbreviations – all in French – is a very widespread practice in Morocco.

2   Keagan, p. 484.

3   CIA, *Morocco: National Intelligence Survey*, March 1973, CIA/FOIA/ERR.

4   Ibid.

5   Pivka, pp. 122-124; Keagan, p. 484 & Dr Ben Kirat, 'The Restructuring of the Moroccan Army since Independence', Sahara-Question.com, 30 May 2016.

6   CIA, *Morocco: National Intelligence Survey*, March 1973, CIA/FOIA/ERR &Tobji, pp.74-75. Notably, the Defence Ministry and the FAR also controlled the Royal Gendarmerie, a 3,500-strong, all-volunteer force responsible for maintaining law and order in rural areas, controlling traffic and for performing military police functions in the armed forces. The Royal Gendarmerie had the secondary role of augmenting the army in ground operations (as it did during the Sand War with Algeria in 1963), but it remains unclear to what degree it became involved in the fighting in Western Sahara.

7   CIA, *Morocco: National Intelligence Survey*, March 1973, CIA/FOIA/ERR; E. C. & N. B., diverse interviews since 2015; Tobji, p. 105 & Dr Ben Kirat, 'The Restructuring of the Moroccan Army Since Independence', Sahara-Question.com, 30 May 2016. Tobji (p. 99) expressed his disagreement with the organisation of the GEBs: in his opinion, this kind of *ad-hoc* unit, combining sub-units of mobile formations with sub-units of fixed formations could never work, because their troops were not trained to cooperate.

8   E. C. & N. B., diverse interviews since 2015 & Tobji, p. 81.

9   Largely based on Pivka, pp. 122.

10 List based on information provided by E.C. and N.E.

11 CIA, *Morocco: National Intelligence Survey*, March 1973, CIA/FOIA/ERR.

12 Ibid.

13 *Third Party Transfer to Morocco*, 'Confidential' telegram from the US Embassy in Amman, Jordan, to the Department of State, 18 May 1976 (retrieved from the Wikileaks, on 25 September 2019).

14 N. B., interview, October 2019.

15 CIA, *Morocco: National Intelligence Survey*, March 1973, CIA/FOIA/ERR; Dr Ben Kirat, 'The Restructuring of the Moroccan Army since Independence', Sahara-Question.com, 30 May 2016; Pivka, pp. 122-124. For further details on all the acquisitions for the FRA in the late 1960s and the early 1970s, see *Volume 1*, pp. 39-43. Additional details by E.C. and N. B., and from Tobji, p. 32.

16 Based on interviews with E.C. and N.B.; Keagan, p. 484; Pivka, pp. 122-123, Flintham. Notably, starting with reforms introduced after the coup attempt of 1972, the FRA stopped using alpha-numeric designations: instead, its units have ever since used names. Furthermore, all reports about the transfer of up to 26 F-5A and 5 F-5Bs from Iran in 1975 remain unconfirmed: although up to half of the fleet listed in Table 3 was shot down over Western Sahara (and mostly over positions held by the POLISARIO), not one serial number of Moroccan aircraft of this type has become known that wasn't originally delivered directly from the USA.

17 CIA, *Morocco: National Intelligence Survey*, March 1973, CIA/FOIA/ERR.

18 For further details on the operations in question and related Moroccan experiences, see Cooper et al, *Arab MiGs Volumes 5 & 6* and Kowalczuk, *Kolwezi*.

19 CIA, *Morocco: National Intelligence Survey*, March 1973, CIA/FOIA/ERR.

Chapter 3

1   Zunes et al, xxviii.

2   CIA, 'Moroccan Campaign to Regain Spanish Sahara', 25 July 1974 & CIA, 'Moroccan Plans to Invade Spanish Sahara', 3 October 1975; CIA/FOIA/ERR. Interestingly, the two documents in question reveal that the CIA expected a much more serious Spanish response, including a significant deployment of air power – in the form of at least two squadrons of F-5s, and four squadrons of Mirage IIIs and McDonnell Douglas F-4C interceptors to Spanish Sahara. On the other hand, the CIA correctly assessed that Algeria would stop short of direct military intervention while creating as many problems for Morocco as possible through waging a sustained insurgency effort.

3   Keagan, pp. 465 & 485. The released Spanish soldiers were evacuated with the help of UH-1H helicopters. These and other machines of the Spanish Army Aviation flew a total of 5,730 flight hours in 371 operational sorties between 9 December 1971 and 21 December 1975.

4   Indeed, although the COIN component of the 46th Composite Wing at the Gando AB – units equipped with types such as the T-6D – was disbanded in April 1976, it was replaced by the 464th Squadron equipped with F-5As and RF-5As. This unit was tasked not only with air defence, but also combat air patrols off the coast of Western Sahara – because the POLISARIO soon began to harass Spanish fishing boats. Such missions were continued until March 1982, when the re-activated 462nd Squadron replaced the F-5As with more advanced Mirage F.1CEs.

5   Ali Najab, 'Ma guerre contre le POLISARIO', Medias24.com, 22 July 2015.

6   Sahara: POLISARIO Claims, French Aircraft to Morocco, Atrocities, 'Unclassified' telegram from the US Embassy in Algiers to the Department of State, 15 January 1976 & *Talk with King Hussein – Moroccco and Military Aid*, 'Secret' telegram from the Department of State to the NATO, 2 February 1976 (both retrieved from the Wikileaks, on 25 September 2019).

7   Bhutani, pp. 251-256 & CIA, *Prospect for Morocco*, Interagency Intelligence Memorandum, NI IIM 82-10004, May 1982, CIA/FOIA/ERR. The figures for the Sahrawi population are based on a census run by Spain in 1974.

8   Zunes et al, p. 6.

9   Zunes et al, p. 6 & Bárbulo, pp. 266-282.

10 S.N., interview provided on condition of anonymity, April 2001; M. A. interview provided on condition of anonymity, June 2004; M. R., interview provided on condition of anonymity, April 2017; N. B. and E. C., interviews provided on condition of anonymity, August-October 2019. US communications disclosed by the Wikileaks confirm that the Algerian unit deployed '200km from Algerian border' (inside Western Sahara) was a 'food and medical supply unit' (for details see *Talk with King Hussein – Moroccco and Military Aid*, 'Secret' telegram from the Department of State to the NATO, 2 February 1976 (both retrieved from the Wikileaks, on 25 September 2019). Contrary to all of the available Moroccan sources, all Algerian sources stress that they never deployed any kind of heavy weapons and especially none of the frequently reported Soviet-made Kvadrat (SA-6) SAM-systems inside Western Sahara as of 1975. As described further below, independent Russian sources confirm this fact beyond any doubt simply by pointing out that no SA-6s had been delivered to Algeria at this point in time.

11 In similar fashion to the French military during the Liberation War in Algeria, so also the Moroccan military – and its allies in the West – became obsessed with the idea that Morocco was fighting a Soviet-instigated conspiracy aimed to gradually bring all of Africa under communist control. An article from December 1979 cited the FAR Brigadier-General Muhammad Abruk's statement: 'We are the last fort protecting Western interests in this part of the world.'

12 M.A. interview provided on condition of anonymity, June 2004.

13 H.B., interview provided on condition of anonymity, November 2005. The fact that Salah's unit abandoned its position did not damage the career of this officer: on the contrary, he subsequently enjoyed a successful career, and was appointed Deputy Minister of Defence of Algeria in 2013. Ever since, he has been one of the most influential figures within top circles of the Algerian armed forces.

14 N. B., interview, October 2019.

15 'Interview with President Hossni Mubarak', Egyptian National TV, 2008; Bhutani, pp. 251-256 & 'Las tropas marroquies ocupan el oasis de Tifariti, en el Sahara', ABC, 7 February 1976.

16 Ibid.

17 S. N., interview provided on condition of anonymity, April 2001; M. A. interview provided on condition of anonymity, June 2004 & M. R., interview provided on condition of anonymity, April 2017. For the Moroccan version of this clash, see Hughes, p. 252 & San Martin, 'El rearme del ejército, un peligro para el trono marroqui', El Pais, 8 May 1976.

18 E.C., interview, February 2019 & 'Interview with President Hossni Mubarak', Egyptian National TV, 2008. Despite countless claims of Algerian combat involvement on the side of the POLISARIO, even the CIA eventually confirmed that there was no evidence of such participation since the January-February 1976 period; see CIA, *Prospect for Morocco*,

Interagency Intelligence Memorandum, NI IIM 82-10004, May 1982, CIA/FOIA/ERR.

19 CIA, 'Viability and Orientation of a Western Saharan State', PA81-10069, March 1981, CIA/FOIA/ERR.

20 CIA, 'The Conflict in Western Sahara', June 1977, CIA/FOIA/ERR.

21 Zunes et al, p. 15; José Ramon Diego Aguirre, Guerra en el Sáhara (Madrid: Istmo, 1991), p. 78 & Fuente Cobo and Fernando M. Marino Menéndez, El conflicto del Sáhara occidental (Madrid: Ministry of Defence, 2006), p. 30.

22 Tobji, pp. 80-81.

23 Ibid, pp. 79-80; Diego Aguirre, pp. 160-161; Keagan, p. 464.

24 El-Djeich (in French), Vol. 003/January-February-March 2007 & Keagan, p. 484. One should keep in mind that the Mauritanian air force was always a very small service. As detailed in Volume 1, it was established in 1962, when the country had only two qualified pilots. French donations and acquisitions elsewhere enabled a significant growth during that decade and then in the early 1970s, but a major tragedy struck in April 1972, when seven fully qualified aircrews (each consisting of one pilot, one co-pilot, and one flight engineer) were killed in the crash of a DC-3 transport (for further details, see Hedi Dahmani, 'Le chamelier du ciel', L'Autre Journal, February 1990). Left with only one qualified pilot (he was on sick leave and thus not on that flight), the FAIM had to start from scratch: a new group of 10 students was then trained on Cessnas and Short Skyvans in Ireland, starting in 1974. Three additional trainees were sent for training on Cessnas a year later, but failed to complete their course. Thus, most of those who flew and fought over Western Sahara and Mauritania 1976-1979 were still from the group of transport-pilots that earned their wings in Ireland.

25 CIA, The Conflict in Western Sahara, June 1977, CIA/FOIA/ERR.

26 Lorell, p. 29; notably, Cap Vert outside Dakar served as the French headquarters for Western Africa.

27 Zunes et al, pp. 11-12, Lorell, p. 29. The Noratlas transports deployed in support of Operation Fanon are known to have been drawn from the AdA's Transport Squadron 55 (ETOM.55), forward deployed to Dakar for this purpose. They picked up Moroccan troops from bases in Guelimine, Agadir and Kenitra, and ferried them to Zouerate and Akiout.

28 Lorell, p. 30; E. C., interview, December 2017; Keagan, p. 466. Obviously, the deployment of FRA F-5s at Nouadibou was because the importance of the local port for Mauritanian exports of iron ore. Ajouit was critical because it was connected to Nouakchott by one of the few well-constructed roads in the country of the time.

29 Keagan, p. 465.

30 Zunes et al, p. 11.

31 E.C., interview, November 2018.

32 E.T. Abdel Kader, 'Guerre du Sahara, 16 Juliet 1977, l'avion du Commandant Kader abattu par le Polisario', cridem.org, 14 July 2015.

33 Lorell, p. 29; Zunes et al, pp. 11-12 & Keagan, p. 465. Notably, as of 1977, export of iron ore provided about 80 per cent of the Mauritanian foreign exchange.

34 Because the earlier French military interventions in Gabon of 1964, and Chad in 1969, caused a public outcry in France, Paris kept the intervention in Mauritania as secret as possible. This resulted in many sources wrongly reporting even the start of this intervention as December 1977.

35 Air et Cosmos, 31 December 1977. The first four French fighter-bombers deployed to Senegal during Operation Lamantin, were single-seat Jaguar As A55/11-RH and A56/11RJ, and two-seat Jaguar Es E29/11-EA and E32/11RG. The reason for the deployment of two-seaters was to keep as many single-seaters as possible back, for the defence of metropolitan France. Moreover, Jaguar Es were able to expose additional pilots to the experience of in-flight-refuelling, overseas and combat operations: one should keep in mind that at the time there were only 20 Jaguar-pilots qualified for IFR-operations in all of the AdA. While these first four aircraft were ready for action immediately upon their arrival, and a suitable target offered itself in the form of an ELPS column that raided the railway in northern Mauritania, no order for an attack was issued. The other four fighter-bombers followed on 23 November. Once again, they included two single-and two two-seaters: single-seat Jaguar As A54/11RT and A59/11-EG, and Jaguar Es E31/11-RF and E33/11RC.

36 Zunes et al, pp. 11-12, Lorell, p. 30; Cobo, p. 112.

37 There is still a great deal of confusion about what exactly was attacked at what point in time. Air et Cosmos (31 December 1977) reported only reconnaissance sorties flown on 3 and 5 December 1977, while other French media provided equally confusing releases. The account here is based on a cross-examination of all contemporary publications – in France and elsewhere. Notably, the third quartet of French fighter-bombers deployed to Senegal in the course of Operation Lamantin included Jaguar As A49/11RM and A51/11-RO, and Jaguar Es E35/11MV and E36/11MW.

38 Contemporary volumes of Air et Cosmos; K.H., interview, July 2004 & Cobo, p. 114. Two Transalls of the AdA deployed the repair crew, spares and tools necessary to repair Jantet's Jaguar. Eventually, the damage was found too massive for in-situ repairs: the aircraft was thus dismantled, loaded into one of the C.160s, and flown back to France for repairs.

39 CIA, The Conflict in Western Sahara, June 1977, CIA/FOIA/ERR; Lorell, pp. 29-31; Hedi Dahmani, 'Le chamelier du ciel', L'Autre Journal, February 1990. Mohammed Ould Bah Ould Abdel Kader was the sole FAIM pilot left after the tragedy that struck this air force in August 1972, and thus the last of the 'first generation' of Mauritanian military fliers.

40 Air et Cosmos, February and March 1978; Hedi Dahmani, 'Le chamelier du ciel', L'Autre Journal, February 1990. Most French Jaguar pilots were trained to fly low altitude attacks with parachute-retarded bombs in central Europe (see Forget, p.40).

41 For details on both affairs in Chad and Zaire, see Cooper et al, Libyan Air Wars, Volumes 1 and 2, and Kowalczuk, Kolwezi.

42 Bouna Moctar, 'Interview with Colonel M Barek' (in French), El-Djeich, No. 001/June-July-August 2006.

43 Ibid; Lorell, pp. 30-31 & Flintham, p. 86.

44 Zunes et al, p. 15.

45 Belkace Hacene-Djaballah, Conflict in Western Sahara: A Study of POLISARIO as an Insurgency Movement (Ph.D. dissertation, Catholic University of America, Washington DC, 1985), pp. 144-145; CIA, The Western Sahara Conflict: Morocco's Millstone, PA 79-10167, April 1979, CIA/FOIA/ERR & Keagan, p. 465.

46 Zunes et al, p. 13 & Keagan, p. 465. According to H.B. and E.C., although subsequently developing friendly relations with the POLISARIO, even late during its involvement in Western Sahara, Nouakchott still took care to warn Rabat about its agreement with the insurgents, and make it clear it had agreed specific dates by which the ELPS was to take over. This in turn enabled the FAR to deploy the troops of the 1st Parachute Brigade with the aim of securing places like Dakhla – before the insurgents could reach them.

Chapter 4

1 Pivka, p. 122; Keagan, p. 465 & E.C., interview, November 2018.

2 Dean pp. 38-39.

3 CIA, The Conflict in Western Sahara, June 1977, CIA/FOIA/ERR.

4 Tobji, p. 166 & E.C., interview, January 2019.

5 Liebert et al, p. 225. Some English-language sources tend to designate the six final Moroccan F.1s as F.1EH-200s because of their IFR-probes. However, such designation was never used by the FRA.

6 H.B., interviews provided on condition of anonymity, November 2005 & E.C., multiple interviews, 2018-2019.

7 Vetter, p. 170.

8 Hollwell, p. 117 & E.C., interview, February 2019.

9 Vetter, p. 170 & Zunes et al, p. 12.

10 Keagan, p. 483.

11 Conclusions based on all available sources (see Bibliography); details on FRA losses in 1976 thanks to E.C., H B. and N.B.

12 E.C., interview, November 2018.

13 CIA, The Conflict in Western Sahara, June 1977, CIA/FOIA/ERR & H. B., interview, April 2004 & E.C. interview, December 2018.

14 Ibid.

15 K.H., P.A., E.C., H.B., and N.B, diverse interviews since 2004.

16 Tobji, pp. 76-68 & E.C., interview, August 2019.

17 Tobji, pp. 76-78, 83, 106-107; H. B., interviews, December 1999 and January 2000; E.C., interviews, December 2018-September 2019.

18 Lovelace, pp. 42-43; Tobji, p87 & 'Polisario's Tan-Tan Attack Renews Algerian-Moroccan Tensions', Cambio 16, 18 February 1979; H.B., interviews, December 1999 and January 2000; K.H., interviews, April 2004 & June 2005; E.C., interview, September 2019; Flintham, p. 86. Obviously shocked by this blow, Rabat first denied it, then downplayed its importance, and finally announced that the FAR had killed 200 'mercenaries'. It took demands for a parliamentary meeting by Morocco's political parties to force King Hassan II to admit in public, that 'the situation was not getting better' – and then introduce a surprisingly wide range of reforms on the political and military level. Especially since the ELPS attack on Tantan, reports surfaced according to which the insurgents had a policy of not taking prisoners, and about summary executions of Moroccan troops – including the injured (for one description of a massacre on injured FAR troops, see Hollwell). According to their own statements, the ELPS was actually advised to take as many Moroccans prisoners of War (POWs) as possible, and bring them back to its own bases alive – not only as 'bargaining chips' for at least indirect negotiations run with Rabat nearly all the time, but also because parading the POWs and loot in front of the Sahrawi refugees and the international press at the camps in the Tindouf area has had a strong psychological and propaganda value.

19 K.H., interview, July 2004.

20 Zunes et al, p. 17 & Dean, p. 39. The same deal originally included the delivery of 24 Hughes 500 Defender attack helicopters and 24 OV-10As, but Morocco turned these down because it was already in the process of receiving the above-mentioned Gazelles from France.

21 Cooper et al, Showdown in Western Sahara, Volume 1; Lake, 'Northrop F-5', World Air Power Journal; E.C. diverse interviews, 2018-2019.

22 Unless stated otherwise, this sub-chapter is based on Tobji, p. 11 & E.C. interviews, 2018-2019. The 1°GEB eventually formed the centrepiece of the future 1°BRIMeca, while the 7°GEB and Task Force Ouhoud grew in size until being split into the 7°BRIMeca (which also included the 3°RIM), and 9°BRIMeca. The reform in question was extremely comprehensive, and went down the chain-of-command too. For example, all the motorised units were broken down along the system named '3-ochra': into teams of 4-5 troops responsible for operating and supporting every combat vehicle, no matter if MBT, APCs, self-propelled or towed artillery piece, truck or a 4WD. Each team was organized by officers, who usually combined two more experienced soldiers with two or three less experienced ones. Each team was autonomous with regards to its supplies of food and other daily needs: only refuelling the vehicles and resupply of water was done in bulk. This system enabled troops a measure of freedom, while welding them together.

23 Zunes et al, p. 16, H.B. and E.C., diverse interviews since 2004.

24 Tobji, p. 113; Lovelace, p. 43; 'Morocco admits fall of Garrison', *The New York Times* (NYT), 27 August 1979; K.H., P.A., E.C., and H.B., diverse interviews since 1999. While the majority of Moroccan sources insisted that the POLISARIO had 'wildly exaggerated' its reports about the damage caused to the 3°GEB, at least one observed, 'the 3°GEB should not have been sacrificed like that' – indicating the unit was actually destroyed. Characteristically, in complete ignorance of the 3°GEB's commander's timely warnings and repeated calls for help, the FAR court-martialled – and draconically punished – him and 76 other officers of this unit for cowardice and negligence of duty. The commander and nine other officers were executed, while 36 were imprisoned. The survivors of the 3°GEB were subsequently reorganized in el-Hajeb and re-equipped with French-made AMX-10RC heavy armoured cars and VAB APCs. This unit was grouped with the 3°RIM, 1°GAR and support units to form the 3°BRIMeca.

25 Lovelace, pp. 43-44; Zunes et al, p. 15 & L Roberts Sheldon, 'Morocco Uses New Muscle in Sahara War', *The Christian Science Monitor*, 18 October 1979; K.H., interview, July 2004 & E.C., interview, August 2019. Ironically, although resulting in some of the worst defeats of the FAR – and although the deputy commander of the Samara garrison subsequently acknowledged a loss of 121 soldiers, the ELPS raids on Ibourate and Samara are next to never, or only very superficially mentioned in Moroccan – or US – histories of this war.

26 N. B., interview, October 2019. For comparison, the official Rabat reported that the insurgents were 'taken by surprise' by the Task Force Ouhoud, and lost 130 killed.

27 Raphael Mergui, 'Sahara: la grande riposte', *Jeune Afrique*, No 985, 21 November 1979.

28 'Morocco Fights a Desert War', *Time Magazine*, 10 December 1979.

Chapter 5

1 Tobji, p. 76-78, 83, 85, 106-107; E.C., interview, August 2019. Although never outright disbanded, as claimed by Tobji, the CMVs eventually proved to have a more dissuasive than an effective combat role: still, after August 1978, they rarely exchanged any shots with the ELPS, and many of their troops defected after their families were kidnapped by the insurgents during the battle for Samara, in 1979. Nevertheless, at least one of their Sahrawi commanders, Aída Ould Tamek, is known to have retired from the FAR with the rank of Colonel-Major. At least two CMVs remain operational (see Table 4 for details).

2 Zunes et al, p. 20.

3 Tobji, p. 85; P.A. and H.B., diverse interviews since 2004.

4 Zunes et al, p. 21.

5 CIA, *The POLISARIO Front: Status and Prospects*, NESA 83-10081, April 1983, CIA/FOIA/ERR & Tobji, pp. 109-110. Who exactly came up with the idea that eventually won the war for Morocco remains unclear: most Moroccans attribute it to Hassan II himself, some to the US, French or other foreign advisors that played an increasingly important role, but at least one of the unofficial sources cited a mere captain in command of one of units deployed in the Western Sahara as the actual source.

6 CIA, *The POLISARIO Front: Status and Prospects*, NESA 83-10081, April 1983, CIA/FOIA/ERR.

7 Department of State, The Director of Intelligence and Research, SECRET/ NOFORN, 28 September 1982; CIA, Probable Libyan Arms Delivery to POLISARIO Forces in Algeria, Mers el-Kebir Naval Base and Shipyard and Oued Tatrat POLISARIO Camp No.1, 16 September 1982; CIA, *The POLISARIO Front: Status and Prospects*, NESA 83-10081, April 1983; K.H., H.B. and E.C., diverse interviews, 2004-2019.

8 Department of State, The Director of Intelligence and Research, SECRET/ NOFORN, 28 September 1982; CIA, Probable Libyan Arms Delivery to POLISARIO Forces in Algeria, Mers el-Kebir Naval Base and Shipyard and Oued Tatrat POLISARIO Camp No.1, 16 September 1982; CIA, *The POLISARIO Front: Status and Prospects*, NESA 83-10081, April 1983; K.H., H.B. and E.C., diverse interviews, 2004-2019; K.H., interview, July 2004. Despite their 'first combat deployment' as of October 1981, it is meanwhile next to certain that the POLISARIO had received its SA-6s at a much earlier date. Some of the Algerian sources stress this happened even before

Algeria received its first examples, in 1979. Considering it takes significant amounts of time – at least six months, often more – to properly train the necessary crews, it is very likely that this was indeed the case.

9 N.B., interview, October 2019.

10 K.H., interview, September 2004.

11 Ibid.

12 Liébert et al, p. 226.

13 K.H., interview, July 2004; H.B., interview, November 2005 & K.H., interview, July 2004.

14 K.H., interviews, July 2004 & May 2017; H.B., interview, November 2005.

15 'Soviet-made missiles down two Moroccan planes', *UPI*, 14 October 1981. According to Algerian sources, members of the QJJ's MiG-21 detachment deployed at Tindouf AB while the battle of Guelta Zemour was raging were constantly listening to the Moroccan radio transmissions. One of these reported that two Mirage F.1s – including one with the radio callsign 'Médi-1' – were shot down that day, but in a clash with Algerian MiGs! Given the number of Algerian pilots deployed at Tindouf AB was very small, and none was airborne that day, this caused quite a surprise. Another intercepted radio transmission cited the Mirages shot down by a 'very dangerous missile…fired from Algerian territory': the truth was that at least some ELPS SAMs were deployed close to, even though not 'within', Algeria.

16 K.H., interview, July 2004.

17 Holeindre & H.B., interview, November 2005. The French press subsequently dubbed the Moroccan commander a 'New Desert Fox'.

18 H.B. interview, November 2005.

19 Liébert et al, p. 226 & K.H., interview, July 2004; Richard Holmes, 'The Battle of Guelta Zammour', *AirEnthusiast*, December 1981 (pp. 19-42).

Chapter 6

1 Department of State, The Director of Intelligence and Research, SECRET/ NOFORN, 28 September 1982; CIA, Probable Libyan Arms Delivery to POLISARIO Forces in Algeria, Mers el-Kebir Naval Base and Shipyard and Oued Tatrat POLISARIO Camp No.1, 16 September 1982; CIA, *The POLISARIO Front: Status and Prospects*, NESA 83-10081, April 1983, CIA/ FOIA/ERR.

2 For details see Cooper et al, *Libyan Air Wars, Volumes 1, 2, and 3*.

3 Zunes et al, p. 19 & Dean p. 39.

4 William E Smith, 'Landing Rights and Help with Unwinnable War', *Time Magazine*, 31 May 1982 & Dean, p. 66.

5 Damis, p. 129 & CIA, *The Western Sahara Conflict: Morocco's Millstone*, PA 79-10167, April 1979, CIA/FOIA/ERR.

6 Dean, p. 69 & US Defense Security Assistance Agency, Department of Defense, 'Cluster Bomb Exports under FMS, FY1970-FY1995', 15 November 1995, obtained in response to FOIA request, 17 February 2001.

7 Dean, p. 70.

8 Ibid, p. 71.

9 CIA, *Royal Moroccan Air Force (RMAF) Electronic Warfare (EW) Support (U)*, 26 February 1982, CIA/FOIA/ERR.

10 CIA, *Probable SA-6 Equipment, Ain el-Bel, Western Sahara*, 4 February 1982; CIA, *SA-6 Firing Unit, Ain el-Bel POLISARIO Camp 3*, Western Sahara, 6 February 1982; CIA, *SA-9 Missile System, Ain el-Bel POLISARIO Camp 5*, Western Sahara, 19 March 1982 & CIA, Fishbed Deployment, Tafaraoui/ Lartigue Airfield, Algeria, January 1982 CIA/FOIA/ERR.

11 The conclusion about deliveries of AN/AAQ-8 pods to Morocco is based on photographs showing FRA F-5Es carrying such systems that appeared since the early 1990s.

12 E. C., multiple interviews in 2017 & M. A., interview, July 2017.

13 CIA, *Airstrike Against SA-6 Equipment, Ain el-Ben POLISARIO Camp 2*, Western Sahara, 6 January 1982, CIA/FOIA/ERR.

14 CIA, *Airstrike Against Polisario Forces, Raudat el-Hach Military Facility, Western Sahara*, 5 March 1982, CIA/FOIA/ERR.

15 Dean, p. 70.

16 Brigadier-General Ahmad Sadik (retired officer of the Intelligence Department of the Iraqi Air Force), interview, March 2006. Sadik not only explained the Moroccan search for solutions that led to the use of Jupiter fuses, but also added that the Iraqis adopted the idea, and began using Portuguese- and Spanish-made Mk.84 bombs with Jupiters on their own Mirage F.1s. For further details to this topic, see Cooper et al, *Iraqi Mirages*.

17 N.B., interview, October 2019 & E.C. interviews, August-September 2019.

18 E.C., interview, August 2019. According to Hadri, he was interrogated by an Algerian officer, who insisted on finding out how the Moroccans knew that the second T-55 survived the first strike and was in the process of being towed away. When Hadri explained to him that this was coincidence, the Algerian refused to believe him, and beat him in an attempt to 'extract the truth'.

19 E.C. & N.B., diverse interviews, January 2018 – September 2019. Delivery-flights of F-5E/Fs were run by US pilots, from the USA, via Canada, Greenland, Iceland and the United Kingdom. The FRA's sole Boeing 707-320C in question was N58937, originally a B707-700C (powered by CFM56 engines), manufactured in 1982 as the last airliner of this prolific

About the Authors

Tom Cooper

Tom Cooper is an Austrian aerial warfare analyst and historian. Following a career in the worldwide transportation business – during which he established a network of contacts in the Middle East and Africa – he moved into narrow-focus analysis and writing on small, little-known air forces and conflicts, about which he has collected extensive archives. This has resulted in specialisation in such Middle Eastern air forces as of those of Egypt, Iran, Iraq, and Syria, plus various African and Asian air forces. In addition to authoring and co-authoring more than 30 books – including an in-depth analysis of major Arab air forces at war with Israel in the 1955-1973 period – and over 1,000 articles, Cooper is a regular correspondent for multiple defence-related publications.

Albert Grandolini

Military historian and aviation-journalist Albert Grandolini was born in Vietnam and gained an MA in history from Paris 1 Sorbonne University. His primary research focus is on contemporary conflicts in general and particularly on the military history of Asia and Africa.

Having spent his childhood in South Vietnam, the Vietnam War has always been one of his main fields of research. He authored the book Fall of the Flying Dragon: South Vietnamese Air Force (1973-1975), two volumes on the Vietnam Easter Offensive of 1972 for Helion's Asia@War Series, and three volumes on Libyan Air Wars for the Africa@War Series. He has also written numerous articles for various British, French, and German magazines.

Adrien Fontanellaz

Adrien Fontanellaz, from Switzerland, is a military history researcher and author. He developed a passion for military history at an early age and has progressively narrowed his studies to modern-day conflicts. He is a member of the Scientific Committee of the Pully-based Centre d'histoire et de prospective militaire (Military History and Prospectives Centre), and regularly contributes for the Revue Militaire Suisse and various French military history magazines. He is co-founder and a regular contributor to the French military history website L'autre coté de la colline, and this is his ninth title for Helion's @War series.

Continued from page 79

family ever. In Morocco, it was re-engined back to Pratt & Whitney JT3D engines and received the Moroccan registration CNA-NR (see the colour section for details). Notably, the FRA was already using another, but slightly smaller Boeing 707: the aircraft with the registration CNA-NS was a B707-138B N58937 manufactured in 1961 and then configured as VIP-transport on behalf of the Saudi millionaire Akram Ojjeh's TAG Group. Ojjeh sold it to Morocco in 1983, where it served as VIP-transport, but also for training of the CNA-NR's crew.

20 CIA, *The POLISARIO Front: Status and Prospects*, NESA 83-10081, April 1983, CIA/FOIA/ERR.

21 K.H., interviews, April 2004 & July 2015; Martin Smisek, interview, July 2015.

22 CIA, *Improved POLISARIO Air Defence Capability Oued Tatrat POLISARIO Camp No.1, Algeria (SWN)*, 20 July 1983 & CIA, *Moroccan Air Strike, Bir Lehmar POLISARIO Camp, southern Western Sahara*, Z-10027/82. Notable is that US intelligence incorrectly identified the radar in question as 'P-18'. Further information from K.H., interview, April 2004 & August 2019.

23 CIA, *The POLISARIO Front: Status and Prospects*, NESA 83-10081, April 1983, CIA/FOIA/ERR.

24 The content of this box is entirely based on interviews with M.A. (active officer of the CFDAT), 25 January 2005 & H.K. several interviews since 2004, and upon online publications by Dr. Aleksander Andreevich Raspletin, foremost *History PVO website* (historykpvo.narod2.ru), 2013.

25 The RMSAs were established in 1979, and totalled five regiments equipped with SA-6s – based at Bechar, Tindouf, Oran, Annaba, and Laghouat – and one equipped with SA-8s at Ain Oussera. Widely published reports about the Algerian army operating '60 batteries' of SA-6s and '48 batteries' of SA-8s belong within the realms of science fiction.

26 K.H., interview, July 2004.

27 Ibid.

28 CIA, *Vacation of POLISARIO Camps, Western Sahara*, 31 August 1983; CIA, *Redeployment of POLISARIO Forces, Western Sahara (SWN)*, 8 September 1983; CIA, The Western Sahara War, 1 December 1983, CIA/FOIA/ERR & Lovelace, p. 50.

29 H. B., interview provided on condition of anonymity, November 2005. Notably, this operation was also clear proof that the Algerians did not participate in the Western Saharan War, then Operation Great Maghreb was run only about 50-60 kilometres away from their border, and the Algerians could at least provide ample early warning about Moroccan fighter-bombers to the ELPS – but they didn't.

30 CIA, *The Western Sahara War*, 1 December 1983, CIA/FOIA/ERR.

31 Jonathan Broder, 'Morocco Checks Revolt with 1,500-mile Earth Wall', *Chicago Tribune*, 16 August 1985 & Lovelace, p. 50.

32 Zunes et al, p. 24 & CIA, *Prospect for Morocco*, Interagency Intelligence Memorandum, NI IIM 82-10004, May 1982, CIA/FOIA/ERR.

33 CIA, *Extension of Moroccan Defensive Berm into Mauritanian and Western Sahara*, N-10004/84.

34 *El Pais*, 15 January 1985.

35 Zunes et al, p. 25.

36 K.H., interview, July 2004.

37 Lovelace, p. 51.

38 Lovelace, p. 49.

39 P.A., interview, November 2004 & E.C., interview, August 2019. The ferocity of fighting was such that in 1987 the FRA is known to have placed an order for 192 additional HOT ATGMs to replenish its depleted stocks: the missiles in question were delivered in 1988-1991. There are reports that the ELPS deployed even a few of the more powerful T-62 MBTs during this engagement. Reportedly, such tanks had been supplied from Algerian stocks during the late 1980s, when the Algerians – for once – may have agreed to replace some of the insurgent losses, because Libya had ceased supporting them. However, currently, it is still unknown if any ELPS T-62s had actually reached the insurgency by the time of this action.

40 'Muerte en el-Sáhara', *El Pais*, 13 August 1991.

41 Lovelace, p. 59.

42 Lovelace, p. 59; Tobji, pp. 80-81; 'El ministerio de la guerra del Sáhara', *El Pais*, 10 September 2006; Ali Najab, 'Ma guerre contre le polisario', *Medias24.com*, 22 July 2015. Sources differ, but either one or two of the downed FRA pilots managed to escape from the POLISARIO's POW-camps, on 17 October 1987.

43 Confirmed losses are printed in bold. The table is based on cross-examination of information collected from all available sources. Notably, five additional FRA pilots are known to have been shot down during the war, but exact dates in question remain unknown. They were:
   • Capitaine Ayoub Ben Ali (type of aircraft unknown)
   • Sergeant-Chef Bel Kaddi (F-5 pilot)
   • Sergeant-Chef el-Mardi (F-5 pilot)
   • Adjutant-Chef Driss el-Yazami (Mirage F.1 pilot), and
   • Raghib el-Matawi (rank and type of aircraft unknown)